Special Occasions

JOHN HADAMUSCIN

Special Occasions

Holiday Entertaining
All Year Round

PHOTOGRAPHS BY RANDY O'ROURKE

ART DIRECTION BY KEN SANSONE

HARMONY BOOKS / NEW YORK

◆

Published by Harmony Books, a division of Crown Publishers, Inc.,
225 Park Avenue South, New York, New York 10003
and represented in Canada by the Canadian MANDA Group
HARMONY and colophon are trademarks of Crown Publishers, Inc.

Manufactured in Japan

◆

Library of Congress Cataloging-in-Publication Data

Hadamuscin, John.
Special occasions: holiday entertaining all year yound
by John Hadamuscin: photographs by Randy O'Rourke.

p.   cm.
1. Entertaining   2. Holiday cookery.   3. Cookery, American
4. Menus.   I. Title
TX731.H2 1988   642′.4—dc19   88-792 CIP

ISBN 0-517-57196-X
10 9 8 7 6 5 4 3 2 1
First Edition

*F*or
my family and friends,
who make any
occasion special

Contents
◆

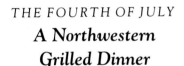

Introduction

♦

I love any kind of celebration, and I look forward to any excuse or reason to plan an event and bring friends and family together. To me a special occasion doesn't have to be confined to one season of the year or even to an official "holiday." It can be any event that later becomes a happy memory —a family tradition or ritual, a season, or even the creation of a memorable event out of an ordinary day. A special occasion is a time when we naturally want to entertain, a time when, even if we do little real cooking anytime else, we cook up a storm. And it's a time when we indulge ourselves, eating richer foods and more courses (and sometimes even more than one dessert!).

My love of special occasions began early. From Christmastime in the winter to our big family reunions each summer, from the coming of spring to Hallowe'en, we would gather together—family, friends, and neighbors—to celebrate. An essential part of each celebration was, of course, the food. There would always be special foods that we didn't eat every day—a jar of my grandmother's peach chutney, wild mushrooms that grew in the woods after the spring rains, or a three-layer chocolate birthday cake.

Living in an Ohio farming community, we always had the best of everything. On our six-hundred-acre farm, Dad grew cash crops of oats, wheat, soybeans, and corn, and he had a herd of beef and dairy cattle, along with a few hogs. For the family, Mom had a one-acre vegetable garden, where she grew everything from acorn squash to zucchini, and she raised chickens for eggs and eating. We also had a small orchard, where we grew apples, peaches, pears, and wild black cherries. And along with our own produce, we shared in the abundance, such as the local maple syrup and fresh fish from Lake Erie, of our area. But the foods I remember most fondly are those that grew wild in the back pastures and alongside the roads: asparagus, elderberries, strawberries, blue raspberries, blackberries, butternuts, chestnuts, black walnuts, and wild mushrooms.

All these foods were a major part of our celebrations, and in some cases were even the reason for them. Our big Christmas dinners always featured specialties from Mom's cellarful of home-canned goods,

and in the spring, the appearance of maple syrup would be the only reason needed for a special breakfast. In the summer, when the corn had reached its peak, Dad would hold a huge corn roast for all the family and neighbors.

My acquaintance with regional American foods and celebrations began with our family vacations. Early each summer, after the crops and garden were planted, my father would announce that vacation time had arrived. My two younger brothers, my younger sister, and I would groan loudly, knowing we would not be going off to some far-off fantastic place of our dreams, such as Africa or the Amazon, but to somewhere slightly more local. And Dad would always respond to our cries of dismay with the same rhetorical question: "Why go see the world, when we haven't seen all there is to see here in America, yet?" So, we would all be packed into the car and take off on one of Dad's whirlwind tours of America.

We covered a lot of ground during those two- and three-week trips, traveling one year to the Grand Canyon, and the next year to the man-made canyons of Manhattan. And along with the sights and sounds there were the wonderful flavors and aromas. I ate grits for the first time in Greenup, Kentucky; I tasted my first lobster in Boothbay Harbor, Maine, on the Fourth of July; and the best buckwheat pancakes I ever had were in Port Allegheny, Pennsylvania.

Along with tasting many American foods, I also discovered how some holidays, such as the Fourth of July, are celebrated differently across the country, and I learned about regional celebrations, such as New Orleans' Mardi Gras. Over the years, I've adopted some of these special occasions, while continuing to celebrate the ones I grew up with. I've even begun a few traditions of my own, such as cooking a comforting supper on the night that income tax returns are due, to help keep things festive throughout the year.

The recipes offered here are American ones; regional specialties from across the country, favorites from my childhood in Ohio, and concoctions of my own that use native American ingredients or cooking techniques in ways that I find particularly appealing.

♦

I've found that a special occasion doesn't just happen; a successful party is the result of careful planning and organization and an awareness of just what makes special occasions memorable. Once I've decided to have a party, the ambience is established right along with the menu. I start making lists of both priorities and details. I keep a running guest list; as my enthusiasm for the event grows, the guest list can tend to grow, too. There's a checklist of how the food will be presented, with table linens, flatware, dishes, glassware, and any special serving pieces that the menu may require. Another list includes details, such as flowers, candles, and other special decorations, along with any appropriate music or other individual touches that help make the occasion special, such as serving soup in a pumpkin on Hallowe'en or decorating shortcakes with miniature American flags on the Fourth of July. If everything's well organized when my guests arrive, I'm in a relaxed frame of mind and enjoy the party as much as they do.

As far as the cooking itself goes, each menu is preceded by a section called "getting ready," to help you plot out your cooking schedule, including as much advance preparation as possible. I like to spread the work out if I can, using a spare few minutes here and there, but you might want to concentrate the work; it depends on how you like to work in the kitchen.

Most of the time, especially for good-sized gatherings, I like the back-to-basics approach to cooking. I leave restaurant cooking to the restaurants. After all, the foundation of American cooking and our seasonal celebrations is home cooking, so again and again you will see references to down-home menus and recipes, some updated and refined and some remaining in their "original" form.

Since this book is about seasonal celebrations, the menus emphasize the use of fresh seasonal ingredients, but try to be flexible. If a menu calls for green beans and they don't look their best at the market, substitute something that does. As far as other ingredients go, I use unsalted "sweet" butter, unbleached white all-purpose flour, and pure flavorings, such as real chocolate and vanilla extract. Herbs are best fresh when available, but in many cases I've listed an alternative quantity for dried ones if you need to use them

(but never use dried parsley, which tastes like green sawdust).

In the photographs throughout the book, I've tried to keep things realistic, practical, and easy to do. I'm all for making pictures pretty, but some things shown in magazines and books, such as using irreplaceable antique quilts as tablecloths or delicate Champagne flutes on a sailboat, just don't make good sense to me. As for all the dishes, glasses, linens, and so on that appear in these pages, I have to admit to being an incurable collector. Since I can't pass the words *Tag Sale Today* without stopping the car, my closets and cupboards are crammed with more things than are found in most households. I certainly don't think anyone *needs* more than one set of dishes, but I enjoy putting together different combinations for different occasions. If I had to keep only one set, it would be the simple creamware that appears several times in these pages, since it's so versatile and almost all food looks good on it, and I'd keep one set of plain wineglasses and the simplest flatware.

I always have flowers in my house and I don't think there can ever be enough of them. Flowers add a note of festivity to any table or room, so they appear at almost every occasion here, whether I've made a simple bouquet of a few tulips, a big basket of wildflowers, or an elaborate wreath of dried flowers and herbs.

I like food that looks like food, not like an art object that's been the subject of endless torture in the kitchen, so the food in the pictures is all "real." Any garnishing here is simple and quickly accomplished. You'll also notice that I don't always take things too seriously; there may be a few "corny" touches here and there, but when something comes to the table I like to see smiles on the faces of my guests along with hearing the *oohs* and *aahs*.

Good organization, great food, and a beautiful table are not the only keys to creating special occasions. The most important ingredients are thought and caring. The food should be fun, the occasion should be fun, and the host should be fun. Memories are what we celebrate.

John Hadamuscin

MENU

Pineapple Sangaree

Hot Bloody Marys

◆

Slivered Smokehouse Ham (page 108)
on Sweet Potato-Pecan Biscuits
with Maple Mustard

Spicy Crab Cakes with
Watercress Mayonnaise

Down East Pork and Sage Handpies

Blue Cheese-Stuffed
Celery Hearts and Grapes

Santa Fe Corn Muffins

Olive and Peppercorn Cheese

Salmon and Caviar Mousse

Crackers and Breads

◆

Creole Porcupines

New Amsterdam New Year's Cookies

Peppermint-Fudge Brownies

Fresh Winter Fruits

OPPOSITE: A welcoming array of finger foods and a bouquet
of carnations and eucalyptus are laid out on a candle-lit,
flowered-chintz-covered table.

My Annual Open House

FOR 50

◆

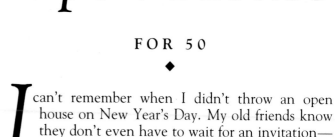

I can't remember when I didn't throw an open house on New Year's Day. My old friends know they don't even have to wait for an invitation—they know where they'll be on January 1. And throughout the year, I find myself inviting new acquaintances who I hope will become new friends.

For me, the New Year's Day afternoon open house is a calm alternative to a frenetic New Year's Eve party with all its forced gaiety. (In fact, I'm usually not aware of the midnight passing of the old year, since I'm almost always in my kitchen, where a ringing bell only means it's time to take something out of the oven.) And as far as the guests go, everyone's usually in a relaxed and happy state of mind, filled with the expectant good cheer of the day and the continuing high spirits of the season.

Through the years, the menu has changed according to my current whims, but the event itself has always remained basically the same. This menu is my favorite at the moment; next year a few dishes will probably disappear and new ones will show up, but most of the real favorites will remain, as they have for years, since everyone expects them. Come to think of it, the menu is kind of like the guest list.

Getting Ready: Most of the work for this menu can be done ahead. On the day of the party, it's helpful to have an extra hand in the kitchen.

Make the mustard at least one week before serving.

Up to two weeks ahead, make the biscuits, muffins, and handpies and freeze them. Or bake a day in advance; store the biscuits and muffins in a cool place and the handpies in the refrigerator. Bake the cookies and store them in tins in a cool place.

Up to five days in advance, cook the ham, but don't do the final trimming, glazing, and baking until a day ahead (page 108). The Olive and Peppercorn Cheese can also be made up to five days ahead and stored in the refrigerator, tightly covered.

The day before, make the syrup base for the Pineapple Sangaree and freeze the pineapple mold; make the crab cakes, assemble them on baking sheets, cover tightly, and store in the refrigerator; make the salmon mousse; and bake the ham. Also, double-check that serving dishes are ready.

On the day of the party, stuff the grapes and celery; assemble the ingredients for the Hot Bloody Marys; arrange the handpies on baking sheets; make the Watercress Mayonnaise; arrange the cookies on trays and the breads in baskets. Set up the coffee and tea pots. Allow at least half an hour for arranging serving dishes on the buffet. Unmold the mousse and slice part of the ham just before serving. Preheat the oven for baking the handpies and crab cakes; put the handpies in the oven about half an hour before serving; put the crab cakes in about fifteen minutes before serving.

Pineapple Sangaree

MAKES ABOUT 30 DRINKS

◆

Sangarees were popular in this country a few centuries before sangría became trendy. This version of the red wine punch incorporates the juice of the pineapple— the colonial symbol of welcome.

2 cups cubed pineapple (see note)
1½ quarts pineapple juice
1 cup orange juice
1 cup lemon juice
1 cup sugar
1 tablespoon whole cloves
1 tablespoon whole allspice
3 liters chilled dry red wine
1 liter chilled club soda

1. Arrange the cubed pineapple in an even layer in the bottom of a 4-cup decorative mold. Pour 2 cups of the pineapple juice over the fruit and freeze until firm.

2. Combine the remaining pineapple juice, the orange and lemon juices, sugar, and spices. Stir until the sugar is dissolved. Refrigerate for 6 hours, or overnight, to allow flavors to blend.

3. To serve, pour the juice mixture into a punch bowl and stir in the wine and club soda. Unmold the frozen pineapple and juice and gently slip it into the punch bowl.

Note: Canned pineapple or cooked fresh pineapple have the best consistency for freezing; do not use raw pineapple.

Hot Bloody Marys

MAKES ABOUT 24 DRINKS

◆

These are great welcomers on a cold, blustery day.

   1 46-ounce can tomato juice
   1 46-ounce can V-8 or Vegemato juice
   4 cups beef stock
 ⅓ cup freshly grated horseradish
 ¾ cup Worcestershire sauce
   2 teaspoons freshly ground black pepper
   1 tablespoon Tabasco sauce
      Juice of 2 limes
      Vodka

1. Combine all the ingredients except the vodka in a kettle, place over medium heat, and bring to just below the simmering point. Reduce heat and keep the mixture warm on the stove.

2. Serve the Bloody Marys directly from the stove or a hot plate, ladled into mugs, with vodka added to individual tastes.

Maple Mustard

MAKES ABOUT 1½ CUPS

◆

I like this sweet and hot mustard on country ham or any smoked meat or mild-flavored smoked sausage. Make the mustard at least a week before you want to serve it; it will keep for several months in the refrigerator.

 ¾ cup cider vinegar
 ¾ cup dry mustard
 ⅔ cup maple syrup
  2 large egg yolks, at room temperature

1. Place the vinegar in a small saucepan and bring to a boil. Remove the pan from the heat and stir in the mustard. Cover and let stand overnight at room temperature.

2. Beat in the maple syrup and egg yolks. Place the pan over low heat and cook, stirring constantly, until thickened. Pour the mustard into two half-pint jars or crocks, cover tightly, and store in the refrigerator.

Sweet Potato-Pecan Biscuits

MAKES ABOUT 3 DOZEN 1½-INCH
BISCUITS

◆

Light in texture yet deep in flavor, these are equally good as part of an hors d'oeuvre buffet or with dinner, piping hot from the oven, split open, and slathered with sweet butter. They're great for breakfast, too, with butter and honey.

   2 cups all-purpose flour
   4 teaspoons baking powder
   2 tablespoons sugar
  ¼ teaspoon ground cinnamon
  ½ teaspoon salt
  ⅔ cup vegetable shortening
1½ cups cooked and mashed sweet potatoes
  ½ cup chopped pecans
  ¼ cup milk

1. Combine the flour, baking powder, sugar, cinnamon, and salt in a large mixing bowl. Using two knives or a pastry blender, cut the shortening into the dry ingredients until the mixture resembles coarse meal.

2. Using a heavy spoon, stir in the sweet potatoes and pecans until the ingredients are just blended. Pour the milk over the mixture and stir until it is just blended in. *Do not overmix.*

3. Preheat the oven to 425°F. Lightly grease two baking sheets. Turn the biscuit dough out onto a well-floured surface and pat it into a rough rectangle about ½ inch thick. Cut the dough into circles with a 1½-inch biscuit cutter and place them on the baking sheets.

4. Bake the biscuits for 10 to 12 minutes, or until the tops are golden brown. Serve warm or at room temperature.

Note: Though they are at their best when freshly baked, the biscuits may be made ahead and frozen. Slightly underbake them, cool, wrap tightly, and freeze for up to a month. To reheat, thaw them completely and place them on a baking sheet in a 350°F. oven for 5 to 7 minutes.

Orange-Sweet Potato Tea Biscuits. For a sweeter version to serve at breakfast or teatime, substitute ¼ cup light brown sugar for the white sugar, substitute golden raisins for the pecans, and add 1 teaspoon grated orange rind. Cut into 2-inch biscuits and bake for 12 to 15 minutes. Makes about 2 dozen.

Spicy Crab Cakes

MAKES 4 DOZEN 1-INCH CAKES

◆

1 cup (2 sticks) butter
1½ cups finely diced celery
2 medium onions, finely chopped
12 thin slices white bread, trimmed and cubed
3 pounds lump crab meat, flaked
2 cups milk, approximately
6 large eggs, lightly beaten
¾ cup chopped parsley
1 teaspoon freshly ground black pepper
1 teaspoon cayenne pepper
1 teaspoon dry mustard
4 cups fine, dry bread crumbs, approximately

1. Melt the butter in a small skillet over medium heat. Add the celery and onions and sauté until crisp-tender, about 10 minutes. Transfer to a large mixing bowl.

2. Place the bread in a shallow bowl or pan with milk to cover. Soak 5 minutes and then remove the bread, squeezing out the milk (reserve the milk). Add the bread and all remaining ingredients except dry bread crumbs to the mixing bowl and toss to mix well. The mixture should have the consistency of raw meat loaf; add some of the reserved milk if necessary.

3. Preheat the oven to 400°F. Lightly grease two baking sheets.

4. Place dry bread crumbs in a shallow bowl. Shape the crab mixture into 1-inch diameter balls and flatten them slightly between your palms. Roll each cake in the dry bread crumbs to lightly coat and place them on the baking sheets, about 1 inch apart. (*May be prepared up to a day ahead to this point, covered with plastic wrap, and refrigerated.*)

5. Bake for 10 minutes, or until golden brown. Arrange the cakes on a platter lined with watercress and serve hot with Watercress Mayonnaise for dipping.

Watercress Mayonnaise

MAKES ABOUT 3 CUPS

◆

2 bunches watercress, stems removed
2 scallions, white and green parts, coarsely chopped
3 tablespoons lemon juice
2 cups Homemade Mayonnaise (page 188)
⅛ teaspoon cayenne pepper
1 cup heavy cream

1. Place the watercress (reserving a few leaves for garnish), scallions, and lemon juice in the bowl of a food processor fitted with the steel chopping blade. Chop well, then scrape out and blend into the mayonnaise. Stir in the cayenne pepper.

2. In a separate bowl, whip the cream until stiff. Fold the whipped cream into the mayonnaise mixture and serve in a small bowl.

Down East Pork and Sage Handpies

MAKES 3 DOZEN HORS D'OEUVRES

◆

A century ago, these fragrant little turnovers were baked in larger versions as a portable lunch for farmers to take out into the fields. I don't know how they ever carried them that far without eating them.

3 tablespoons butter
1 small onion, finely chopped
2 pounds lean ground pork
2 medium potatoes, boiled, peeled, and cubed
2 medium baking apples, peeled and diced
3 tablespoons all-purpose flour
1 tablespoon dark brown sugar
½ teaspoon salt
1 teaspoon freshly ground black pepper
4 tablespoons rubbed sage
Basic Pastry for a 10-inch pie, tripled (page 188)
2 large egg yolks mixed with 2 tablespoons water

1. Melt the butter in a skillet over medium heat. Add the onion and sauté 5 minutes. Add the ground pork and sauté until well browned, about 10 minutes. Stir in the potatoes and apples. Add the flour, toss to blend, and cook 2 minutes longer. Stir in the brown sugar, salt, pepper, and sage. Remove from heat.

2. Preheat the oven to 400°F. Using half the pastry at a time, roll out to ⅛ inch thick. Cut the pastry into circles with a 2½-inch biscuit cutter. Place a heaping teaspoon of the pork mixture on one side of each circle. Moisten the edges with water and fold each circle into a semicircle. Press the edges lightly with a fork to seal. (*May be made ahead up to this point, tightly wrapped, and refrigerated or frozen. Thaw and bring to room temperature before baking.*)

3. Lightly brush the surface of the pies with the egg yolk mixture. Place the pies on ungreased baking sheets and bake for 20 to 25 minutes, or until golden brown. Serve warm or at room temperature.

A still life of Blue Cheese-Stuffed Grapes is arranged
on a Victorian pressed-glass cakestand and
garnished with bunches of purple grapes and lemon
leaves. Down East Pork and Sage Handpies are
served on an old silver hotel tray.

TOP TO BOTTOM:
Slivers of this spectacular ham are delicious served on
Sweet Potato-Pecan Biscuits with a dab of Maple Mustard.

Blue Cheese-Stuffed Celery Hearts are served on
an antique hammered silver tray.

Spicy Crab Cakes, arranged on a bed of watercress, are
ready for dipping in Watercress Mayonnaise.

Sweet bites: star-shaped New Amsterdam New Year's
Cookies, Creole Porcupines, and Peppermint-Fudge
Brownies. A Revere bowl filled with pears is offered for
those who've made New Year's dieting resolutions.

Blue Cheese-Stuffed Celery Hearts and Grapes

◆

Cream cheese
Blue cheese
Celery hearts
Seedless grapes
Finely chopped walnuts

1. Mix 2 parts softened cream cheese with 1 part crumbled blue cheese.

2. For celery, use a pastry tube fitted with a large star tip to flute the cheese mixture into 2-inch lengths of celery ribs. Arrange on a serving platter and chill until the cheese is firm. Cover with plastic wrap and store in the refrigerator.

3. For grapes, press a thin layer of the cheese mixture around seedless grapes, then roll the grapes in finely chopped walnuts. Arrange on a serving plate with bunches of grapes, cover with plastic wrap, and refrigerate until serving.

BELOW: To make this winter wreath, I used flowers and herbs collected from my garden and the Connecticut countryside and dried in the cellar.

Santa Fe Corn Muffins

MAKES 4 DOZEN MINIATURE MUFFINS
OR 1½ DOZEN REGULAR MUFFINS

◆

Perfect as an hors d'oeuvre or as a bread served with a simple supper, these muffins combine a wonderful mixture of textures, colors, and flavors: grainy yellow cornmeal, smoky brown bacon, piquant green jalapeños and scallions, and sharp yellow Cheddar.

These muffins are at their best when made no more than a few hours before serving, but they can be made up to a day ahead or made well in advance and frozen.

    6 thin slices streaky bacon
    ¾ cup stone-ground yellow cornmeal
    1 cup all-purpose flour
    1 tablespoon baking powder
    ½ teaspoon baking soda
    2 teaspoons sugar
    ½ teaspoon salt
    2 tablespoons cold butter
    1 cup buttermilk
    2 large eggs
    ⅔ cup coarsely grated sharp yellow Cheddar cheese
    2 tablespoons finely chopped jalapeño peppers
    3 scallions, white and green parts, finely chopped

1. Coarsely chop the bacon and place it in a skillet over medium heat. Sauté for 10 to 12 minutes, or until most of the fat has been rendered. Remove the bacon from the skillet with a slotted spoon and drain it on paper towels. Cover the bacon and reserve. Pour off the bacon fat from the skillet into a crock, place it in the refrigerator, and chill until firm, about 2 hours.

2. Preheat the oven to 400°F. Grease 4 miniature 1-dozen muffin pans or 1 regular 1-dozen muffin pan.

3. In a large mixing bowl, sift the dry ingredients together. Cut in the butter and 2 tablespoons of the chilled bacon fat until fats are just blended in. (Discard the remaining bacon fat or store in the refrigerator for another use.)

4. In a small separate mixing bowl, beat together the buttermilk and eggs. Pour this mixture over the dry ingredients and stir with a wooden spoon or rubber spatula until the dry ingredients are just moistened; the batter should be slightly lumpy. Fold in the grated Cheddar cheese, jalapeños, scallions, and the reserved bacon all at once.

5. Drop the batter by spoonfuls into the cups of the prepared pans, filling each until almost full. Bake miniature muffins for 15 to 20 minutes and regular muffins for 20 to 25 minutes, or until the muffins are golden brown. Serve hot or at room temperature.

Olive and Peppercorn Cheese

MAKES ABOUT 3 CUPS

◆

    1 pound Monterey Jack cheese, finely grated
    ¾ cup finely chopped black California olives
    ¾ cup finely chopped green olives
    2 tablespoons green peppercorns
    1 teaspoon black peppercorns, cracked
    ½ cup Homemade Mayonnaise (page 188)
       Whole olives, for garnish

Combine all ingredients, mound into a small bowl, and chill overnight. Bring to room temperature before serving with crackers or Melba toast.

Salmon and Caviar Mousse

MAKES ONE 4-CUP MOUSSE

◆

Every New Year's Day I serve a salmon mousse in one form or another. This version is my current favorite. Make two of these for a large party.

    1 tablespoon (1 envelope) unflavored gelatin
    ¼ cup cold water
    ⅓ cup boiling water
    ⅔ cup sour cream
    4 scallions, white and green parts, finely chopped
    3 tablespoons finely chopped dill
    1 tablespoon lemon juice
    ½ teaspoon salt
    1 cup heavy cream
    1¾ cups flaked poached salmon (or one 15½-ounce can red salmon, picked over to remove skin and bones)
    2 ounces salmon caviar

1. In a large mixing bowl, soften the gelatin in the cold water and let stand for 2 to 3 minutes. Gradually stir in the boiling water and stir until the gelatin is dissolved. Refrigerate for a few minutes, until the mixture has cooled.

2. Add the sour cream, scallions, dill, lemon juice, and salt and whisk until blended. Return to the refrigerator and chill about 15 minutes, or until the mixture is slightly thickened. (If the mixture becomes too thick, whisk for a few seconds until smooth.)

3. While the gelatin mixture is chilling, whip the cream in a separate chilled bowl. When the gelatin mixture has chilled and thickened, stir in the salmon. Gently fold in the whipped cream and caviar.

4. Oil a 4-cup mold and transfer the mousse to it,

cover with plastic wrap, and refrigerate until firm, at least 3 hours. To serve, unmold the mousse onto a platter and garnish with dill sprigs. Serve with thinly sliced squares of pumpernickel bread or cucumber slices.

Creole Porcupines

MAKES ABOUT 6 DOZEN COOKIES

◆

⅓ cup (⅔ stick) butter, melted and cooled
1½ cups firmly packed light brown sugar
3 large eggs
1½ cups chopped dates
2 cups coarsely chopped pecans
3½ cups shredded coconut, approximately

1. Preheat the oven to 325°F. Lightly grease baking sheets.

2. Beat together the butter and sugar, then beat in the eggs. Stir in the dates, pecans, and 1½ cups of the coconut. Allow the mixture to stand 20 minutes.

3. Form the mixture into balls about ¾ inch in diameter and roll the balls in the remaining coconut to coat (use more coconut if needed).

4. Place the balls onto the baking sheets about 2 inches apart and bake until lightly browned, about 20 minutes. Cool on wire racks and store in tightly covered containers.

New Amsterdam New Year's Cookies

MAKES ABOUT 6 DOZEN, DEPENDING
ON THE SIZE OF CUTTERS

◆

I imagine that a few centuries ago these unusual cookies were being baked in a farm kitchen in my Manhattan neighborhood, and I'm happy to pick up the tradition.

2 large eggs
1¼ cups sugar
1 cup heavy cream
3 cups all-purpose flour
2 teaspoons baking powder
¼ teaspoon salt
1 teaspoon grated nutmeg
½ teaspoon ground cinnamon
4 teaspoons caraway seeds

1. In a large mixing bowl, beat the eggs until light and foamy. Gradually beat in the sugar, then beat in

the cream. In a separate bowl, sift together the flour, baking powder, salt, and spices. Gradually stir this mixture into the wet mixture, then stir in the caraway seeds. Cover the bowl and refrigerate the dough until it is firm but pliable, about 2 hours.

2. Preheat the oven to 350°F. Roll out the dough on a lightly floured surface and cut out with cookie cutters (I use star-shaped cutters). With a spatula, place the cookies on baking sheets and generously sprinkle the surface of the cookies with sugar.

3. Bake the cookies for about 10 minutes, or until the edges are lightly browned. Transfer to wire racks to cool, then store in tightly covered containers.

Peppermint-Fudge Brownies

MAKES ABOUT 5 DOZEN

BITE-SIZE BROWNIES

◆

½ cup (1 stick) butter, melted
2 squares unsweetened chocolate, coarsely chopped
2 large eggs
½ cup sugar
⅛ teaspoon salt
½ cup all-purpose flour
1 teaspoon vanilla extract
½ cup coarsely chopped peppermint stick candy

Frosting
2 tablespoons butter
4 ounces semisweet chocolate
¼ teaspoon peppermint extract
½ cup coarsely chopped peppermint stick candy

1. Preheat the oven to 325°F. Lightly grease an 8-inch square baking pan.

2. Melt the butter in a small heavy saucepan over low heat. Add the chocolate and stir until just melted. Remove from the heat, add the eggs, and beat well. Beat in the sugar and salt and then the flour. Stir in the vanilla and the candy.

3. Pour the batter into the baking pan and bake for 40 minutes, or until a cake tester comes out clean. Cool in the pan on a wire rack.

4. To make the frosting, melt the butter in a small heavy saucepan over low heat. Add the chocolate and stir until just melted. Remove from heat and stir in the peppermint extract. Spread this mixture evenly over the cooled brownies. Sprinkle the candy over the frosting. Allow the frosting to cool and set.

5. Cut the cake into 1-inch squares.

A TV Supper

FOR 8

◆

MENU

Freshly Popped Popcorn

American Beers

◆

Ohio Eight-Way Chili

◆

Hudson Valley Apple Crumb Bars

Vanilla Custard Ice Cream (page 119)
with Crushed Praline

Fan or not, no one in America can escape Super Bowl Sunday. I like to have a few friends over for this simple, relaxed winter menu that can be served easily whenever I'm ready. Popcorn should hold everyone over until halftime, which seems like the best time to serve the chili and all its accompaniments. The timing for serving dessert depends on the game; if I'm glued to the television, dessert comes afterward.

Getting Ready: The ice cream can be made a week or two ahead, no more, and stored in the freezer. The chili can be made up to three days in advance (it tastes better if made ahead) and stored in the refrigerator, or made earlier and frozen.

The crumb bars can be baked up to a day in advance, covered well, and stored in a cool place. Cut them just before serving.

Most of the chili condiments can be made ready early in the day but cut up the avocado and cook the rice and spaghetti just before serving.

Pop some popcorn while you're watching the game.

Ohio Eight-Way Chili

SERVES 8

◆

Five-way chili is a Cincinnati specialty, developed half a century ago by the cooks in Greek-owned chili parlors. In addition to the fact that the chili includes some very *un*southwestern ingredients, the classic southern Ohio five-way preparation must be layered in the following order: spaghetti, chili, kidney beans, chopped onions, and grated Cheddar cheese.

I, being from *northern* Ohio, take a more liberal approach. This chili is loosely based on the "chili soup" my mother always made and served over rice. And the eight ways here are only suggestions—anything goes. In any case, I like putting everything out as a buffet and letting my guests construct their own.

4 tablespoons vegetable oil
3 medium onions, coarsely chopped
1 cup finely diced celery
4 large garlic cloves, chopped
1 pound beef chuck, ground
1 pound lean pork, ground fine
2 16-ounce cans red kidney beans
5 cups canned tomatoes
2 large green peppers, coarsely chopped
2 teaspoons ground cumin seed
4 tablespoons chili powder
1 teaspoon ground cinnamon
½ teaspoon ground cardamom
1 bay leaf

The Eight Ways

1 pound spaghetti, broken in half, cooked, and tossed
   with 3 tablespoons olive oil
4 medium red onions, coarsely chopped
1 pound sharp Wisconsin Cheddar cheese, grated
3 cups long-grain white rice, cooked
6 cups shredded iceberg lettuce
1 pint sour cream
4 ripe avocados, coarsely chopped and tossed with the
   juice of 1 lime
   Tostados (tortilla chips)

1. Heat the oil in a large heavy kettle or Dutch oven over medium heat. Add the onion, celery, and garlic and sauté 15 minutes. Add the meats and brown.

2. Add the remaining chili ingredients and bring to a boil. Reduce the heat and simmer uncovered, stirring occasionally to prevent sticking, for 2 hours.

3. To serve, arrange the eight ways in serving bowls surrounding the pot of chili.

ABOVE: Ohio Eight-Way Chili and all the fixings are arranged buffet-style in front of the TV before halftime.

BELOW: Ohio Eight-Way Chili piled mile high.

RIGHT: A simple dessert of vanilla ice cream sprinkled with Crushed Praline and served with cinnamon-scented Hudson Valley Apple Crumb Bars.

Hudson Valley Apple Crumb Bars

MAKES ABOUT 3 DOZEN

◆

Crust

  2/3 cup (1 1/3 sticks) butter
  1 3-ounce package cream cheese, softened
  1/4 cup firmly packed dark brown sugar
  1 large egg
  1 teaspoon vanilla extract
  2 cups all-purpose flour
  1/4 teaspoon salt

Filling

  1/3 cup sugar
  2 tablespoons all-purpose flour
  1 teaspoon ground cinnamon
  1/4 teaspoon grated nutmeg
  8 cups thinly sliced tart baking apples

Topping

  1 cup all-purpose flour
  3/4 cup firmly packed dark brown sugar
  1 tablespoon ground cinnamon
  1/2 cup (1 stick) cold butter

1. Preheat the oven to 375°F. Lightly grease a jelly roll pan (approximately 10½ x 15 inches).

2. For the crust, cream the butter, cream cheese, and brown sugar together in a mixing bowl, then beat in the egg and the vanilla. Stir in the flour and salt until just blended in. Using your fingers, press the dough into the pan in an even layer.

3. For the filling, mix the sugar, flour, and spices in a small bowl and toss this mixture with the apples. Arrange the apples in an even layer over the dough.

4. For the topping, combine the flour, brown sugar, and cinnamon in a small mixing bowl. Cut in the butter until coarse crumbs are formed. Sprinkle the crumbs evenly over the apples.

5. Place the pan in the oven and bake for about 40 minutes, or until the apples are tender and the topping is nicely browned. Cool in the pan on a wire rack and cut into 2-inch-square bars.

Crushed Praline

MAKES ABOUT 1 CUP

◆

I always have a batch of this topping stashed away for sprinkling over homemade or even store-bought ice cream.

  3/4 cup sugar
  2 tablespoons water
  3/4 cup chopped pecans

1. Combine the sugar and water in a small heavy saucepan and stir over low heat until the sugar has dissolved. Raise the heat and boil rapidly without stirring until the syrup turns a light golden brown, 5 to 7 minutes.

2. Stir in the pecans, pour the mixture out onto a lightly greased baking sheet, and cool thoroughly. Chop the cooled praline fine in the bowl of a food processor fitted with the steel chopping blade. Store in a covered jar at room temperature.

Breakfast in Bed

FOR 2

◆

MENU

Cranberry Mimosas Morning Ambrosia

Quick Cinnamon Sticky Buns

I have a friend who, when asked what her favorite meal is, immediately says "room service." I agree completely. There is nothing more luxurious than breakfast in bed, but you don't have to stay in a hotel to enjoy it. This simple menu is planned so the bedcovers will still be warm by the time you climb back in with the breakfast tray, and you can indulge yourself and that very special person any day of the week.

Getting Ready: The Cranberry Mimosas are from my previous book, *The Holidays.* Simply fill Champagne flutes one quarter full with chilled cranberry juice cocktail and add chilled California Champagne to about three-quarters full. The ambrosia should be prepared the night before. The sticky buns are best prepared just before eating, but they really don't take very long. Put on a pot of coffee while the buns are baking and mix the mimosas just as you're ready to climb back into bed for breakfast.

Morning Ambrosia

SERVES 2

◆

1 small pink grapefruit, peeled, halved, and sectioned
1 tangerine, peeled and sectioned
¼ cup shredded coconut
1 tablespoon sugar

Combine the grapefruit, tangerine, coconut, and sugar and chill overnight. To serve, spoon the ambrosia into footed dessert glasses.

Quick Cinnamon Sticky Buns

MAKES ABOUT 1½ DOZEN MINIATURE BUNS

◆

To make regular-size buns, simply double the recipe and roll the dough out into an 8 x 10-inch rectangle in step 4. Extras can be frozen and rewarmed in a slow oven.

2 tablespoons butter
1 tablespoon dark brown sugar
24 pecan halves

2 tablespoons butter, softened
¼ cup sugar
1 large egg
1 cup all-purpose flour
1 teaspoon baking powder
   Pinch of salt
½ teaspoon ground cinnamon
¼ cup milk

1 tablespoon butter, melted
1 tablespoon dark brown sugar
   Cinnamon
2 tablespoons dried currants

1. To make the topping, melt the butter in a small saucepan over low heat, remove from heat, and stir in the brown sugar. Grease a 12-cup miniature muffin tin and spoon ¾ teaspoon topping into each cup. Lay 2 pecan halves into each cup. Preheat the oven to 375°F.

2. To make the dough, cream the butter and sugar together in a mixing bowl, then beat in the egg (use a fork for all mixing). In a separate bowl, sift together the flour, baking powder, salt, and cinnamon. Pour the dry mixture over the wet mixture, add the milk, and beat until all ingredients are just blended.

3. With well-floured hands, pat the dough out on a well-floured surface into a rectangle about 5 x 8 inches and ¼ inch thick. Brush the dough with the melted butter and sprinkle the sugar, cinnamon, and currants on top.

4. Roll the dough up lengthwise into a long slender cylinder. Cut the dough into ½-inch slices and gently press one slice, cut side down, into each muffin cup. Bake for about 20 minutes, or until lightly browned. Turn the pan onto a rack, rap the pan hard, and lift it off. Serve the buns warm.

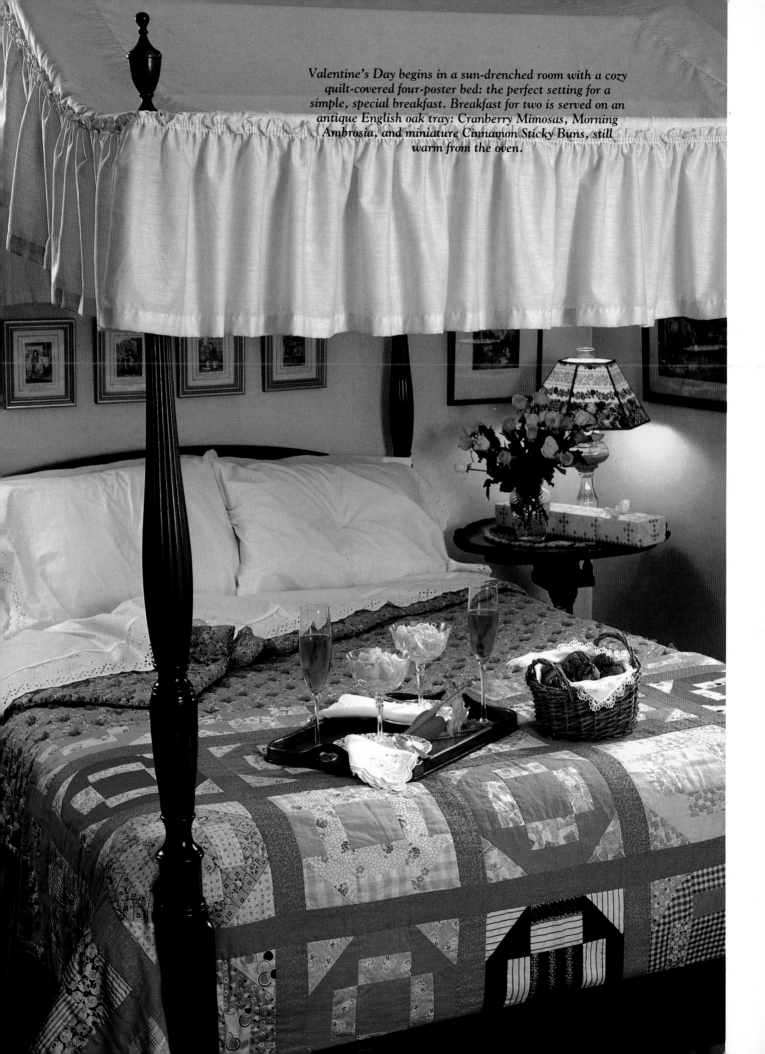

Valentine's Day begins in a sun-drenched room with a cozy quilt-covered four-poster bed: the perfect setting for a simple, special breakfast. Breakfast for two is served on an antique English oak tray: Cranberry Mimosas, Morning Ambrosia, and miniature Cinnamon Sticky Buns, still warm from the oven.

The day ends with a romantic dinner with a low table and big plump pillows set before a crackling fire. The main course, served with California Champagne, is a celebration of extravagant tastes: Roasted Quail with Hazelnut Stuffing and Pear Sauce, Asparagus Tips and Wild Mushrooms in Brown Butter, and Braised White Radishes.

A Romantic Fireside Dinner

FOR 2

◆

MENU

*Oysters on the Half Shell and Shrimp with
Tomato-Horseradish Sauce*

◆

*Roasted Quail with Hazelnut Stuffing
and Pear Sauce*

Oven-Braised White Radishes

*Asparagus Tips and Wild Mushrooms in
Brown Butter*

◆

Frozen Grapes

*Chocolate Sweethearts with Orange Custard
and Raspberries*

Outside, icy winds are blowing, but indoors a fire is glowing in the fireplace. A low table is set by the hearth and soft cushions are laid on the floor. Here's a simple dinner of extravagant tastes for that most romantic day of the year.

Getting Ready: This dinner was designed to keep the cook in the kitchen for no more than an hour on the night it is served, as long as a few things are made ahead. The Tomato-Horseradish Sauce for the first course can be made several days ahead, and it takes only a few minutes. The Chocolate Sweethearts can be made early in the day, or even a day in advance if need be, and stored, tightly wrapped, in a cool place (not refrigerated). The orange custard sauce can be made while the chocolate cakes are baking and can be stored in the refrigerator.

About an hour before serving, cook the shrimp and chill them while you make the stuffing and stuff the quail. Next, trim the asparagus and assemble the radish dish. Shuck the oysters and arrange them on a plate with the shrimp.

The quail take about half an hour to roast, so put them into the oven as you're sitting down to the first course. When you turn down the oven temperature for the quail, pop the radishes into the oven. About fifteen minutes before serving, start the asparagus and mushrooms.

Beverages: With the main course I like Champagne or a rich, full-bodied Chardonnay. Espresso goes perfectly with the richly flavored dessert, and afterward it's nice to linger over small glasses of a Late Harvest Zinfandel.

Oysters on the Half Shell and Shrimp with Tomato-Horseradish Sauce

SERVES 2

◆

½ dozen oysters, shucked and on the half shell
6 jumbo shrimp, cooked and peeled

Tomato-Horseradish Sauce
¼ cup tomato paste
¼ cup prepared horseradish
2 tablespoons lemon juice
1 tablespoon snipped chives
¼ cup vodka

Combine all sauce ingredients in a small saucepan over medium-high heat. Bring to a boil, reduce the heat, and simmer 5 minutes. Transfer to a small serving bowl and chill several hours.

Roasted Quail with Hazelnut Stuffing and Pear Sauce

SERVES 2

◆

2 quail
  Salt and freshly ground black pepper
½ cup hazelnuts
2 tablespoons butter
¼ cup finely chopped celery
1 small shallot, finely chopped
1 tablespoon finely chopped parsley
½ teaspoon dried tarragon
⅔ cup coarse fresh bread crumbs
2 very ripe pears, peeled and quartered
½ cup Madeira wine
½ cup heavy cream, at room temperature

1. Preheat the oven to 450°F. Rinse the quail in warm water, pat dry with a towel, and sprinkle inside and out with salt and pepper.

2. Place the hazelnuts on a baking sheet and toast in the oven for about 10 minutes, or until the skins split. Remove from the oven and allow to cool. Rub the nuts between your fingers to remove the skins, then coarsely chop the nuts. Reserve.

3. Melt the butter in a small skillet over medium heat; add the celery and shallot and sauté 10 minutes. Add the parsley, tarragon, bread crumbs, and reserved hazelnuts and toss well. If necessary, stir in a tablespoon or so of water to make the mixture hold together. Use this mixture to stuff the quail.

4. Place the quail, breast side up, on a rack in a small, shallow roasting pan and arrange the pear quarters around it. Pour the Madeira over the quail and dot the skin with butter. Roast 5 minutes, reduce the oven temperature to 300°F., and bake an additional 20 to 25 minutes, basting the quail and pears frequently with the pan juices.

5. Remove the quail to warmed dinner plates. Transfer the pears and pan juices to a food processor fitted with the steel chopping blade. Add the cream and puree until smooth. Spoon this sauce around the quail and serve.

Oven-Braised White Radishes

SERVES 2

◆

8 white radishes, washed and trimmed
1 tablespoon butter
2 tablespoons hot water

1. Preheat the oven to 300°F. Drop the radishes into boiling water for 30 seconds and drain. Place the radishes in a small baking pan or casserole, toss with the butter until melted, and sprinkle the water over them.

2. Place the pan in the oven, cover, and bake for 20 minutes, or until the radishes are crisp-tender. Serve immediately.

Asparagus Tips and Wild Mushrooms in Brown Butter

SERVES 2

◆

12 asparagus
¼ cup (½ stick) butter
1 teaspoon lemon juice
4 small wild mushrooms, thinly sliced

1. Trim the tender tips from the asparagus, approximately the top 2 or 3 inches (reserve the stalks for another use, such as soup).

2. Melt the butter in a skillet over medium-low heat and stir in the lemon juice. Add the mushrooms and sauté until the mushrooms begin to darken and release their liquid, about 10 minutes. Add the asparagus to the skillet and continue cooking 3 to 5 minutes, or until the asparagus are crisp-tender and a bright emerald green.

Frozen Grapes

◆

These are great as a palate-cleanser or a refreshing nibble. And there's nothing complicated to do—just loosely pack washed and dried seedless red or green grapes in a freezer container, cover, and freeze.

ABOVE: *A first course of oysters and shrimp, served with Tomato-Horseradish Sauce on a bed of watercress.*

Chocolate Sweethearts with Orange Custard and Raspberries

MAKES 2 SMALL CAKES

♦

1 large egg, at room temperature, separated
¼ cup sugar
2 ounces semisweet chocolate, melted and cooled
¼ cup (½ stick) butter, melted and cooled
1 tablespoon all-purpose flour
Orange Custard Sauce (recipe follows)
¼ cup raspberries

1. Preheat the oven to 350°F. Generously butter two small heart-shaped or round shallow pans or oven-proof molds (about ¾-cup capacity), line the bottoms with wax paper, and butter the wax paper.

2. In a small mixing bowl, beat the egg yolk and sugar until thick and lemon-colored. Gradually beat in the chocolate and butter, then beat in the flour. In a separate bowl, whisk the egg white until stiff but not dry. Fold the egg white into the chocolate mixture.

3. Spoon the batter into the prepared pans and bake for about 30 minutes, or until the center springs back when depressed with a finger. Cool the cakes in the pans and gently unmold just before serving.

4. To serve, spoon custard sauce around the cakes and garnish with raspberries.

Orange Custard

⅓ cup milk
1 large egg yolk, at room temperature
1 tablespoon sugar
¼ teaspoon vanilla extract
½ teaspoon grated orange rind

1. Scald the milk in a very small saucepan, remove from the heat, and set aside.

2. In the top of a double boiler, not yet over the heat, whisk together the egg yolk and sugar until thick and lemon-colored. Gradually whisk in the milk. Place the mixture over simmering water and cook, whisking constantly, until the custard is thick enough to coat a spoon, about 10 minutes.

3. Remove from the heat and stir in the vanilla and orange rind. Serve the sauce warm or transfer it to a small bowl, place plastic wrap directly onto the surface of the sauce, cool, and chill thoroughly.

LEFT: *For dessert, sinfully rich Chocolate Sweethearts with Orange Custard and Raspberries are served on dinner plates rimmed with heart-embossed gold bands.*

MENU

Pontchartrain Punch

*Andouille Sausage Baked in Corn Bread
with Cumin Mustard*

Cheese-Pecan Coins

◆

Salad of Bitter Greens with Red Onions

◆

Low Country Shrimp and Chicken Étouffée

Baked Green Rice

◆

*Banana-Praline Pudding with Bourbon
and Rum*

Mississippi Mud Squares

Café Brulot   Café au Lait

A Cajun Buffet Dinner

FOR 12

◆

M ardi Gras always seems to come at the right time of year, just when I'm getting a little cranky. The winter doldrums are at their lowest and spring, even though the calendar says it's just around the corner, is usually nowhere in sight. So, despite the fact that I live a thousand miles from New Orleans, I put together a Mardi Gras party, and I've got enough transplanted Louisiana friends to make the event seem authentic. One year I served this menu around Mardi Gras time

and, lacking the real festivities, we had a Mardi Gras hatmaking contest. I supplied all kinds of colored papers, foils, and feathers, along with tape and glue, and everyone went to it. I don't remember who the winner was, but I do remember that we laughed till we cried (and the food was pretty good, too).

Plan on starting late in the afternoon or early in the evening and serve dinner at a leisurely pace. To keep festivities at a fever pitch, play plenty of Dixie-

*Colorful masks, foil garlands, and votive candles, along
with beads and doubloons—souvenirs from a real Mardi
Gras celebration in New Orleans—add the spirit of
"Fat Tuesday" to a Manhattan apartment.*

land jazz, and if anyone starts to dance during dinner, don't stop them.

Getting Ready: This menu is a good one for a good-size group, because there are no fussy details to deal with just before serving. While a lot of the preparation can be done ahead, a good deal needs to be done a few hours before serving, but it leaves you relatively free from the kitchen at dinnertime.

The Cumin Mustard can be made several weeks in advance. The Cheese-Pecan Coins can be baked up to a week in advance and stored in tins.

A day in advance: bake the Mississippi Mud Squares, but do not cut until serving; bake the sausage corn bread; prepare the base for the étouffée; make the custard for the banana pudding; chill the punch ingredients.

A few hours before dinner, assemble the banana pudding (top with whipped cream no more than three hours ahead); clean salad greens and make the dressing; peel and devein the shrimp for the étouffée. As soon as guests arrive, make the punch. An hour before serving, assemble and begin baking the rice. A half hour before serving, start reheating the étouffée; add the shrimp fifteen minutes before serving. Last, dress the salad.

Beverages: With the hearty main course, I like a Medium Zinfandel. An alternative to the punch with the hors d'oeuvres and wine with the main course might be a good southern beer all the way. After dessert, serve Café Brulot or Café au Lait.

Pontchartrain Punch

SERVES 12, WITH REFILLS

◆

1 liter Southern Comfort liqueur
2 cups light rum
¼ cup fresh lemon juice
1 6-ounce can frozen concentrated limeade
1 6-ounce can frozen concentrated orange juice
¼ cup grenadine
3 liters lemon-lime soda
1 liter club soda
1 lemon, sliced
1 lime, sliced
1 orange, sliced

Have all ingredients well chilled, leaving the limeade and orange juice frozen. Combine them all in a punch bowl just before serving, adding the sodas last. Float the lemon, lime, and orange slices on top and serve.

Note: For a nonalcoholic punch, eliminate the Southern Comfort and rum and add a liter of ginger ale.

Andouille Sausage Baked in Corn Bread

MAKES ONE 8½ x 4½ x 3½-INCH LOAF

◆

Andouille is a native Louisiana smoked pork sausage that is becoming more and more available across the country. If you can't find it, kielbasa or a similar smoked sausage made in your area can be substituted.

This recipe should be doubled for this menu, but it's best to make the batter in two separate batches.

2 7½-inch lengths andouille or *kielbasa or other smoked sausage (about 1 pound)*
1⅓ cups stone-ground yellow cornmeal
⅔ cup all-purpose flour
2 teaspoons baking powder
1 teaspoon baking soda
1 teaspoon sugar
½ teaspoon salt
3 large eggs
¼ cup (½ stick) butter, melted and cooled
1 cup buttermilk

1. Prick the skin of the sausage all over with a fork and place the pieces in a skillet with water to cover over medium-high heat. Bring to the simmer, turn the heat down, and simmer for 10 minutes. Remove the sausage, wrap it in paper towels to absorb excess fat, and allow it to cool. (If the sausage is curved, flatten it with a skillet as it cools). Discard the water.

2. Preheat the oven to 425°F. Grease an 8½ x 4½ x 3½-inch loaf pan very well.

3. Combine the cornmeal, flour, baking powder, baking soda, sugar, and salt in a large mixing bowl. In a separate bowl, beat the eggs lightly with a fork, then beat in the butter and buttermilk. Using a large fork, gradually stir this mixture into the dry ingredients until just moistened throughout.

4. Pour about half the batter into the prepared pan. Lay the sausage pieces on the batter, leaving about ½ inch between them. Cover the sausage with the remaining batter. Place the pan on the center rack of the oven and bake for about 35 minutes, or until the surface of the bread is well browned and a toothpick or cake tester inserted into the center of the bread comes out clean.

5. Remove the pan from the oven, place it on a wire rack, and allow it to stand for 15 minutes. Remove the bread from the pan and cool it completely on the rack. Just before serving, cut the bread into ¼-inch-thick slices with a sharp bread knife. Serve with a crock of Cumin Mustard.

Cumin Mustard

MAKES 1½ CUPS

◆

½ cup dry mustard
¼ cup boiling water
½ cup dry white wine
½ cup white wine vinegar
1 tablespoon all-purpose flour
1 tablespoon dried cumin
¼ teaspoon cayenne pepper
1 teaspoon salt

1. Combine the mustard and water in a small bowl and let the mixture stand for 1 hour.

2. In a small heavy saucepan, combine the mustard mixture with the remaining ingredients and bring to a simmer over medium heat, stirring constantly. Lower heat and simmer, stirring constantly, until the mixture has thickened, about 5 minutes.

3. Remove from heat, transfer the mustard to a small bowl, and allow to cool. Cover tightly and refrigerate overnight.

4. Remove the mustard from the refrigerator and whisk it with a fork until smooth. Transfer the mustard to crocks or jars and store, tightly wrapped, in the refrigerator.

Cheese-Pecan Coins

MAKES ABOUT 10 DOZEN CRACKERS

◆

Coins and beads play a large part in the festivities of Mardi Gras as symbols of riches and good fortune, hence the name for these savory, crunchy crackers. Traditionally, these crackers are round like coins, but an alternative method for making more decorative shapes is given at the end of the recipe.

1 cup (2 sticks) butter, softened
1 pound sharp Cheddar cheese, finely grated
2 cups all-purpose flour
½ teaspoon salt
¼ teaspoon cayenne pepper
1¾ cups finely chopped pecans

1. Combine the butter and cheese in a large mixing bowl and mix well. Gradually blend in the flour, salt, and cayenne pepper, then blend in 1 cup of the pecans.

2. Form the dough into 4 cylinders about 1½ inches in diameter and about a foot long. Roll the cylinders in the remaining ¾ cup pecans and wrap them tightly in wax paper or plastic wrap. Chill the dough for 8 hours or overnight (or freeze it and then thaw overnight in the refrigerator).

3. Preheat the oven to 350°F. Remove the dough from the refrigerator and unwrap it. Cut the cylinders into ¼-inch slices with a sharp, wet knife. Place the slices onto lightly greased baking sheets, prick well with a fork, and bake 12 to 15 minutes, or until the crackers are lightly browned.

4. Cool the crackers on a wire rack and store them in a tightly covered container up to three weeks.

Variation Rather than shaping the dough into cylinders and rolling them in pecans, the dough may also be formed into a ball at the end of step 1. Chill and roll out into a rectangle ⅛ inch thick. Cut it into crackers with cookie cutters; stars, hearts, crescents, and diamonds are good choices for Mardi Gras.

Salad of Bitter Greens with Red Onions

SERVES 12

◆

2 cups torn chicory
2 cups torn spinach leaves
1 cup arugula leaves
1 cup watercress leaves
1 small red onion, thinly sliced and separated into rings
½ cup Red Wine Vinaigrette (page 188)

Wash and dry the greens well and toss them together with the sliced onion in a large serving bowl. Just before serving, pour the vinaigrette over the salad and toss well.

ABOVE: *To start the party off, a platter of sausage corn bread with spicy Cumin Mustard, a tray of Cheese-Pecan Coins, and Pontchartrain Punch served from a fish bowl.*

BELOW: *Low Country Shrimp and Chicken Etouffée and a mound of Baked Green Rice look wonderful in a black-and-white enamelware soup plate.*

BELOW: *Banana-Praline Pudding with Bourbon and Rum, capped with a mountain of whipped cream, and a platter of dense, chocolaty Mississippi Mud Squares.*

Low Country
Shrimp and Chicken Étouffée

SERVES 12

◆

"Étouffée" means "smothered," and the shrimp and chicken are smothered here in a piquant tomato-based sauce fragrant with onions, green peppers, celery, shallots, and herbs. It's become fashionable lately to serve shrimp in their shells, no matter what the prep-aration, but I find this a silly (and messy) pretention. Peel the shrimp before cooking, so they can mingle with the sauce.

My friend William Barnard says "The only way you know you've used enough hot pepper sauce is when your eyes burn and your nose starts to run." You be your own judge.

- ¼ cup olive oil
- 8 chicken thighs, boned but not skinned
- 8 small chicken breast halves, boned but not skinned
- ¼ cup (½ stick) butter
- ½ cup flour
- 3 medium onions, coarsely chopped
- 2 large green peppers, coarsely chopped
- 1½ cups chopped celery, stalks and leaves
- 4 shallots, finely chopped
- 1 6-ounce can tomato paste
- 4 cups chicken stock
- 1 tablespoon lemon juice
- 4 bay leaves
- 1½ teaspoons dried thyme
- ½ teaspoon freshly ground black pepper
- 1 teaspoon hot pepper sauce (or more to taste)
- 2 pounds jumbo shrimp, peeled and deveined
- ½ cup chopped parsley
- 3 scallions, white and green parts, thinly sliced
  Lemon slices

1. Pour the oil into a large Dutch oven (8 quarts) over medium-high heat and heat until oil is sizzling. A few pieces at a time, add the chicken and brown it on all sides. Remove the chicken and reserve.

2. Add the butter to the Dutch oven and turn the heat down to medium. Add the flour, stirring well to combine it with the fats. Continue stirring the mix-ture over medium heat until the flour is lightly browned, about 20 minutes, making a brown roux. Stir in the onions, green peppers, celery, and shallots and sauté for about 10 minutes.

3. Stir in the tomato paste, chicken stock, lemon juice, herbs, ground pepper, and hot pepper sauce, then stir well to blend. Simmer for about 10 minutes. Add the reserved chicken to the sauce and cook slowly, uncovered, for about 30 minutes, or until the chicken is cooked through. Stir frequently to prevent sticking. (*The étouffée may be made ahead up to this point, cooled, covered, and refrigerated. Allow it to come to room temperature before reheating.*)

4. Add the shrimp to the Dutch oven and simmer for 10 to 12 minutes, or until the shrimp turn pink. Stir in half of the chopped parsley, remove from the heat, and let stand for 10 minutes.

5. Serve the étouffée in shallow soup plates spooned around mounds of Baked Green Rice. Sprinkle the remaining chopped parsley and the sliced scallions over each serving and garnish each with a lemon slice. Pass hot pepper sauce at the table.

Baked Green Rice

SERVES 12

◆

- ¼ cup (½ stick) butter
- 6 scallions, white and green parts, finely chopped
- 3 cups long-grain rice
- 1 cup chopped parsley
- 4 cups hot, well-seasoned chicken stock
- 2 cups hot water
  Salt

1. Preheat the oven to 375°F. Put the butter in the bottom of a 3-quart flameproof casserole or Dutch oven, place over medium heat, add the scallions, and sauté until golden, about 5 minutes.

2. Add the rice and parsley to the casserole and toss to coat with the melted butter. (*May be made several hours ahead up to this point.*) Add the chicken stock, water, and salt to taste; stir well. Cover the casserole, place it in the oven, and bake for 45 to 50 minutes, or until the rice is fluffy and has absorbed all the liquid. Stir the rice gently once with a fork about halfway through the baking process. This rice will hold for an hour in a turned-off oven.

Variations This basic method for preparing baked rice can be varied in many ways to serve as an accom-paniment to simple grilled chops or fish steaks. Try any of the following:

Substitute 2 garlic cloves for the scallions, use all chicken stock rather than chicken stock and water, and stir in ¾ cup freshly grated Parmesan cheese; sauté 1 cup mushrooms, substitute 4 medium shallots for the scallions, and use beef broth instead of the chicken stock and water; add ½ cup toasted sliced almonds, ½ cup golden raisins, and 1 tablespoon curry powder; eliminate the scallions and add 2 tea-spoons grated orange rind.

Banana-Praline Pudding with Bourbon and Rum

SERVES 12

When I was a kid I always looked forward to any "potluck" occasion, because I knew Donna Carnihan would be bringing her specialty, banana pudding, a dessert well loved throughout the Midwest and the South. This is my own version, incorporating the crunch and flavor of New Orleans pralines and just a touch of "likker." Go ahead and use store-bought vanilla wafers—that's the way banana pudding is done.

Custard

1¼ cups sugar
¾ cup all-purpose flour
½ teaspoon salt
4 cups milk
8 large egg yolks
2 teaspoons vanilla extract

1 12-ounce box vanilla wafers
¼ cup light rum
¼ cup bourbon
6 very ripe bananas
1 cup Crushed Praline (page 20)
3 cups heavy cream
2 tablespoons sugar
½ teaspoon vanilla extract
  Pinch of salt
1 ounce semisweet chocolate, grated

1. To make the custard, combine the sugar, flour, and salt in the top of a double boiler. Stir in the milk, place mixture over simmering water, and bring to just below the simmering point.

2. While the milk mixture is heating, beat the egg yolks, in a mixing bowl until they thicken and lighten in color. Gradually pour the hot milk mixture into the eggs, beating continuously.

3. Pour the mixture back into the top of the double boiler and cook, stirring continuously, until the custard has thickened and thickly coats the back of the spoon. *Do not allow the custard to simmer at any point.*

4. Remove the top of the double boiler from the heat and dip it into a large bowl of cold water to stop the custard from cooking any further. Beat the custard briskly for 5 minutes to help it cool off rapidly; then beat in the 2 teaspoons vanilla. Allow the custard to cool. (*May be made up to a day ahead and stored, very tightly covered, in the refrigerator.*)

5. To assemble the pudding, spread the vanilla wafers on a sheet of wax paper. Combine the rum and bourbon and sprinkle the cookies lightly with this mixture.

6. Arrange a layer of the doused cookies in the bottom of a glass serving bowl 10 to 12 inches in diameter and 5 to 6 inches deep (a trifle bowl is perfect). Thinly slice a layer of bananas over the cookies and cover the bananas with a third of the custard. Sprinkle about one fourth of the Crushed Praline over the custard.

7. Repeat step 6 twice more, reserving the final fourth of the Crushed Praline for garnish. (*The pudding may be assembled early on the day when it will be served and stored in the refrigerator, tightly wrapped.*)

8. No more than 3 hours before serving, whip the cream in a chilled bowl until stiff peaks form, then beat in the sugar, vanilla, and salt. Spoon the whipped cream onto the assembled pudding in mounds, completely covering the top custard layer. Sprinkle the reserved Crushed Praline over the whipped cream and top with a sprinkling of grated chocolate.

Mississippi Mud Squares

MAKES 2 DOZEN 2½-INCH SQUARES

◆

Rich, dense, and a chocoholic's dream, Mississippi Mud is an old favorite in the deep South. With the addition of the classic liqueur, Southern Comfort, it becomes even more sinful. I like to serve these after dinner and dessert with coffee and liqueurs in the living room, but if you're serving them as the only dessert, top each serving with Southern Comfort-spiked whipped cream, which only adds insult to injury. In the summer, serve Mississippi Mud topped with vanilla ice cream and fresh raspberry puree.

    1 cup (2 sticks) butter
    6 squares unsweetened chocolate
    1 cup Southern Comfort liqueur
    1 cup strong coffee
    2 cups sugar
    2 cups all-purpose flour
    ¾ teaspoon baking soda
    ⅛ teaspoon salt
    1 teaspoon ground cinnamon
    2 large eggs
    1½ teaspoons vanilla extract

    1 pint heavy cream
    2 tablespoons sugar
    2 tablespoons Southern Comfort liqueur
    ¼ teaspoon vanilla extract
      Unsweetened cocoa powder, for dusting

1. Preheat the oven to 275°F. Grease a shallow rectangular baking pan (approximately 10 x 15 inches) *very well.*

2. Melt the butter in a heavy medium saucepan over low heat (or the top of a double boiler over simmering water), then add the chocolate, stirring until it is melted. Add the 1 cup Southern Comfort and the coffee and stir well to blend all ingredients. Remove the pan from the heat.

3. Gradually add the sugar to the chocolate mixture, beating constantly with a fork until the sugar is melted and blended in completely.

4. Combine the flour, baking soda, salt, and cinnamon in a small bowl, then gradually beat this mixture into the chocolate mixture. Beat the eggs lightly in a bowl, then beat them into the chocolate batter. Stir in the 1½ teaspoons vanilla until well blended.

5. Pour the batter into the prepared pan and bake for 1 hour and 10 minutes, or until the cake shrinks away from the sides of the pan and a cake tester or toothpick inserted into the center of the cake comes out clean. Remove the cake, in its pan, to a baking rack, and allow it to cool completely. Cut into 2½-inch squares just before serving.

6. No more than 3 hours before serving, whip the cream with chilled beaters in a chilled bowl until stiff peaks form, then beat in the sugar, Southern Comfort, and vanilla. Serve each cake square with a large dollop of whipped cream and a light dusting of cocoa.

Café Brulot

SERVES 12

◆

Café Brulot is a must after-dinner drink in many Louisiana dining rooms. Here's an easy method for making a big batch all at once. While the favored coffee blend in New Orleans is the local one that includes chicory, French roast coffee, available almost everywhere, is equally good.

    2 cups brandy
    ½ cup sugar
      Peel of 1 orange, cut into strips
      Peel of 1 lemon, cut into strips
    1 teaspoon whole cloves
    1 cinnamon stick, broken in half
    2 quarts hot, freshly brewed strong coffee

1. Combine all ingredients except the coffee in a small heavy saucepan over low heat and stir well to dissolve sugar. Bring mixture to just below the simmering point and then ignite. Allow the mixture to flame for 30 seconds so just part of the alcohol in the brandy burns off.

2. Pour the brandy mixture into the coffeepot and stir to blend. Serve immediately in small coffee cups.

Café au Lait

◆

There's no secret to making café au lait, the coffee that New Orleanians seem to consider essential morning, noon, and night.

Combine equal amounts of piping hot, very strong coffee and hot scalded milk, pouring them simultaneously into a warmed coffee cup, then stir in sugar to taste.

A Hearty Farmhouse Breakfast

FOR 6 TO 8

◆

MENU

Freshly Squeezed Orange Juice

Pan-Glazed Country Ham Steaks

Home-Fried Sweet Potatoes

Cornmeal Griddle Cakes

Warm Maple-Pecan Syrup

Cinnamon-Blueberry Jam (page 122)

A big breakfast in a sun-filled kitchen: All mornings should start like this, with a heaping platter of Cornmeal Griddle Cakes and Pan-Glazed Country Ham Steaks, jars of Cinnamon-Blueberry Jam and Maple-Pecan Syrup, and a bowl of Home-Fried Sweet Potatoes.

When I was growing up, we always celebrated the first signs of spring. The birds would begin returning to the north, the maple sap would start running, the winter snows would begin melting away to reveal small green patches of grass, and the cows would start wending their way back to the pastures. The sprouting of the first crocus, the blossoming of the first forsythia, and the greening of the weeping willow out back were signals to open the windows and

let in some of that first clean, fresh spring air. We always knew that spring had "officially" arrived when, on the first warm day, my mother would serve breakfast on the big screened-in back porch.

This breakfast is like those special ones we had then. Our own ham, sliced and fried up in a skillet, sweet potatoes from the root cellar, Mom's homemade jam, and the first precious maple syrup of the season gave us all a wonderful feeling of well-being and anticipation of the next season's coming abundance.

Getting Ready: The syrup can be made a few days ahead.

First thing before breakfast, put on a big pot of coffee. If you keep a few skillets going on the stove, this menu can be prepared in less than an hour. Start the sweet potatoes first, since they take the longest. Mix the batter for the griddle cakes and start cooking them and the ham. Keep them warm in a low oven while you start the next batch. Pour the syrup into a small heavy saucepan and warm it over very low heat.

Pan-Glazed Country Ham Steaks

SERVES 6 TO 8

◆

3 to 4 tablespoons bacon fat or butter
6 to 8 ¾-inch ham slices, about ⅓ pound each
¼ cup apple or orange juice

Melt the fat in a large skillet (or two skillets) over medium-high heat. Add the ham and sauté on both sides until browned. Add the juice, turn the heat up to high, and continue cooking until most of the juice has evaporated and the ham is glazed.

Home-Fried Sweet Potatoes

SERVES 6 TO 8

◆

4 large sweet potatoes
3 tablespoons bacon fat or butter
1 small onion, chopped
2 to 3 tablespoons brown sugar

1. Place whole sweet potatoes in a large pot with water to cover. Salt the water and place the pot over high heat. Parboil the sweet potatoes 10 minutes.

2. Peel the sweet potatoes and cut them into ⅛-inch-thick slices. Heat the fat in a large skillet until sizzling, add the onion and sweet potatoes, and sauté until sweet potatoes are well browned. Add more fat if necessary.

Cornmeal Griddle Cakes

MAKES ABOUT 3 DOZEN MINIATURE PANCAKES

◆

1½ cups stone-ground yellow cornmeal
½ cup all-purpose flour
2 tablespoons sugar
2 teaspoons baking powder
1 teaspoon salt
3 large eggs
1½ cups milk
4 tablespoons butter, melted

1. Preheat a large skillet or griddle over medium-high heat.

2. In a large mixing bowl sift together the cornmeal, flour, sugar, baking powder, and salt. In a separate bowl, blend together the eggs, milk, and butter, then gently stir the wet mixture onto the cornmeal mixture until just moistened. Do not overmix; the batter should be somewhat lumpy.

3. Test the griddle by splashing a few drops of water onto it. If the water sizzles, the griddle is ready. Lightly grease the griddle and drop batter by tablespoonfuls onto it, several inches apart. Cook until the surface of the griddle cake begins to bubble, 3 to 4 minutes. Turn and cook an additional 2 or 3 minutes, or until lightly browned.

4. Serve immediately or keep warm while making more by placing onto a baking sheet in a single layer in a warm oven.

Corn Pancakes Add 1 cup raw corn kernels and cook as large pancakes, using 3 tablespoons batter for each. Serve with plain maple syrup or honey.

Warm Maple-Pecan Syrup

MAKES ABOUT 2 CUPS

◆

1¾ cups pure maple syrup
¼ cup coarsely chopped pecans

Combine all ingredients in a small heavy saucepan, place over low heat, and simmer gently for 5 minutes. Pour the syrup into a bottle or jar, cover tightly, cool, and refrigerate for 2 or 3 days. Gently rewarm in a small heavy saucepan before serving.

A Dinner to Celebrate Spring

FOR 8

◆

MENU

*Chilled Steamed Asparagus with
Chervil Dressing*

◆

*Roasted Herb-Stuffed Leg of Lamb with
Pan-Roasted New Potatoes and Baby Onions*

Sugar Snap Peas with Morels

◆

*Bittersweet Lemon Tart
with Almond Shortbread Crust*

Maple-Walnut Tart

Come spring, I can't wait for the outdoor Greenmarket to open on Union Square in Manhattan. I love to get up early in the morning and walk through the market to see the just-picked early produce that the farmers of rural New Jersey, eastern Long Island, and upstate New York have brought in and set up in abundant displays. Even in the country, it's hard to find the incredible selection and impeccable quality that can be found at the Greenmarket.

This dinner is composed of some of the first spring flavors I find at the market—tender young vegetables and fresh herbs, along with succulent young lamb, and in the dessert, freshly tapped maple syrup.

Getting Ready: The tarts can be made early in the day, or even a day in advance. The lamb should be marinated the day before serving.

The lamb goes into the oven about three hours before serving; add the potatoes and onions about an hour before serving. The asparagus can be steamed and the dressing made in the morning or as close as an hour in advance. Begin cooking the peas and morels about ten minutes before you want to serve them.

Beverages: Try a Chardonnay with the first course, followed by a Cabernet Sauvignon or medium-bodied Merlot with the main course.

Chilled Steamed Asparagus with Chervil Dressing

SERVES 8

◆

One of the sure signs of spring when I was young was wild asparagus growing abundantly along the back roads. They were very thin, tender, and incredibly flavorful—if you ever have the chance to eat wild ones, don't pass it up.

    Juice of 2 lemons
 2 *tablespoons chopped chervil*
 1 *large egg yolk*
 ⅔ *cup olive oil*
 2 *pounds tender young asparagus*

1. Whisk together the lemon juice, chervil, and egg yolk in a small bowl. Gradually whisk in the oil until the mixture is creamy and smooth. Cover and chill. Whisk for a minute or so just before serving.

2. Trim the asparagus of any fibrous ends and steam it in a vegetable steamer over simmering water until it is crisp-tender and turns a bright emerald green, no more than 5 minutes. Remove to a colander and place under cold running water until it is cool. Drain the asparagus and chill it until serving time.

3. To serve, arrange asparagus spears on a salad plate and drizzle a small amount of dressing over them.

Roasted Herb-Stuffed Leg of Lamb,
Pan-Roasted New Potatoes and Baby Onions,
and Sugar Snap Peas with Morels.

Chilled Steamed Asparagus with Chervil Dressing.

Maple-Walnut Tart served with whipped cream.

Roasted Herb-Stuffed Leg of Lamb with Pan-Roasted New Potatoes and Baby Onions

SERVES 8 TO 10

◆

A leg of young lamb soaked in a simple marinade, stuffed with a delicate mixture of herbs, and then roasted is a wonderful way to welcome spring. The most difficult and time-consuming part of this recipe is boning and trimming the lamb, so I let my butcher earn his keep by having him do the dirty work. Rolling and tying the lamb isn't tedious as long you use a little patience and care.

1 6-pound leg of lamb, boned and trimmed

Marinade
> 1 cup dry white wine
> ¼ cup fresh lemon juice
> ½ cup light olive oil
> 3 medium shallots, finely chopped
> ½ teaspoon salt
> ½ teaspoon freshly ground black pepper

Stuffing
> 1 cup fine dry bread crumbs
> ½ cup chopped parsley
> ¼ cup chopped fresh mint
> 2 teaspoons fresh or 1 teaspoon dried rosemary leaves
> 6 scallions, white and green parts, finely chopped
> ½ cup (1 stick) butter, melted
> 1 large egg

> 2 pounds small new potatoes
> 1½ pounds baby yellow onions, peeled
> Parsley or mint, for garnish

1. Place the lamb in a shallow bowl. Combine the marinade ingredients in a small bowl, blend them well, and pour them over the lamb. Cover tightly and refrigerate for 6 hours or overnight.

2. About 1 hour before roasting, remove the lamb from the refrigerator. About 20 minutes before roasting, preheat the oven to 450°F. Oil a shallow roasting pan.

3. Remove the lamb to a clean work surface and pat it dry with paper towels. Reserve the marinade for the potatoes (step 6). Combine the stuffing ingredients in a small bowl and mix well. Spread the stuffing out in a thin layer over the surface of the lamb.

4. To roll the lamb, turn it so one edge is parallel to the edge of the work surface. Roll the edge away from you over the stuffing, keeping the roll as tight as possible. Secure the roll temporarily with trussing skewers and then tie it at 2-inch intervals with kitchen string.

5. Remove the skewers, place the lamb, edge down, in the pan, and insert a meat thermometer. Place the lamb in the oven and reduce the oven temperature to 325°F. Roast for 2 to 2½ hours for rare to medium rare (20 to 25 minutes a pound, or until the thermometer reads 160°F.); about 3 hours for well done (30 minutes a pound, or until the thermometer reads 180°F.).

6. Immediately after placing the lamb in the oven, scrub the potatoes well under cold running water. Using a sharp knife or a vegetable peeler, cut away a strip of skin about ¼ inch wide around each potato. Place the potatoes and the peeled baby onions in a nonmetallic bowl and pour the reserved marinade over them. Cover the bowl and set aside.

7. About 1 hour before the lamb will be done, remove it from the oven. Remove the potatoes and onions from the marinade and arrange them in an even layer around the lamb. Baste the vegetables with the pan juices, then return the pan to the oven. After 30 minutes, turn the potatoes so they brown evenly, then continue roasting until the lamb is done.

8. When the lamb is done, remove it to a carving board and allow it to rest for 20 minutes. Slice the lamb into ½-inch slices to serve.

Sugar Snap Peas with Morels

SERVES 8

◆

My brothers and I used to hunt for morels in the back woods behind the farm right after the spring rains; nowadays I hunt for them every spring at the Greenmarket.

> ¼ cup (½ stick) butter
> 16 small morels, washed and patted dry
> 2 pounds sugar snap peas, trimmed and washed

Melt the butter in a medium skillet over medium heat and add the morels. Sauté the morels until tender and darkened, about 10 minutes. Add the sugar snap peas to the skillet and continue sautéing a few minutes longer, until the peas are crisp-tender and a bright emerald green. Serve immediately.

Bittersweet Lemon Tart with Almond Shortbread Crust

MAKES ONE 9½-INCH TART

◆

The refreshing flavor of lemon is as fresh as spring and satisfies my yearning for the fresh fruit that won't be available until later on in the year. I've always loved lemon pies—from lemon chess to lemon meringue—and this tart, with a toothsome almond shortbread crust and a surprise hint of bittersweet chocolate under the lemon filling, is my latest favorite.

Almond Shortbread Crust
  1 cup all-purpose flour
  ¼ teaspoon salt
  ¼ cup confectioners' sugar
  ⅓ cup ground almonds
  ½ cup (1 stick) butter, melted and cooled
  ½ teaspoon almond extract

  1½ squares bittersweet chocolate

Lemon Filling
  1 cup granulated sugar
  2 tablespoons flour
  ½ teaspoon baking powder
  3 large eggs, lightly beaten
  Juice of 1 lemon
  Grated rind of 1 lemon

  Confectioners' sugar, for decorating

1. Preheat the oven to 350°F. Lightly butter a 9½-inch tart pan with a removable bottom (or use a 9-inch pie pan).

2. To make the crust, sift together the flour, salt, and confectioners' sugar in a small mixing bowl. Blend in the almonds, and then beat in the cooled melted butter and almond extract until thoroughly combined, forming a thick dough.

3. Using your fingers, press the dough into the tart pan, evenly lining the bottom and sides. Place the pan in the oven and bake for 15 to 20 minutes, or until lightly browned, and then transfer the tart pan to a wire rack.

4. While the crust is prebaking, melt the chocolate in a small, heavy saucepan over low heat or in the top of a double boiler over simmering water. While the crust is still warm, brush the chocolate in an even layer over it, coating the bottom completely, and allow the chocolate to cool.

5. To make the filling, sift the granulated sugar, flour, and baking powder together in a small mixing bowl, and then beat in the eggs, lemon juice, and lemon rind. Pour this mixture into the cooled, chocolate-coated crust.

6. Carefully return the filled crust to the oven and bake for about 20 minutes, or until the filling is set and very lightly browned. Remove to the wire rack and allow the tart to cool completely. Remove the outer ring of the tart pan, leaving the tart on the pan bottom.

7. To decorate the tart, center a round paper doily on it and lightly sprinkle confectioners' sugar over it, gently holding the doily down against the tart's surface with your other hand. Carefully remove the doily, leaving a lacy pattern of sugar on the tart. Transfer the tart to a serving plate or cakestand and decorate with a perfect spring blossom just before serving.

Maple-Walnut Tart

MAKES ONE 11-INCH TART

◆

I can't think of a better way to make use of the first syrup of the season. Serve thin slivers of this rich tart with dollops of unsweetened whipped cream.

  Basic Pastry for a 10-inch pie (page 188)
  3 large eggs
  1 cup sugar
  ¼ teaspoon salt
  ⅓ cup (⅔ stick) butter, melted and cooled
  1 cup maple syrup
  1 teaspoon vanilla extract
  1 cup chopped walnuts

1. Preheat the oven to 450°F. Line an 11-inch tart tin with the pastry and line it with aluminum foil weighted with dry beans. Bake the pastry crust for 7 minutes and remove from the oven. Place the crust on a wire rack, remove the beans and foil, and cool. Reduce the oven temperature to 375°F.

2. In a mixing bowl beat together all the remaining ingredients except the walnuts until thoroughly blended. Stir in the walnuts.

3. Place the crust on the oven rack and carefully spoon the filling into it (this is easier than filling the crust first and then transferring it to the oven.) Bake for 35 to 40 minutes, or until a knife inserted in the filling comes out clean. Remove the tart to a wire rack to cool. Serve warm or at room temperature.

OSCAR NIGHT

"Hooray for Hollywood" Buffet Supper

FOR 10 TO 12

◆

MENU

Hollywood Popcorn
Beverly Hills "Pizzas"
Brown Derby Cobb Salad

◆

Orange Cookie Stars (page 105)
Macadamia Nut Brownies
White Zinfandel Ice

ABOVE: *A big bowl of spicy and nutty Hollywood Popcorn.*

RIGHT: *Colorful Beverly Hills "Pizzas," each topped with a different combination of garnishes, are great finger foods.*

Brown Derby Cobb Salad combines an unusual mixture of flavors and textures.

Macadamia Nut Brownies—the best ones ever.

LEFT: Tall glasses of White Zinfandel Ice topped with Orange Cookie Stars, with one of my favorite cookie jars, commemorating one of Hollywood's legends.

When I moved to New York, I discovered that "Oscar" parties, where a group gathers to watch the annual televised Academy Awards presentations, are a popular form of entertaining. A good group of friends can help make even the most uneventful show more fun as they argue over who really gave the best performance or why X wasn't nominated, or even wonder why Z was chosen as a presenter, having never appeared in anything but TV game shows.

This menu is an eclectic one, and is loosely California-inspired in honor of the locale of the event. Little "pizzas" and a composed Cobb Salad comprise the main course, which, once the advance preparation is done, can be served pretty quickly. The dessert course can likewise be served whenever you're ready.

Getting Ready: The Oscars are always televised on a Monday night, leaving Sunday to do all the advance preparation. The sauce and the toast bases for the pizzas can be made then, or made well in advance, the toasts stored in tins and the sauce frozen. The cookies and brownies, too, can be made either a day ahead or earlier and frozen. The ice, of course, should be made at least a day, but no more than a week, ahead. Poach the chicken breasts, hard-boil the eggs, and cook the bacon for the salad a day ahead. Also toast the nuts for the popcorn.

On the night of the party, assemble the pizza toppings in individual small bowls and cover them. Prepare and assemble the salad ingredients and make the dressing. As soon as the first guest arrives, enlist him or her as a helper to assemble the pizzas.

Beverages: I like to offer a few hearty, inexpensive California jug wines; nothing so delicate that it would be overpowered by the food. Sodas and beers are an alternative.

Hollywood Popcorn

MAKES 2 QUARTS

◆

Popcorn and the movies go hand-in-hand, so it seems only natural to munch it while watching "the Oscars."

- 1 cup slivered almonds
- ½ cup (1 stick) butter
- 2 tablespoons snipped chives
- 2 teaspoons ground cumin
- ½ teaspoon cayenne pepper
- 2 quarts freshly popped popcorn
  Salt

1. Preheat the oven to 350°F. Place the almonds in an even layer on a baking sheet and toast until lightly browned, about 10 minutes.

2. Melt the butter in a small skillet and stir in the chives, cumin, and cayenne.

3. Place the popcorn in a serving bowl and add the almonds. Pour the butter mixture over and toss well to coat. Add salt to taste and serve.

Beverly Hills "Pizzas"

SERVES 12

◆

- 2 loaves good-quality white bread, thinly sliced
  Olive oil

Sauce

- 2 tablespoons olive oil
- 1 large garlic clove, finely chopped
- 1 medium onion, finely chopped
- 1 28-ounce can imported crushed plum tomatoes
- 1 6-ounce can tomato paste
- 1 tablespoon fresh oregano leaves or 1 teaspoon dried oregano
- 2 teaspoons sugar

Toppings

- 1½ pounds whole milk mozzarella cheese, shredded
- ½ pound soft goat cheese
  Tiny broccoli flowerets
  Steamed asparagus tips
  Strips of sun-dried tomatoes
  Thinly sliced wild mushrooms
  Sliced black California olives
  Julienned green pepper
  Sliced artichoke hearts
  Strips of pimiento
  Thinly sliced pepperoni
  Anchovy fillets, halved lengthwise

1. Preheat the oven to 300°F. Cut the bread into quarters, either strips or triangles. Brush both sides of the bread very lightly with olive oil and arrange on baking sheets. Toast until the bread begins to dry out and the edges are lightly brown, 15 to 20 minutes. Cool on wire racks and store in tightly covered containers at room temperature up to 2 weeks.

2. To make the sauce, place the oil, garlic, and onion in the bottom of a heavy saucepan over medium heat and sauté 5 minutes. Add the tomatoes, tomato paste, oregano, and sugar and simmer uncovered, stirring occasionally, until thick and smooth, about 30 minutes. Cool. (*Sauce may be made several days in advance and stored in the refrigerator or made far in advance and frozen.*)

3. Just before serving, preheat the oven to 400°F. Arrange the bread on baking sheets. Generously brush the surface of each piece of bread with the sauce and cover with mozzarella or goat cheese.

4. Enlisting a helper or two, assemble the "pizzas" by arranging a different assortment of toppings on each. *(The pizzas may be assembled an hour or so in advance and covered tightly with plastic wrap.)* Bake the pizzas for about 10 minutes, or until the cheese has melted.

Brown Derby Cobb Salad

SERVES 12

◆

This salad offers a wide spectrum of flavors and textures. According to legend, it was created in 1936 by Robert Cobb at the Brown Derby restaurant at the corner of Hollywood and Vine, apparently improvised from the contents of the refrigerator. You can vary the ingredients according to your own taste, but the list here is pretty much the classic.

- ½ head iceberg lettuce, shredded
- 1 head romaine, shredded
- 2 cups spinach, shredded
- 1 bunch watercress, stems removed and shredded
  Red Wine Vinaigrette (page 188)
- 3 large chicken breast halves, poached and cut into strips
- 8 slices of smoked bacon, cooked and crumbled
- 4 large eggs, hard-boiled and coarsely chopped
- 3 scallions, white and green parts, cut into ¼-inch lengths
- 3 ounces blue cheese, crumbled
- 3 ripe tomatoes, seeded and coarsely chopped
- 2 ripe avocados, peeled, sliced, and tossed with the juice of 1 lime

Place the greens in the bottom of a large shallow bowl and toss with ½ cup of the vinaigrette. Arrange the remaining ingredients in rows or in some other pattern over the greens. Toss the salad at the table and serve. Pass additional dressing and the pepper grinder.

Macadamia Nut Brownies

MAKES ABOUT 18

◆

These are just about the fudgiest brownies there are, since they have so little flour in them. The flavor and texture of macadamia nuts complements this fudginess perfectly.

- 2 squares unsweetened chocolate
- ½ cup (1 stick) butter
- 1 cup sugar
- 2 large eggs
- ½ teaspoon vanilla extract
- ¼ cup all-purpose flour
- ¼ teaspoon salt
- 1 cup coarsely chopped macadamia nuts

1. Preheat the oven to 325°F. Butter an 8-inch square baking pan.

2. Melt the chocolate and butter in a heavy saucepan over low heat or in the top of a double boiler over simmering water. Remove the pan from the heat and stir in the sugar. Gradually beat in the eggs and then beat in the vanilla. Stir in the flour, salt, and nuts.

3. Transfer the batter to the prepared pan and bake for about 40 minutes, or until the cake comes slightly away from the edges of the pan. Remove to a wire rack and cool. Cut into 1½-inch squares before serving.

White Zinfandel Ice

SERVES 12

◆

- 3 cups sugar
- 3 cups water
- 3 cups white Zinfandel
- 2 cups white grape juice
  Juice of 2 lemons

1. Combine the sugar and water in a saucepan and bring to a boil. Simmer for 5 minutes. Stir in the Zinfandel and simmer 5 minutes longer. Remove from the heat and cool to room temperature.

2. Stir in the grape juice and lemon juice. If using an ice cream maker, freeze according to the manufacturer's instructions. Or freeze as follows.

3. Pour the mixture into a shallow metal pan and place in the freezer. Freeze for 4 hours, breaking up the layers of ice with a fork once an hour. Remove the pan from the freezer and cut the ice into chunks. In batches, place the chunks in a blender or the bowl of a food processor fitted with the steel chopping blade. Blend at low speed or process using short pulses until the mixture becomes smooth. Return to the pan and freeze until firm.

A Comforting Supper

FOR 4 TO 6

◆

MENU

Baked Tomato Spaghetti

Wilted Lettuce with Hot Bacon Dressing

◆

*Steamed Chocolate Pudding
with Brandy and Almond Whipped Cream*

A rich and fragrant slice of Steamed Chocolate Pudding is served with a big dab of almond-flavored whipped cream spiked with brandy.

Special occasions don't always have to mean happy ones, and April 15 is not exactly my favorite day of the year. But I'm always one for making the best of any situation, so I offer this supper of easy and wonderfully comforting foods to help pull in the purse strings and to make swallowing the pill just a little bit easier.

Getting Ready: The spaghetti can be assembled and the salad greens can be washed and torn a few hours in advance. The chocolate pudding should be begun about three hours before serving or made a day in advance and reheated a half hour before serving. Make the salad dressing and whip the cream for the pudding just before serving.

Beverages: With the main course, I like either beer or a dry red wine, such as an inexpensive Zinfandel or Barbera. With the dessert, a bracing cup of strong hot coffee, and afterward maybe a snifter of good brandy.

Baked Tomato Spaghetti

SERVES 4 TO 6

◆

Don't try to gussy up this humble old-fashioned dish; its beauty lies in its honest simplicity.

> 1 pound spaghetti
> 2 28-ounce cans tomatoes
> ½ pound sharp Cheddar cheese, coarsely grated
> ⅓ cup (⅔ stick) butter, cut into ½-inch slices

1. Cook the spaghetti in boiling salted water until *al dente* and drain it well. Preheat the oven to 350°F. and generously butter a 2-quart baking dish.

2. Place the tomatoes in a bowl and crush them against the side of the bowl with the back of a large spoon; reserve. Arrange a third of the spaghetti in the bottom of the baking dish, followed by a third of the tomatoes, a third of the grated cheese, and a third of the butter. Continue layering with the remaining ingredients, ending with butter.

3. Bake 50 to 60 minutes until the top is very well browned (the crusty top is the best part).

OPPOSITE: *There's nothing more satisfying than a mound of Baked Tomato Spaghetti served with Wilted Lettuce with Hot Bacon Dressing.*

Wilted Lettuce with Hot Bacon Dressing

SERVES 6

◆

6 *thin slices bacon, coarsely chopped*
3 *tablespoons cider vinegar*
1 *teaspoon sugar*
½ *teaspoon freshly ground black pepper*
2 *heads Boston lettuce, washed and torn into bite-size pieces*

1. Place the bacon in a skillet over medium heat and cook until crisp, about 10 minutes. Add the vinegar, sugar, and pepper to the skillet and bring to a boil.

2. Place the lettuce in a serving bowl, pour the dressing over it, and toss quickly to distribute the dressing. Serve immediately.

Steamed Chocolate Pudding with Brandy and Almond Whipped Cream

SERVES 6 GENEROUSLY

◆

One of the most comforting of comfort foods. Serve it immediately after reading the bottom line of your income tax return.

¼ *cup (½ stick) butter*
3 *ounces semisweet chocolate*
1 *cup sugar*
2 *large eggs*
⅔ *cup milk*
2 *teaspoons vanilla extract*
1½ *cups all-purpose flour*
¼ *teaspoon salt*
2 *teaspoons baking powder*
1 *teaspoon baking soda*

1 *pint heavy cream*
2 *tablespoons confectioners' sugar*
¼ *cup brandy*
¼ *teaspoon almond extract*
½ *cup slivered almonds, toasted*

1. Melt the butter and chocolate in a large heavy saucepan over low heat, stirring occasionally. Remove from the heat, beat in the sugar, and allow to cool 15 minutes. Put on a kettle of water to boil.

2. Beat the eggs into the chocolate mixture, and then the milk and vanilla. In a small mixing bowl, sift together the flour, salt, baking powder, and baking soda; gradually beat this into the wet mixture until just blended in.

3. Transfer the batter to a well-greased 6-cup pudding mold and cover with the lid. Place the mold in a large pot and pour boiling water halfway up the sides of the mold. Cover the pot and place it over medium-high heat. Steam the pudding, keeping the water at a gentle boil, for 2 hours. Replenish the pot with more boiling water as necessary. Allow the pudding to cool for half an hour before serving. (*The pudding can be made ahead, cooled completely, and stored in the mold in the refrigerator; bring to room temperature and then reheat by steaming for about half an hour.*)

4. Whip the cream until soft peaks form, beat in the confectioners' sugar, and gently fold in the brandy and almond extract. Unmold the pudding and cut it into thick slices. Garnish each serving with a generous dollop of the whipped cream and a sprinkling of toasted almonds.

A Special Dinner for Mom

FOR 8

◆

MENU

Hot Buttermilk Biscuits

Roasted Loin of Pork with Garlic, Apples, and Thyme

Pan-Roasted Baby Carrots

Sautéed Cabbage and Egg Noodles

Spring Vegetable Salad

◆

Rhubarb-Pineapple Crumble

The second Sunday of May was set aside by President Wilson in 1914 as a national holiday to honor America's mothers. The idea of Mother's Day was first conceived by Anna Jarvis in 1907, and was celebrated for the first time in May 1908. Even though the day has become a major excuse for greeting card companies to peddle their wares, we can still celebrate it with the original simple sentiments.

I suppose I could write pages of wonderful things about my mother, but I'll stick to one sentence: "My mother is just about perfect." This dinner, which should please just about any mother, is composed of Mom's favorite dishes.

Getting Ready: Though most of the preparation for this dinner should be done on the same day, this is an easy menu to prepare.

The fruit for the crumble can be pared a day in advance, covered tightly, and stored in the refrigera-

tor. Bake the crumble early on the day of serving.

The vegetables for the salad can be pared and cooked, the lettuce washed and torn, and the dressing made early in the day.

The pork should be begun about two and one-half hours before serving. The carrots should be assembled and put into the oven about an hour before serving. Begin cooking the noodles and cabbage about one hour before serving. After taking the roast and carrots out of the oven, turn the oven to low and reheat the crumble.

Beverages: For the non-wine drinkers, serve a hard or sweet cider; for the wine drinkers, a light-bodied dry Grênache Rosé or Gamay.

Hot Buttermilk Biscuits

MAKES ABOUT 1 DOZEN

◆

Hot-from-the-oven homemade biscuits take only a few minutes to make, so I can't imagine why anyone would want to bake those hot-air things that come in a cardboard can.

> 2 cups all-purpose flour
> 2 teaspoons baking powder
> ½ teaspoon baking soda
> ½ teaspoon sugar
> ½ teaspoon salt
> ¼ cup (½ stick) butter
> ¼ cup vegetable shortening
> ¾ cup buttermilk

1. Preheat the oven to 450°F. Lightly grease a baking sheet.

2. In a mixing bowl, blend together the flour, baking powder, baking soda, sugar, and salt. Using two knives or a pastry blender, cut in the butter and shortening until the mixture resembles coarse meal. Pour the buttermilk over the mixture and stir with a fork until just blended in, forming a soft dough.

3. Turn the dough out onto a floured work surface and, with floured hands, knead the dough for half a minute. Pat the dough into a rectangle about ½ inch thick and cut out biscuits with a floured 2-inch biscuit cutter or a decorative cookie cutter and place about an inch apart on the baking sheet.

4. Bake the biscuits until golden brown, about 15 minutes. Serve hot with sweet butter.

ABOVE: Heirloom silver and vibrant African violets against the backdrop of a treasured family quilt provide the perfect setting for Mother's Day dinner.

RIGHT: The main course is served family-style on a big ironstone platter.

ABOVE: Roasted Loin of
Pork with Garlic, Apples,
and Thyme; Pan-Roasted
Baby Carrots; Sautéed
Cabbage and Egg Noodles;
a Buttermilk Biscuit; and
a salad of spring
vegetables.

LEFT: Mom's favorite
spring dessert, Rhubarb-
Pineapple Crumble, baked
in a heart-shaped,
ovenproof glass pan.

Roasted Loin of Pork with Garlic, Apples, and Thyme

SERVES 8

◆

2 tablespoons vegetable oil
1 5-pound boned and rolled pork loin roast
2 tablespoons butter
8 large garlic cloves, finely chopped
3 large tart baking apples, peeled and thickly sliced
1 tablespoon fresh thyme leaves or 1 teaspoon dried thyme
Salt and freshly ground black pepper
2 tablespoons cider vinegar
¾ cup applejack or apple cider
Thyme sprigs, for garnish

1. Preheat the oven to 350°F. Place the oil in a flameproof casserole or Dutch oven and place over medium-high heat. When the oil is hot, add the pork roast to the pan and brown it on all sides. Remove the roast and reserve.

2. Add the butter to the pan, and when it has melted add the garlic and apples. Reduce the heat to low, cover the pan, and cook for 10 minutes, stirring occasionally.

3. Press the thyme onto the surface of the roast, season it with salt and pepper, and return it to the pan. Place in the preheated oven and roast for about 1¾ hours, or until the pork is tender and cooked through; baste the roast occasionally with the pan juices.

4. Remove the pan from the oven. Transfer the roast to a cutting board and cover it loosely with foil. Stir the vinegar and applejack or cider into the pan and place the pan over medium-high heat. Cook, gently stirring the mixture, until the liquid is reduced and thickened, 10 to 15 minutes. Season with salt and pepper to taste.

5. To serve, remove the strings and excess fat from the roast and cut it into ½-inch-thick slices. Spoon the sauce over each serving and garnish with sprigs of thyme.

Pan-Roasted Baby Carrots

SERVES 8

◆

This simple preparation is ideal for fresh baby carrots, allowing their delicate flavor to shine.

2 pounds baby carrots, peeled
1 teaspoon dried basil
¼ cup chicken stock
¼ cup (½ stick) butter

Preheat the oven to 350°F. Place the carrots in a shallow baking dish and sprinkle the basil over them. Pour the chicken stock over the carrots and dot them with butter. Cover the casserole loosely and roast for 45 minutes, or until the carrots are very tender.

Sautéed Cabbage and Egg Noodles

SERVES 8

◆

8 ounces egg noodles
¼ pound sliced smoked bacon, coarsely chopped
1 medium onion, coarsely chopped
5 cups shredded cabbage
1 teaspoon caraway seeds
Salt and freshly ground black pepper

1. Put a large pot of salted water onto the stove and bring to a boil. Add the noodles, cook until *al dente* (time depends on thickness of noodles), and drain.

2. Meanwhile, brown the bacon in a large heavy skillet over medium heat. Add the onion and sauté 10 minutes, or until tender. Add the cabbage to the skillet and continue sautéing until crisp-tender, about 8 minutes.

3. Stir in the cooked and drained noodles and the caraway seeds, toss well to mix, lower heat, and cook an additional 5 minutes. Season with salt and pepper to taste and serve.

Spring Vegetable Salad

SERVES 8

◆

1 pound asparagus
1 pound sugar snap peas
3 cups torn leaf lettuce
1 cup Red Wine Vinaigrette (page 188)

Trim the asparagus and cut it into 1½-inch lengths. Place the asparagus and peas in a vegetable steamer over simmering water, cover, and steam 5 minutes, or until crisp-tender and a vivid emerald green. Remove from heat, rinse with cold water, drain, and chill. Just before serving, toss all the ingredients together in a salad bowl.

Rhubarb-Pineapple Crumble

SERVES 8

◆

On our farm, the rhubarb grew along a picket fence next to the smokehouse, and among the tall, lush stalks grew delicate lilies-of-the-valley—one of my favorite signs of spring. When we were kids, we used to just snap off the rhubarb stalks, run into the kitchen for the salt shaker, and then sit out on the back stoop and dig in!

Mom's favorite way of eating rhubarb is this sweet and tart crumble, served warm from the oven with whipped cream.

4 cups diced rhubarb (see note)
1 large ripe pineapple, cored and cut into ½-inch cubes or 2 20-ounce cans cubed pineapple, drained
1½ cups sugar
2½ cups all-purpose flour
1 cup (2 sticks) butter

1. Preheat the oven to 375°F. Butter a shallow 2-quart baking pan, preferably ovenproof glass or ceramic.

2. Place the rhubarb, pineapple, and ½ cup of the sugar in a saucepan over medium heat and cook, stirring occasionally, until the fruit begins to release its juices and a syrup begins to form, about 10 minutes. Transfer the fruit mixture to the prepared baking pan.

3. In a mixing bowl, sift the flour and remaining 1 cup sugar together, then cut in the butter, forming coarse crumbs. Sprinkle the crumbs over the fruit and bake until the crumbs are well browned, about 40 minutes. Serve warm with sweetened whipped cream.

Note: If the rhubarb is tender, there is no need to peel it; otherwise peel away the stringy outer skin before dicing it.

Derby Cocktails and Mint Juleps are served with Blue Cheese Horseshoes.

A Kentucky Bluegrass Buffet Dinner

FOR 12

◆

When I was very young, part of my summers were spent at my grandparents' horse and sheep farm in Indiana. My stepgrandfather had retired by that time and started a new career—racing horses. Every weekend, my grandmother and I would drive to a county or state fair to help out and watch the races. Grandpa's prize horse was Calico, a small mare who always would stay back until the final stretch, and then she would open up and win. My grandmother had the secret: she would whisper encouragement to Calico before she went onto the track.

For my twelfth birthday, my parents bought me Maisie, who I hoped would win races like Calico (I didn't realize that Maisie was only a farmhorse) and some day the Kentucky Derby would be hers. But, alas, Maisie was as stubborn as any other member of the Hadamuscin family. I couldn't even get her to go across the tiny creek in the back woods, let alone win a race.

Anyway, that's why I'm fascinated with horse racing and one of the reasons why I always make a big deal of Derby Day (the other reason is that the Derby takes place right around my birthday). The core of this menu is based on the dishes that are as classic to Kentuckians on Derby Day as turkey and fixings are on Thanksgiving. I like to serve this dinner late in the afternoon, after the race.

Getting Ready: The Blue Cheese Horseshoes and the Deviled Nuts can be made up to a week in advance and stored in tins in a cool place.

MENU

Derby Cocktails   Mint Juleps

Blue Cheese Horseshoes

Deviled Nuts (page 84)

◆

Sweet Potato Corn Pones

Kentucky Burgoo

*Molded Perfection Salad with
Horseradish Mayonnaise*

◆

Louisville Pie   Strawberry Tartlets

The flavor of burgoo only improves if it is made a day or two in advance; in fact it can be made well in advance and frozen. The Molded Perfection Salad can be made a day (or at least six hours) in advance, as can the Horseradish Mayonnaise, which takes only a few minutes. The Sweet Potato Corn Pones can be made ahead and frozen, but they're best made no more than a few hours before serving.

The two desserts really should be assembled no earlier than on the day they are to be served, but you can make the pastry ahead and freeze it, and the crusts can be baked a day in advance.

Beverages: I limit the length of the cocktail hour, since the drinks here are pretty potent. With the main course, I switch to a hearty dry red wine, such as a Pinot Noir or a Barbera. With dessert, a strong black coffee, such as French roast or espresso, is perfect, with cordials served afterward.

Derby Cocktails

◆

Here's my (less potent) adaptation of a classic cocktail from the thirties.

For each drink, combine a jigger of gin, a half jigger of peach brandy, and a crushed mint sprig in a cocktail shaker. Shake well, strain over shaved ice, and add a generous splash of sparkling water.

Mint Juleps

◆

It seems that every Kentuckian I've ever met has his own "secret," "classic," or "authentic" method for mixing the state's most famous drink, but the basic ingredients remain the same. In other states, the liquor may vary somewhat; for example, Louisianans may use rum, or Virginians may add a splash of Cognac to the basic Kentucky recipe. Southerners traditionally serve their juleps in silver julep cups, but I serve them in my collection of annual Kentucky Derby souvenir glasses.

1. For each drink, crush 4 or 5 mint leaves with the back of a spoon in the bottom of an 8- to 10-ounce beverage glass. Add 1 to 2 teaspoons superfine sugar to taste (I prefer 2) and 1 tablespoon cold water and stir until the sugar dissolves.

2. Fill the glass with shaved ice and pour 2 jiggers of Kentucky bourbon over the ice. If you've got the time or the patience, chill the drinks in the freezer for 20 minutes or so, until each glass is coated with a thin layer of frost. Serve each drink with a stirrer and garnished with a sprig of mint.

Blue Cheese Horseshoes

MAKES ABOUT 3 DOZEN

◆

Here's a savory version of the classic cheese straw, a perfect accompaniment to before-dinner drinks.

- ¾ pound blue cheese, softened
- 1 3-ounce package cream cheese, softened
- ½ cup (1 stick) butter, softened
- 2 tablespoons half-and-half or milk
- ¼ teaspoon cayenne pepper
- ¼ teaspoon salt
- 3 cups sifted all-purpose flour
- ½ cup finely chopped pecans

1. Preheat the oven to 400°F. Cream the cheeses and butter together in a mixing bowl. Beat in the remaining ingredients until blended.

2. On a floured board, roll the dough into a rectangle approximately ¼ inch thick. Cut the dough into strips approximately ¼ inch by 4 inches. Holding each strip between your thumbs and forefingers, twist the strips several times. Bend the strips into a horseshoe shape and place them onto ungreased baking sheets.

3. Bake until golden brown, 5 to 7 minutes. Remove to wire racks to cool and store in tightly covered containers in a cool place.

Sweet Potato Corn Pones

MAKES ABOUT 2 DOZEN

◆

- 1 cup stone-ground yellow cornmeal
- 1 cup all-purpose flour
- 2 teaspoons baking powder
- ½ teaspoon grated nutmeg
- 1 teaspoon salt
- 2 large eggs
- ½ cup light corn syrup
- 2 cups buttermilk
- 3 cups grated raw sweet potatoes

1. Preheat the oven to 450°F. Grease corn stick pans well (or use heavy muffin pans).

2. In a large bowl, sift together the cornmeal, flour, baking powder, nutmeg, and salt. Beat in the eggs, corn syrup, and buttermilk until just blended, then stir in the sweet potatoes.

3. Fill the corn stick pans almost to the top (fill muffin tins about two-thirds full) and bake for 30 minutes, or until well browned and a cake tester comes out clean. Serve the pones hot with sweet butter.

Kentucky Burgoo

SERVES 12 TO 16

◆

There are many different stories, all "authentic," that detail the origins of this rich, thick country stew. Burgoo traditionally was made with squirrel, but the squirrel has recently been replaced by chicken. I like using rabbit, which adds a bit more character than chicken does. Burgoo is also traditionally cooked forever, to develop its unique flavor. By making it a day in advance and allowing it to stand overnight before serving, I have cut down quite a bit on the cooking time. Another burgoo tradition is that it be fiery hot —this recipe is for a somewhat milder version, but I put the bottle of Tabasco out on the table and let everyone make his or her own adjustment. (By the way, the winner of the 1932 Derby was none other than Burgoo King.)

2 pounds veal shank
1 pound beef shank
1 pound lamb shank
1 4-pound rabbit, quartered or 1 4-pound chicken, quartered
1 quart chicken stock
2 quarts water
4 medium boiling potatoes, peeled and quartered
2 medium onions, coarsely chopped
1 large green pepper, coarsely chopped
4 carrots, peeled and cut into ⅛-inch slices
1 cup okra, cut into ⅛-inch slices
1 cup shredded green cabbage
1 cup thinly sliced celery
2 cups corn kernels
3 cups canned plum tomatoes
3 cups tomato puree
3 tablespoons Worcestershire sauce
1 teaspoon freshly ground black pepper
2 teaspoons Tabasco sauce
½ teaspoon salt
1 cup chopped parsley
2 cups peas

1. Place all the meats in a large, heavy kettle or Dutch oven and add the chicken stock and water. Place the kettle over low heat and bring the contents to a simmer. Cook slowly until the meats fall from the bones, about 2 hours.

2. Remove the meats from the kettle and cut them into chunks. Discard the bones and return the meat to the kettle along with all remaining ingredients except the parsley and peas.

3. Simmer slowly over low heat, stirring frequently, until the mixture is very thick, about 2 hours (or bake in a 250°F. oven, stirring occasionally). Stir in the parsley and peas and let the stew cook another 10 minutes. Serve the burgoo right from the cooking pot.

Molded Perfection Salad

SERVES 8 TO 10

◆

Some rather bizarre concoctions using ghastly green, yellow, and red flavored gelatins along with tiny marshmallows and who knows what all else have given "congealed" salads a bad name; I think it's time the good ones fight back. This classic southern congealed salad is a perfect foil to the rich burgoo and it deserves to regain its past popularity. To fill a deep Turk's head mold, double the recipe.

2 envelopes unflavored gelatin
½ cup cold water
1 20-ounce can crushed pineapple with juice (see note)
½ cup sugar
½ teaspoon salt
¼ cup cider vinegar
2 tablespoons lemon juice
1½ cups finely grated cabbage
1 large carrot, peeled and grated
1 tart apple, unpeeled and grated

1. Mix the gelatin and cold water in a large mixing bowl. Drain the pineapple over a large measuring cup and add enough water to the juice to measure 2 cups. Pour this mixture into a small saucepan and bring it to a boil over medium heat.

2. Stir the sugar and salt into the gelatin mixture, then pour in the juice mixture and stir well to combine. Stir in the vinegar and lemon juice. Put the bowl in the refrigerator to cool.

3. When the gelatin mixture has begun to thicken, remove it from the refrigerator and blend in the grated cabbage, carrot, and apple. Pour the mixture into a ring mold and chill until firm, at least 4 hours. Serve the salad on a lettuce-lined platter with a small bowl of Horseradish Mayonnaise.

Note: Use canned pineapple, since fresh raw pineapple can prevent the gelatin from congealing.

Horseradish Mayonnaise

◆

No elaborate recipe is needed for this. Simply blend 1 tablespoon prepared horseradish and 3 tablespoons milk or cream into 1 cup Homemade Mayonnaise (page 188).

Top to bottom: Kentucky Burgoo, a rich, traditional country stew; Molded Perfection Salad with Horseradish Mayonnaise; and Sweet Potato Corn Pones and sweet butter.

Louisville Pie

MAKES ONE 9-INCH PIE

◆

A Derby Day tradition, this sinfully rich pie has as many different variations as does burgoo. This is the one I like best.

Basic Pastry for a 9-inch pie (page 188)
1 envelope unflavored gelatin
¼ cup cold very strong coffee, preferably espresso
4 large eggs, separated
½ cup sugar
4 teaspoons cornstarch
2 cups milk
1½ ounces unsweetened chocolate, finely chopped
½ teaspoon vanilla extract
⅓ cup bourbon
¼ teaspoon cream of tartar
¼ cup sugar
1 cup heavy cream
Shaved semisweet chocolate, for garnish

1. Preheat the oven to 450°F. Line a 9-inch pie pan with the pastry crust, prick with a fork, and line the crust with aluminum foil weighted with dry beans. Bake the crust until it begins to brown, about 10 minutes. Remove the foil and beans, lower the oven temperature to 400°F, and continue baking until crust turns a rich, golden brown, about 10 minutes longer. Remove crust from the oven and cool in the pan on a wire rack.

2. Stir together the gelatin and coffee in a bowl and set aside. In the top of a double boiler over simmering water, stir together the egg yolks, ½ cup sugar, and cornstarch until the sugar is dissolved. Gradually add the milk and cook, stirring constantly, about 15 minutes, or until the mixture thickens and coats the back of the spoon. Remove from the heat.

3. Transfer half of the custard mixture to a bowl and stir in the chocolate until melted and blended in, then stir in the vanilla. Cool the mixture, then pour it into the baked pie crust.

4. Stir the reserved gelatin mixture into the remaining custard mixture, allow to cool, then stir in the bourbon. Beat the egg whites until soft peaks form, then beat in the cream of tartar and, gradually, the sugar. Fold this into the custard, then spoon this over the pie. Chill until firm.

5. No more than three hours before serving, whip the cream and spoon it over the pie in mounds, covering all but the very center of the pie. Garnish with the shaved chocolate.

Strawberry Tartlets

MAKES 8

◆

Orange Pastry (page 188), divided and chilled
4 squares semisweet chocolate
1 tablespoon vegetable shortening
3 tablespoons Southern Comfort liqueur
2 pints strawberries, hulled
½ cup currant jelly

1. Roll out half the chilled pastry between two sheets of wax paper to a thickness of ⅛ inch. Cut out 4 generous pieces to fit four 3-inch tartlet pans. Fit each into the pans, taking care not to stretch the pastry. Cut away excess. Repeat with the other half of the dough. Prick the bottoms of the pastry shells well with a fork and chill until firm.

2. Preheat the oven to 400°F. Line the pastry shells with aluminum foil weighted with dry beans. Bake until lightly brown, about 7 minutes, and remove the foil and beans. Return to the oven and bake until a rich golden brown, an additional 5 to 7 minutes. Remove from the oven and cool in the pans on wire racks.

3. In the top of a double boiler over simmering water, melt the chocolate and shortening, stirring until smooth. Stir in 1 tablespoon of the liqueur and remove from the heat. Spoon the chocolate mixture into the bottom of the tartlet shells and allow the chocolate to set. Remove the shells from the pans.

4. Slice the strawberries slightly more than ⅛ inch thick. Starting from the outer edge of the shells, arrange the slices, narrow ends out, in concentric circles to create a rose petal effect.

5. Melt the jelly in the top of the double boiler. Add the remaining 2 tablespoons liqueur and stir until smooth and syrupy. While the mixture is still hot, brush it lightly over the berries. If the mixture becomes too thick, warm it up again. Allow the tarts to cool and serve with a dollop of sweetened whipped cream.

A Picnic by the Bay

FOR 6 TO 8

◆

MENU

Fresh Limeade with Rum

*Cold Sliced Herbed Salmon Loaf
and Cucumbers on Grandma Wynn's
Tomato Bread*

Hard-Boiled Brown and White Eggs

Steamed Asparagus and Radishes

◆

Black Bottom Cupcakes

Snickerdoodles   Strawberries

The three-day Memorial Day weekend signals the unofficial beginning of summer and the return of lazy country weekends. Last year, while spending the weekend at the home of a friend on Cape Cod, we had salmon one night for dinner. The conversation turned to foods that made us nostalgic and I was reminded of the delicious salmon loaf my grandmother used to make years ago. I volunteered to make one from the leftover salmon, and this menu was born. The next morning, we all ventured across the road to enjoy a sail on the bay and the first picnic of the season.

Getting Ready: Since this is a picnic, everything is prepared ahead and packed in a cooler. The bread, Snickerdoodles, and cupcakes can be made well in advance and frozen. A day in advance, make the salmon loaf, hard-boil the eggs, and steam and chill the asparagus. The limeade, too, can be mixed up a day ahead.

The rest of the preparation simply involves packing things to travel. Wrap the salmon loaf and the bread well in plastic wrap and don't forget to bring along a cutting board and a few sharp knives. Pack the asparagus, radishes, strawberries, and cupcakes in airtight containers. Pack the cookies in a tin cushioned with crumpled paper towels to avoid breakage. The eggs can be put right back into the cardboard carton they came in. Transport the limeade in an insulated jug.

Fresh Limeade with Rum

MAKES 2 QUARTS
(EIGHT 1-CUP SERVINGS)

◆

1½ cups sugar
6½ cups water
 ¾ cup lime juice
 ¾ cup light rum

1. Combine the sugar and 1 cup of the water in a 3-quart saucepan, place the pan over medium-high heat, and bring the mixture to a boil. Remove from heat and allow to cool.

2. Stir in the remaining 5½ cups water, the lime juice, and the rum. Pour the limeade into a shallow metal pan or bowl, cover with plastic wrap, and freeze for 2 hours, breaking up the ice every half hour or so. Transfer the slushy limeade to an insulated jug to transport it and keep it icy cold.

A midday picnic overlooking Cape Cod Bay is the perfect way to start off the summer.

Left to right: Fresh Limeade with Rum, Grandma Wynn's Tomato Bread, Herbed Salmon Loaf with cucumbers, hard-boiled brown and white eggs, and a colorful combination of steamed asparagus and radishes.

Strawberries, Black Bottom Cupcakes, and Snickerdoodles.

Grandma Wynn's Tomato Bread

MAKES ONE 9x5x3-INCH LOAF

◆

When tomatoes were at the height of their season, my grandmother seemed to put them into just about everything, and this pretty bread was a family favorite. The scallions are my own addition. This is an easy recipe to double, and the bread freezes well; use the extra loaf later for making grilled Cheddar cheese or chicken or turkey club sandwiches.

    1 cup peeled, seeded, and chopped tomatoes
    1 package active dry yeast
    ¼ cup warm water
    3 scallions, white and green parts, finely chopped
    1 tablespoon butter
    1 cup milk, at room temperature
    4½ cups all-purpose flour
    1 teaspoon sugar
    1½ teaspoons salt

1. Place the chopped tomatoes in a sieve over a bowl. Press the tomatoes against the sides and bottom of the sieve and allow them to drain.

2. Stir together the yeast and the warm water in a large mixing bowl. Allow to stand for 15 minutes. Meanwhile, sauté the scallions in the butter in a small skillet for about 5 minutes. Let the mixture cool to room temperature.

3. Stir the milk into the yeast mixture, then stir in the sautéed scallions. In a separate bowl, sift together the flour, sugar, and salt. Stir this mixture, about a cup at a time, into the wet mixture. Fold in the chopped tomatoes, saving the juice that has drained off for another use.

4. Turn the dough out onto a floured board and knead, using floured hands, until the dough is satiny and elastic. (Add a bit more flour, if necessary, to achieve the right texture.)

5. Form the dough into a ball, place it in a lightly oiled bowl, and cover the bowl with a damp cloth. Place the bowl in a warm, draft-free place and allow the dough to rise until doubled in bulk, about 1 hour and 15 minutes.

6. Punch down the dough and knead it for a few minutes in the bowl. Shape the dough into a rectangular loaf. Lightly oil a 9 x 5 x 3-inch loaf pan and place the dough in it. Cover the loaf and allow it to stand for about 50 minutes, or until it again doubles in bulk.

7. Preheat the oven to 450°F. Lightly brush the surface of the loaf with milk and place the pan in the oven. Bake the bread for 10 minutes, reduce the heat to 375°F, and continue baking 20 minutes more, or until the bread is nicely browned and sounds hollow when rapped with a finger.

8. Remove the pan from the oven, remove the bread from the pan, and place the loaf on its side on a wire rack to cool completely.

Herbed Salmon Loaf

MAKES ONE 9x5x3-INCH LOAF

◆

    1 cup fine, dry bread crumbs
    4 large eggs, separated
    1 cup milk
    6 cups flaked poached salmon or 3 15½-ounce cans red salmon, picked over and flaked
    2 teaspoons lemon juice
    ¼ teaspoon freshly ground black pepper
    2 tablespoons chopped fresh dill
    2 scallions, white and green parts, finely chopped
    2 tablespoons chopped parsley
    1 cup uncooked fresh or frozen peas
    5 tablespoons butter, melted

1. Preheat the oven to 350°F. Lightly grease a 9 x 5 x 3-inch loaf pan.

2. Combine all the ingredients except the egg whites, the peas, and 1 tablespoon of the butter in a large mixing bowl and mix well with your hands. Mix in the peas. In a separate bowl, beat the egg whites until stiff but not dry. Fold a few tablespoonfuls of the salmon mixture into the egg whites, then fold the egg whites into the salmon mixture.

3. Spoon the mixture into the greased loaf pan. Place the pan in a larger shallow pan filled with 1 inch of boiling water and place the pans in the oven. Bake for about 50 minutes, or until the center of the loaf is firm to the touch and the surface is lightly browned.

4. Remove the pan from the oven and brush the surface of the loaf with the remaining melted butter. Allow to rest for 10 minutes in the pan, then remove the loaf from the pan and cool to room temperature on a wire rack. Cut into ¼-inch slices just before serving.

Note: Salmon loaf may also be served hot as a main course, sliced and garnished with sour cream and chopped dill or scallions.

Black Bottom Cupcakes

MAKES 2 DOZEN REGULAR CUPCAKES,
OR 3 TO 4 DOZEN MINIATURE CUPCAKES

◆

These rich and easy cupcakes from my editor, Harriet Bell, are perfect picnic fare; they keep well and, since they have no icing, they pack well.

    1½ cups all-purpose flour
    1 cup sugar
    ¼ cup unsweetened cocoa powder
    1 teaspoon baking soda
    ½ teaspoon salt
    1 cup water
    ½ cup corn or vegetable oil
    1 tablespoon distilled white vinegar
    1 teaspoon vanilla extract

Filling
    1 8-ounce package cream cheese
    1 large egg
    ⅓ cup sugar
    ¼ teaspoon salt
    1 cup semisweet chocolate chips
    Sugar

1. Preheat the oven to 350°F. and line muffin tins with fluted paper cups.

2. In a large mixing bowl, sift together the flour, sugar, cocoa, baking soda, and salt. Add the water, oil, vinegar, and vanilla and beat together until well blended. To make the filling, combine the cream cheese, egg, sugar, and salt in a separate mixing bowl and beat well to blend. Stir in the chocolate chips.

3. Fill each muffin cup one-half full with chocolate batter and top with 1 teaspoon of the cream cheese filling (use ½ teaspoon cream cheese mixture for miniature cupcakes). Sprinkle the batter with sugar.

4. Bake for 20 to 25 minutes for miniature cupcakes and 25 to 30 minutes for regular cupcakes, or until a cake tester comes out clean. Remove the cupcakes to a wire rack to cool.

Snickerdoodles

MAKES ABOUT 4 DOZEN COOKIES

◆

Almost forgotten, these old-fashioned crispy and cinnamony morsels are the perfect "go-with" cookies: they go wonderfully with fruit, puddings, ice cream, or even just a glass of cold milk.

    1 cup (2 sticks) butter
    1¾ cups sugar
    2 large eggs
    ½ teaspoon vanilla extract
    2¾ cups sifted all-purpose flour
    1 teaspoon baking soda
    2 teaspoons cream of tartar
    ½ teaspoon salt
    1 tablespoon ground cinnamon

1. In a mixing bowl, cream together the butter and 1½ cups of the sugar, then beat in the eggs and vanilla until the mixture is light and smooth.

2. In a separate bowl, sift together the flour, baking soda, cream of tartar, and salt. Beat this mixture into the wet mixture until a stiff dough has formed. Wrap the dough in wax paper and chill until firm, about 30 minutes.

3. While the dough is chilling, preheat the oven to 400°F. and lightly grease baking sheets. Combine the remaining ¼ cup sugar with the cinnamon in a small bowl and reserve.

4. Tear off small pieces of dough and roll into small balls about ½ inch in diameter. Roll the balls in the cinnamon sugar, then place them on the prepared sheets. Bake for about 7 minutes, or until the cookies are lightly browned. Remove to wire racks to cool; store, tightly wrapped, up to a month at room temperature.

A JUNE WEDDING DAY

A Simple Wedding Breakfast

FOR 20

◆

MENU

Strawberry Champagne Punch   Coffee

◆

*Banana Bread-and-Butter Pudding
with Raspberries and Blueberries*

Honey-Lemon Muffins with Peach Butter

*Apple-Cinnamon Muffins
with Maple-Almond Butter*

Much ado is made about wedding receptions, but usually not much thought is given to creating a sane and stylish beginning to the day and providing sustenance to the family and assorted others who gather at the bride or groom's house during the last-minute preparations before the event itself. A few years ago when a cousin was getting married, I volunteered to fix breakfast for two reasons: one, we would have to eat something, anyway; and two, it would make me useful in what would surely be a hectic household.

In planning the food, I quickly realized that the possibility of a relaxed sit-down breakfast was pretty slim. Any time I've been around a house where a bride was getting ready there hasn't been much calm. So I devised this menu, where bread pudding and berries could be eaten from plates or tiny muffins could be picked up on the run. We set up a buffet on the back lawn (the rain plan was on the screened-in porch) so as family members and friends arrived at the house, they could have a glass of punch, a cup of coffee, or a bite to eat well out of the way of all the activity indoors.

I don't know how well anyone remembers the reception, but I do know that every once in awhile a member of the family remarks on what a nice time they had at breakfast that day.

Getting Ready: The muffins can be made well in advance and frozen, tightly wrapped. Or bake them the night before or early in the morning.

A day in advance: freeze whole strawberries in an ice ring; make the strawberry puree for the punch and chill the other ingredients; make the flavored butters.

Two hours before serving: start making the bread pudding (it can be made a day ahead if need be, but it's best made the same day); once the bread pudding goes into the oven, pare and sugar the berries and get a large coffeepot or urn ready.

ABOVE: Strawberry-Champagne Punch, with a heart-shaped block of ice afloat, catches the morning sunlight.

OPPOSITE ABOVE: Flowered chintz, a Deco coffee urn, a big bouquet of gladioli and hydrangeas, and old wicker give this simple wedding breakfast the air of a Thirties garden party.

OPPOSITE BELOW: Honey-Lemon Muffins and Apple-Cinnamon Muffins in a white wicker basket, Peach Butter, Banana Bread-and-Butter Pudding, and berries.

Strawberry Champagne Punch

MAKES THIRTY 4-OUNCE SERVINGS

◆

This punch recipe from Charleston, where it has been served at daytime receptions for generations, is light enough to be served early in the day, yet it still has the fizzy features befitting a happy celebration.

2 quarts strawberries, hulled
½ cup confectioners' sugar
2 liters chilled Champagne
2 liters chilled sparkling mineral water

1. Puree the strawberries in a blender or in the bowl of a food processor fitted with the steel chopping blade; add the sugar and process until it is dissolved. Strain this mixture through cheesecloth into a wide-mouthed pitcher and chill.

2. At serving time, pour the strawberry puree into a punch bowl over a molded block of whole berries in ice. Gently stir in the Champagne and sparkling water.

Banana Bread-and-Butter Pudding with Raspberries and Blueberries

◆

This is a custardy-rich bread pudding, flavored with bananas and lightly scented with cinnamon and nutmeg—the perfect vehicle for perfect in-season berries. This recipe makes 20 servings for this menu or as a dessert, or 10 to 12 servings as a breakfast main course.

> 2 pints raspberries
> 1 pint blueberries
> 2 tablespoons sugar
> ½ cup (1 stick) butter, softened
> 1 1-pound loaf stale good-quality white bread, sliced
> 2 to 3 large ripe bananas, thinly sliced
> 5 large eggs
> 4 cups half-and-half
> 2 teaspoons vanilla extract
> ¾ cup sugar
> 1 teaspoon ground cinnamon
> ¼ teaspoon grated nutmeg
> Confectioners' sugar

1. Combine the berries and 2 tablespoons sugar and chill several hours.

2. Preheat the oven to 350°F. Butter a shallow 9 x 12-inch baking/serving dish.

3. Lightly butter both sides of the bread slices (using additional butter if necessary). Arrange the banana slices on half the bread slices, top with the remaining bread, and cut the "sandwiches" diagonally in half. Arrange the sandwich halves, overlapping them slightly, in the baking pan.

4. In a large mixing bowl, beat together the remaining ingredients except the confectioners' sugar until well blended. Pour this mixture over the sandwiches, completely moistening all the bread. Gently press the bread down into the liquid and let stand for 10 minutes.

5. Place the baking pan in a larger pan and pour hot water into the larger pan to come halfway up the sides of the pudding pan. Place in the oven and bake for 30 to 35 minutes, or until the custard is set and the bread is golden brown. Sprinkle lightly with confectioners' sugar and serve slightly warm or at room temperature. Spoon some of the berry mixture over each serving.

Honey-Lemon Muffins

◆

> 2 teaspoons baking soda
> 1½ cups buttermilk
> 1 cup (2 sticks) butter, softened
> 1½ cups honey
> 4 large eggs
> 4 cups all-purpose flour
> 2 tablespoons grated lemon rind
> Sugar

1. Preheat the oven to 375°F. and grease two 12-cup muffin tins or four 12-cup miniature muffin tins. Combine the baking soda and buttermilk in a small nonmetallic bowl.

2. In a large mixing bowl, beat the butter and honey together, then beat in the eggs, one at a time. Gradually fold in the flour, then fold in the buttermilk mixture and the lemon rind until just blended in. Do not overmix.

3. Spoon the mixture into the prepared muffin tins and sprinkle the surface of the batter generously with sugar. Bake for about 20 minutes (12 to 15 minutes for miniature muffins), or until the muffins are golden brown and a cake tester or toothpick inserted in the center comes out clean. Cool on wire racks and serve with Peach Butter.

Peach Butter

◆

> 1 cup (2 sticks) butter, softened
> 2 large, very ripe peaches, peeled and finely chopped
> 1 tablespoon confectioners' sugar
> ¼ teaspoon ground cinnamon

Combine all the ingredients in a small mixing bowl. Mound the butter into a serving dish, cover, and refrigerate. Bring to room temperature before serving.

Apple-Cinnamon Muffins

MAKES 2 DOZEN REGULAR MUFFINS,
OR 4 DOZEN MINIATURE MUFFINS

◆

- 4 cups sifted all-purpose flour
- 2 tablespoons baking powder
- 1 teaspoon salt
- ½ cup sugar
- 1 teaspoon ground cinnamon
- 2 large eggs, lightly beaten
- 1½ cups milk
- ½ cup vegetable oil
- 1 cup finely chopped tart baking apples

Topping

- ⅓ cup sugar
- 1 tablespoon ground cinnamon
- 1 teaspoon grated nutmeg
- 2 cups thinly sliced tart baking apples

1. Preheat the oven to 400°F. Lightly grease two 12-cup muffin tins or four 12-cup miniature muffin tins.

2. In a large mixing bowl, sift together the flour, baking powder, salt, sugar, and cinnamon. In a separate bowl, stir together the eggs, milk, and oil. Fold this mixture into the dry mixture until just moistened, then gently fold in the chopped apples.

3. Spoon the mixture into the prepared muffin tins, filling them about two-thirds full.

4. To make the topping, combine the sugar and spices in a small bowl, then toss in the apples, coating them evenly. Press the coated apple slices vertically into the tops of the batter, making stripes.

5. Bake the muffins 20 to 25 minutes (about 15 minutes for miniature muffins), or until they are lightly browned and a cake tester or toothpick inserted in the center of a muffin comes out clean. Remove the muffins from the pans and serve hot, or cool on wire racks and serve at room temperature. Serve with Maple-Almond Butter.

Variations In season, substitute firm, ripe peaches or pears for the apples.

Maple-Almond Butter

MAKES ABOUT 1½ CUPS

◆

- ½ cup sliced blanched almonds
- ½ cup maple syrup
- ½ teaspoon almond extract
- 1 cup (2 sticks) butter, softened

1. Preheat the oven to 350°F. Arrange the almonds in a single layer on a baking sheet. Toast them in the oven for 10 to 12 minutes, or until nicely browned. Finely chop the almonds.

2. Combine the almonds and the maple syrup in a small heavy saucepan and place over medium heat. Simmer the mixture for 5 minutes, remove from heat, and stir in the almond extract. Allow the mixture to cool to room temperature.

3. In a small mixing bowl, beat together the butter and the maple-almond mixture until very well blended. Transfer the mixture to crocks or jars, cover tightly, and chill.

FATHER'S DAY

A Lakeside Fisherman's Supper

FOR 8 TO 10

◆

MENU

Vel's Cornmeal-Fried Perch

Catawba Island Fish Sauce

Dad's Famous Baked Tomato Rice

Green and Yellow Bean and Pepper Salad

◆

Apple Pandowdy with
Cinnamon-Ginger Ice Cream

Hot-from-the-oven Dad's Famous Baked Tomato Rice
cools off a bit on the end of the dock.

If anyone ever went looking for my father on a day off, they'd have to take a boat out onto Lake Erie to find him. Off he would go at the crack of dawn, for a relaxing day of fishing. Father's Day was never any different, so off to the lake we'd all go. When we came back ashore, we'd get out the Coleman stove and start frying up the fish as quickly as Dad could clean them.

Though it's not really a picnic, this menu can travel in the same way (in fact, when we took the pictures, I was right out of camera range at the Coleman stove), as long as you don't have to travel too far and you eat fairly soon. The rice should be baked in a heavy crockery baking dish with a cover and it will stay pretty hot; the ice cream should be packed in ice in a cooler. The salad can be packed in the cooler as well. If you take the Apple Pandowdy out of the oven just before leaving home, it might even still be warm when you're ready to eat it.

Getting Ready: The ice cream can be made up to a week ahead. The salad can be made a day in advance. The Apple Pandowdy is best baked no sooner than a few hours before it is to be eaten, but it can be baked a day in advance if need be. The rice should be put into the oven about two hours before you want to serve it, but it can be made a day in advance and reheated. Fry the fish just before you're ready to eat it.

Beverages: Nothing goes better with this supper than a pitcher of not-too-sweet homemade lemonade, but if you're so inclined, you might want to have beer or a chilled dry white wine. With this dessert, piping hot coffee seems the obvious choice.

Catawba Island Fish Sauce

MAKES 1¼ CUPS

◆

This recipe comes from the Catawba Islands in Lake Erie, one of America's oldest wine-producing areas. Fish is a lesser-known local specialty, and this sauce makes it taste even better.

   ½ cup sour cream
   ½ cup Homemade Mayonnaise (page 188)
   1 teaspoon lemon juice
   2 tablespoons grated onion
   1 tablespoon finely chopped parsley
   1 tablespoon finely chopped green olives
   1 tablespoon well-drained capers

Combine all ingredients in a small bowl and stir well to blend. Serve chilled.

*After a day of fishing, Dad's favorite supper
is served from a wooden bench by the side
of the lake just before sunset.*

Vel's Cornmeal-Fried Perch

SERVES 8 TO 10

◆

You don't have to use perch for this recipe if it's not available or fresh enough; in fact, the success of this simple method for fixing fish depends more on the freshness of the fish than the variety. Catfish is delicious fried this way, too, and you can also try any thin, white, firm fish fillets.

½ cup stone-ground yellow cornmeal
¼ teaspoon salt
⅛ teaspoon cayenne pepper
¾ cup milk, approximately
3 pounds fresh perch fillets
  Vegetable oil for frying
  Lemon wedges

1. In a shallow bowl, combine the cornmeal, salt, and cayenne. Pour the milk into another shallow bowl.

2. Dip the fish fillets one at a time into the milk and then dip them into the cornmeal mixture, turning them to coat completely (mix up more cornmeal, salt, and cayenne if necessary). Remove fillets to wax paper, wrap them loosely, and chill for about 15 minutes.

3. Pour oil into a large skillet to a depth of about ¼ inch, place over medium-high heat, and heat the oil until it sizzles, about 350°F. Add the fish to the skillet in one layer (fry in batches or two skillets if necessary) and fry about 3 minutes on each side, or until the fish is firm and the coating is golden brown.

4. Remove the cooked fillets to a warm platter and keep warm while frying the remaining fish. Serve fish fillets warm with Catawba Island Fish Sauce and lemon wedges.

Dad's Famous Baked Tomato Rice

SERVES 8 TO 10

◆

This is one of my favorite dishes that my father made when I was a kid; it was always a favorite of everyone else's, too. It's a simple dish, dependent on only a few simple flavors, so use the best quality bacon you can find. Smoky, lean, real country bacon is what my father always used, since he cured it himself. And, of course, he always used homegrown tomatoes that Mom had put up. Canned imported Italian plum tomatoes are the best store-bought substitute.

1 28-ounce can Italian plum tomatoes
1 15½-ounce can tomato puree
¼ cup chopped parsley
¼ teaspoon salt
½ teaspoon freshly ground black pepper
¼ teaspoon cayenne pepper
1½ cups long-grain rice
1 large onion, chopped
¼ pound very lean country bacon, coarsely chopped

1. Preheat the oven to 350°F. Lightly butter 2½-quart baking dish.

2. Coarsely chop the tomatoes and place them, with their juice, in a mixing bowl. Add the tomato puree, parsley, salt, and peppers and stir until blended.

3. Spread about one quarter of the tomato mixture on the bottom of the casserole, layer about a third of the rice over the sauce, then spread about a third of the onion and bacon over the rice. Continue layering the ingredients until they're all used, ending with tomato sauce.

4. Bake for 1½ hours, or until the rice has absorbed most of the sauce and is soft and fluffy. Serve hot, garnished with a sprinkling of chopped parsley.

Green and Yellow Bean and Pepper Salad

SERVES 8

◆

¾ pound green beans
¾ pound wax beans
1 large green bell pepper, cut into ¼-inch strips
1 large yellow bell pepper, cut into ¼-inch strips

Dressing
½ cup olive oil
  Juice of ½ lemon
1 tablespoon white wine vinegar
1 small garlic clove, crushed
1 teaspoon prepared mustard
1 tablespoon chopped dill
½ teaspoon salt
½ teaspoon freshly ground black pepper

1. Layer the vegetables in a steamer rack, place over a kettle of simmering water, cover, and steam the vegetables for 10 to 12 minutes, or until crisp-tender.

2. Meanwhile, combine the dressing ingredients in a screwtop jar, cover, and shake well to mix.

3. When the vegetables are done, transfer them to a bowl, pour the dressing over them, and allow the salad to cool. Cover tightly and refrigerate for a few hours before serving. Remove the garlic clove before serving the salad.

Apple Pandowdy

SERVES 8

◆

Here's a time-honored favorite that seems to be in everyone's family recipe file, whether it's called apple cobbler, pudding, or even Jonathan. I always made a different version until I came across this one.

Filling

    8 to 9 tart baking apples, pared and sliced
  ¼ cup freshly pressed or reconstituted frozen apple juice
  ¼ cup pure maple syrup
  ½ teaspoon ground cinnamon
  ¼ teaspoon ground cloves
  ⅛ teaspoon grated nutmeg
  ¼ cup firmly packed dark brown sugar
    1 teaspoon grated lemon rind
  ¼ cup (½ stick) soft butter

Topping

  1¾ cups sifted all-purpose flour
    1 tablespoon sugar
    1 tablespoon baking powder
  ¼ teaspoon salt
  ½ teaspoon ground cinnamon
    6 tablespoons cold butter
    1 cup milk
    1 large egg, lightly beaten.

1. Preheat the oven to 375°F. Butter a 9 x 13-inch baking/serving dish, preferably ovenproof glass or earthenware.

2. Layer the sliced apples in the bottom of the baking dish. Combine the remaining filling ingredients, except butter, in a small mixing bowl and pour the mixture over the apples. Dot the surface with the butter.

3. To make the topping, sift together the flour, sugar, baking powder, salt, and cinnamon. Cut in the butter with a pastry blender (or in the bowl of a food processor fitted with the steel chopping blade) until the mixture is the consistency of coarse meal.

4. Pour in the milk and beat with a fork until the milk is just blended in, forming a stiff, sticky dough.

5. Drop the dough by large tablespoonfuls onto the filling, leaving a few spaces for the juices to bubble up and for steam to escape. Brush the surface of the dough with beaten egg and bake for 40 to 45 minutes, or until the top is golden brown and the apples are tender.

6. Serve warm in small bowls or on dessert plates with a scoop of Cinnamon-Ginger Ice Cream or a dollop of sweetened whipped cream.

Cinnamon-Ginger Ice Cream

MAKES ABOUT 1½ QUARTS

◆

  ½ cup sugar
  1½ teaspoons ground cinnamon
      Pinch of salt
    2 cups scalded milk
    4 egg yolks, lightly beaten
    2 teaspoons vanilla extract
  ½ cup chopped preserved ginger
    2 tablespoons ginger syrup (from preserved ginger)
    2 cups (1 pint) heavy cream

1. Stir together the sugar, cinnamon, and salt in the top of a double boiler. Whisk in the scalded milk and place the pan over simmering water. Gradually whisk in the egg yolks and cook, whisking constantly, until the mixture coats the back of a spoon, about 10 minutes. Remove from heat and cool to room temperature.

2. Gradually whisk in the remaining ingredients. Pour the mixture into an ice cream maker and freeze according to the manufacturer's instructions.

*Dad's Famous Baked Tomato Rice, Catawba Island
Fish Sauce, Vel's Cornmeal-Fried Perch, and
Green and Yellow Bean and Pepper Salad*

Supper is served on a spongeware pottery plate on an old Adirondack chair, with a big red bandana for a napkin.

Dessert doesn't get much better than this: warm fragrant Apple Pandowdy and melting Cinnamon-Ginger Ice Cream.

A New England Clambake in the Country

FOR 8 TO 10

◆

MENU

Rhode Island Clam Chowder

◆

Clambake: Clams, Lobster, Mussels, Potatoes, Scallions, and Corn on the Cob

Freezer Cabbage Slaw

◆

Red, White, and Blueberry Shortcakes

Fourth of July Weekend and clambakes seem to go hand in hand here on the East Coast. I love clambakes as much as the next person, but I don't have a beach in my backyard in the country. So I devised this method of having an inland, indoor clambake, with lobsters fresh-caught from the tank at my fish market. I set up the table on the back deck, and when everything is ready, we open the foil packets. As the fragrant steam reaches our nostrils, we can almost hear the sound of waves lapping at the shore. As far as dessert goes, there's nothing more American than real homemade shortcake.

Getting Ready: A good deal of the work can be done ahead. It does help, however, if you can enlist an assistant when you're ready to assemble the clambake.

The slaw can be made up to 3 months in advance and stored in the freezer; it really does taste better if made well ahead. The base for the chowder can be made a day in advance.

As far as the shortcakes go, the fresher the better; bake them and prepare the berries no sooner than early in the day. Whip the cream for the shortcakes a few hours before serving or just as you're ready to serve. Remember to transfer the slaw to the refrigerator early in the day so it thaws.

For the clambake, scrub the mussels and clams and husk the corn no more than an hour or two ahead. Assemble the foil packets for the clambake just as you're ready to cook them. As soon as they're in the oven, finish off the chowder.

Beverages: Beer, lemonade, or iced tea are the best bets, though if you'd prefer wine, Sauvignon Blanc goes nicely with shellfish. Serve iced tea or iced coffee with dessert.

Rhode Island Clam Chowder

SERVES 10 AS A FIRST COURSE, 4 TO 6 AS A MAIN COURSE

◆

For generations, the battle has been waged: Cape Codders maintain that if it has tomatoes, it's not chowder, and New Yorkers turn their noses up at the inclusion of cream. In the smallest state, the perfect compromise has been made, and I think this is the tastiest chowder of all.

¼ *pound streaky salt pork, diced*
2 *tablespoons butter*
2 *medium onions, chopped*
1 *garlic clove, finely chopped*
1 *cup diced celery*
3 *cups diced potatoes*
½ *teaspoon salt*
1½ *teaspoons fresh thyme or ½ teaspoon dried thyme*
1 *cup tomato juice*
1 *cup fish stock or clam broth*
3 *large ripe tomatoes, peeled, seeded, and chopped*
2 *dozen chowder clams, ground, and their liquor*
2 *cups half-and-half*
2 *cups milk*
½ *cup chopped parsley*
   Salt and freshly ground black pepper

1. Place the salt pork in a small heavy saucepan with water to cover and bring the water to a boil over medium-high heat. Lower the heat and simmer the salt pork 5 minutes, then drain it.

2. Put the salt pork in a large heavy kettle and place the kettle over medium heat. When some of the fat is rendered, add the butter; when the butter is melted and bubbling, add the onion, garlic, and celery. Sauté the vegetables 5 minutes.

3. Add the potatoes, salt, thyme, tomato juice, and fish stock and simmer about 15 minutes, or until the potatoes are just tender. Add the tomatoes and the clams and their liquor and simmer 5 minutes. (May be made up to a day ahead up to this point and cooled, covered, and stored in the refrigerator.)

4. Bring the mixture to a simmer again. Stir in the half-and-half, the milk, and the parsley, and return the chowder to just below the simmering point. Season with salt and freshly ground pepper to taste and serve immediately.

Clambake in the Oven

SERVES 1; MULTIPLY AS NEEDED

◆

This alternative method for having a clambake is the easiest one of all; it can be done in the country or in the city, and a dozen servings can be baked in just about any oven.

    3 or 4 spinach leaves, washed
    ½ dozen steamer clams, scrubbed
    ½ dozen mussels, debearded and scrubbed
    3 whole scallions, trimmed
    2 small russet potatoes, scrubbed and halved
    1 ear of corn, husked and broken into thirds
    1 1¼-pound live lobster
      Sprigs of rosemary or thyme
    ¼ cup clam broth
      Melted butter
      Lemon wedges

1. Preheat the oven to 350°F. Have all ingredients at hand.

2. Cut a 24-inch length of heavy-duty aluminum foil and lay it out flat on the work surface. Arrange the spinach leaves in the center of the foil. Place the clams and mussels in a mound in the center of the foil. Scatter the scallions, potatoes, and corn pieces.

3. Carefully place the lobster on a cutting board and, with a sharp knife, quickly sever the vein at the base of the neck. Place the lobster on top of the mound and pull up the sides of the foil. Tuck in a few herb sprigs, pour the clam broth over the mound, and secure the foil, making a watertight packet by using triple folds and crimping the folds.

4. When all the packets are assembled, place them on baking sheets and put them in the oven. Bake for 1 hour.

5. To serve, place the packets onto large serving plates and, at the table, cut the packets open with a very sharp knife or with heavy scissors. Pass small bowls of melted butter, wedges of lemon, and the pepper mill.

Freezer Cabbage Slaw

SERVES 8 TO 10

◆

Simple and delicious, and it can be prepared up to three months ahead.

    1 large head green cabbage, grated
    1 teaspoon salt
    2 large carrots, peeled and grated
    2 large green peppers, seeded and grated
    1 cup cider vinegar
    1 cup sugar
    ¼ cup chopped parsley
    ¼ cup water
    1 teaspoon dry mustard
    1 teaspoon celery seeds

1. Combine the cabbage and salt in a heavy saucepan and toss. Cover and let stand at room temperature for 1 hour, then drain off any liquid that accumulates. Return the cabbage to the saucepan and add the carrots and peppers.

2. Combine the remaining ingredients in a jar, cover, and shake well to blend. Pour this mixture over the vegetables and toss well. Place the pan over medium-high heat and bring the slaw to a boil. Boil 1 minute, remove from heat, and cool to room temperature.

3. Transfer the slaw to airtight containers or bags and freeze at least 24 hours and up to 3 months. Thaw several hours in the refrigerator before serving. Any leftover slaw can be refrozen.

ABOVE LEFT: *Dinner is served on the lantern-lit deck as evening falls across the trees beyond the backyard. A basket of American flags and Queen Anne's lace and a barrel of red and white vining geraniums, blue petunias, and more flags provide a colorful backdrop.*

ABOVE: *A glorious Red, White, and Blueberry Shortcake, decorated with a tiny American flag.*

OPPOSITE: *An indoor clambake is a colorful packet of lobster, clams, mussels, butter and sugar corn on the cob, new potatoes, scallions, and herbs, hot from the oven. Red-and-white plaid dish towels serve as oversized napkins.*

Red, White, and Blueberry Shortcakes

MAKES 10

◆

Every June, I start counting the days until the strawberry festivals are held all over central and western Connecticut. Shortcakes, the real ones combining layers of feathery fresh-baked biscuits, sweet ripe berries, and mounds of whipped cream, are served up on big paper plates and devoured with ease. Sometimes we manage to make it to three or four festivals in one weekend (for scientific testing purposes only, of course).

Home-baked shortcakes are among the quickest and easiest things in the world to mix up and pop into the oven, so I can't figure out why anyone would use those flavorless patty shells from the supermarket instead of the real thing.

> 2 pints strawberries, washed, hulled, and halved
> 1 pint blueberries, washed and picked over
> ½ cup sugar, approximately
> 1 teaspoon lemon juice
>
> 2 cups heavy cream
> ½ teaspoon vanilla extract
> ⅛ teaspoon salt
> 1 tablespoon sugar
>
> 12 Shortcakes (recipe follows)
> ¼ cup (½ stick) soft butter, approximately

1. In a large nonmetallic mixing bowl, combine the berries, ½ cup sugar, and lemon juice. Cover and refrigerate for 2 to 3 hours. If you think of it, toss the berries occasionally. Taste the berries and add more sugar to taste if you think they need it.

2. No more than 2 hours before serving, place the cream, vanilla, salt, and sugar in a chilled mixing bowl and beat with chilled beaters until *soft* peaks form—don't overbeat. Cover and refrigerate until using.

3. Split the shortcakes and butter them lightly (this keeps them from getting soggy). Place the bottom halves in individual serving dishes and spoon the berries onto them. Divide the whipped cream among the Shortcakes, then place the top halves on each one. Serve immediately with soup spoons.

Shortcakes

> 1¾ cups sifted all-purpose flour
> 1 tablespoon sugar
> ¼ teaspoon salt
> 1 tablespoon baking powder
> ¼ cup (½ stick) cold butter
> ¾ cup half-and-half or milk
> 1 egg, lightly beaten

1. Preheat the oven to 425°F. Lightly grease a large baking sheet.

2. In a large mixing bowl, combine the flour, sugar, salt, and baking powder, then cut in the butter with a pastry blender (this can also be done in the bowl of a food processor fitted with the steel chopping blade). Stir in all but 1 tablespoon of the milk until just blended and the dry ingredients are just moistened. *Do not overmix.*

3. Lightly pat out the dough on a floured board to a thickness of about ⅜ inch. Using a 3-inch round biscuit cutter or a cookie cutter (I like using star-shaped cutters for the Fourth) cut out shortcakes and gently place them on the baking sheet. Combine the reserved 1 tablespoon milk with the beaten egg and brush the surface of the shortcakes with this mixture.

4. Bake the shortcakes for about 15 minutes, or until they are well-risen and lightly browned. Remove to a wire rack to cool before serving.

Variations Try different varieties of fruit, such as peaches and raspberries later on in the summer, or sliced bananas and pears tossed in a little lemon juice in the fall.

A Down-Home Southern Barbecue

FOR 12

◆

MENU

Sweet Potato Chips   Deviled Nuts

◆

Pulled Pork Barbecue on Soft Onion Rolls

Fire Engine Red Sauce

Horseradish Jelly (page 121)

Barbecued Sweet Corn on the Cob

Hoppin' John Salad

*Chopped Lettuce Salad
with Celery Seed Dressing*

◆

Iced Watermelon

Raspberry Festival Pie

"Fourth of July Barbecue" is a group of words I hear strung together as often as any other I can think of. Even though cooking and eating outdoors reaches its height during this long weekend, most barbecues aren't "real" barbecue at all. A few years ago, friends from North Carolina were visiting over the Fourth. I had never performed the ritual of making authentic southern-style barbecue, so I coerced them into teaching me their secrets, and the results can be some of the best eating there is.

As for the rest of the menu, it includes other southern influences picked up here and there when visiting the South and from transplanted southern friends here in New York. After the full-flavored main course, slices of icy watermelon make a perfect natural palate cleanser before the delicate dessert.

Getting Ready: There's a bit of work to do on the day of the barbecue, but it can be done at a leisurely pace. Here are the things that can be done in advance: A few days ahead, make the barbecue sauce (or make it sooner, since it freezes well). Make a batch of Horseradish Jelly any time. Sweet Potato Chips and Deviled Nuts can be made up to a week ahead and stored in tins.

Hard-boil the eggs and make the dressing for the lettuce salad a day or two ahead. The day before, cook the black-eyed peas and marinate in the dressing.

Early on the day of the barbecue, bake the pie, so it has plenty of time to chill and firm up. The watermelon should be chilling, too, at this point.

About three hours before you plan to eat, start the charcoal fire and soak the corn. Cook the rice for the Hoppin' John Salad and toss it with the marinated black-eyed peas.

About two hours ahead, put the pork on the grill. Next, garnish the pie with the whipped cream. Enlist a volunteer to shuck the corn and get it ready for the grill.

About a half hour before serving, put the corn on the grill. Make the lettuce salad, but don't dress and garnish it until you're ready to serve.

Beverages: Even though beer is a more usual accompaniment to barbecue, I like a robust dry jug wine on the rocks.

Pulled Pork Barbecue on a soft onion roll with Fire Engine Red Sauce, Hoppin' John Salad, and Barbecued Sweet Corn on the Cob.

OPPOSITE: *Sweet Potato Chips and Deviled Nuts.*

Sweet Potato Chips

◆

Cut peeled raw sweet potatoes into very thin slices and fry them in one-layer batches in about 5 inches of hot vegetable shortening or oil (about 365°F. on a frying or candy thermometer) until nicely browned, about 10 minutes. With a slotted spoon, transfer the chips to absorbent paper to drain and salt them lightly. When cool, store in a tightly covered container up to a week.

Deviled Nuts

MAKES 2 POUNDS

◆

½ cup (1 stick) butter, melted
2 tablespoons Worcestershire sauce
1 teaspoon Tabasco sauce
1 teaspoon onion juice
1 teaspoon salt
½ teaspoon cayenne pepper
1 large garlic clove, peeled and crushed
1 pound shelled roasted pecan halves
1 pound shelled roasted peanuts (unsalted)

1. Combine the butter, Worcestershire and Tabasco sauces, onion juice, salt, cayenne, and garlic in a large bowl. Cover and let stand at room temperature for 1 hour.

2. Preheat the oven to 300°F. Remove the garlic clove from the above mixture, add the nuts, and toss to coat them well. Arrange the nuts in a single layer on large baking sheets and bake for 20 minutes, stirring once or twice to brown all sides.

3. Transfer the nuts to absorbent brown paper or paper towels to cool, then store up to 3 weeks in a tightly covered container.

Pulled Pork Barbecue on Soft Onion Rolls

MAKES 18 SANDWICHES

◆

4 cups cider vinegar
1 tablespoon freshly ground black pepper
1 tablespoon cayenne pepper
6 pounds boneless pork butt and/or shoulder
18 store-bought soft onion rolls

1. Combine the vinegar and peppers in a jar, cover and shake well, and let stand for at least 1 hour.

2. Meanwhile, prepare and light a charcoal fire around a small shallow aluminum foil roasting pan. When the coals are coated with white ash, position the grill 4 to 5 inches above the coals and fill the aluminum foil pan halfway with hot water. Place the pork on the grill and brush it with the sauce. Keep a spray bottle of water handy to extinguish any flames that may flare up during cooking.

3. Cover the meat loosely with aluminum foil (or put the cover on the grill if it has one), and cook the meat for 1½ to 2 hours, or until it is very, very tender and almost falling apart. During cooking, turn the meat and keep it very moist by brushing it liberally with the sauce every 15 or 20 minutes, replacing the cover each time.

4. Remove the meat from the grill and place it on a large cutting board. Using two large forks, pull the meat into large shreds. Heap it onto warmed soft onion rolls and pass Fire Engine Red Sauce and Horseradish Jelly as condiments.

Fire Engine Red Sauce

MAKES ABOUT 1 PINT

◆

There are barbecue sauces and there are *barbecue sauces.* This is one of the latter.

½ cup (1 stick) butter
2 large garlic cloves, finely chopped
1 medium onion, finely chopped
1 small green pepper, finely chopped
4 cups tomato juice
Juice of 3 lemons
⅓ cup dark molasses
1 teaspoon dry mustard
1 teaspoon cayenne pepper
1 teaspoon celery seeds

Melt the butter in the bottom of a medium-size heavy saucepan over low heat, add the garlic and onion, and sauté for 5 minutes. Raise the heat, stir in the remaining ingredients, and bring the mixture to a simmer. Simmer uncovered, stirring occasionally, for 2 hours, or until sauce is thick.

Barbecued Sweet Corn on the Cob

♦

My Louisiana friend Dana Landry taught me this method for grill-roasting corn. The real secret is to start out with the freshest, sweetest corn you can find.

1. Soak the unhusked corn in water to cover for about 2 hours. Remove the darker outer layer of husks from the cobs. Gently peel back the inner husks, but do not pull them off. Then remove the cornsilk.

2. Brush each ear liberally with Fire Engine Red Sauce (page 84), pull the husks up to rewrap the cobs, and secure the husks at the tips with wet twine or thin wire.

3. Place the corn on the grill and cook over hot coals for about 30 minutes, turning occasionally.

Grilled Corn with Green Onion Butter For 1½ dozen ears, substitute a mixture of 1 stick soft butter and ¼ cup finely chopped scallions for the sauce in step 2.

Hoppin' John Salad

SERVES 12

♦

In the South, Hoppin' John—a mixture of black-eyed peas and rice—is traditionally served as a hot dish on New Year's Day to bring good luck. This cold salad, made a day ahead, turns the classic combination into a perfect summer dish. If you happen to have a ham-bone handy, add it to the water when cooking the peas.

   2 cups dried black-eyed peas, picked over and rinsed
   1 medium onion, coarsely chopped
   2 bay leaves
   1 teaspoon salt
   ¼ cup diced smoked ham
   4 scallions, white and green parts, chopped
   1 small red or green pepper, chopped

   ½ cup olive oil
   ½ cup vegetable oil
   ½ cup red wine vinegar
   2 large garlic cloves, finely chopped
   ¼ teaspoon cayenne pepper
   1 cup raw long-grain white rice, cooked

1. Place the black-eyed peas in a large kettle with water to cover. Place over medium-high heat and bring to the boil. Reduce heat and simmer for 2 minutes. Remove kettle from heat, cover, and let stand for 1 hour.

2. Drain the peas, rinse, and return to the pot. Cover with fresh water and add the onion, bay leaves, and salt. Return the kettle to the stove and bring the mixture to a boil. Reduce heat and simmer the peas for 1 hour, or until tender but not mushy. Drain the peas, remove the bay leaves, and cool.

3. Place the peas, ham, scallions, and pepper in a large bowl. To make the dressing, combine the oils, vinegar, garlic, and cayenne in a jar; cover and shake well to mix. Pour the dressing over the peas and toss well to mix all ingredients.

4. Cover the bowl and allow the mixture to marinate overnight. A few hours before serving, remove the peas from the refrigerator and bring to room temperature. Add the rice, toss the salad again, and chill until serving time.

Chopped Lettuce Salad with Celery Seed Dressing

SERVES 12

Use crunchy iceberg lettuce rather than tender leaf lettuce—it's the only kind that has the right texture and mild flavor to complement hot, spicy barbecue.

Dressing
   ½ cup Homemade Mayonnaise (page 188)
   1 tablespoon prepared yellow mustard
   1 tablespoon sugar
   ¼ cup cider vinegar
   1 tablespoon finely chopped onion
   ½ cup vegetable oil
   1 teaspoon celery seeds

   8 cups shredded iceberg lettuce, loosely packed
   4 hard-boiled eggs, peeled and coarsely chopped
   1 hard-boiled egg, peeled and sliced
   12 large pimiento-stuffed green olives

1. In a blender or in the bowl of a food processor fitted with the steel chopping blade, combine the mayonnaise, mustard, sugar, vinegar, and onion and process to blend. With the blender or processor on, gradually add the oil until it is completely blended in. Stir in the celery seeds, transfer the dressing to a jar, cover tightly, and refrigerate for at least 2 hours.

2. Place the shredded lettuce in a large serving bowl and top with the chopped eggs. Pour the dressing over them and toss well. Scatter the sliced egg and the olives over the salad.

Raspberry Festival Pie

MAKES ONE 10-INCH PIE

◆

While I was visiting my sister in Georgia a few years ago, we attended a raspberry festival and tasted a heavenly old-fashioned raspberry and cream pie. The baker wouldn't divulge her secret recipe, but a few months later my sister sent me this recipe, which is almost a duplicate, and I've been making it ever since.

> *Basic Pastry for a 10-inch crust (page 188)*
> 6 *cups raspberries*
> ½ *cup all-purpose flour*
> 1 *cup sugar*
> ½ *teaspoon ground cinnamon*
> ¼ *teaspoon salt*
> 2 *cups heavy cream*
> ½ *cup strained raspberry jam, approximately*

1. Preheat the oven to 400°F. Line a 10-inch pie pan with the pastry crust and arrange the raspberries evenly in it (reserve about 8 of the most perfect berries for garnishing).

2. In a small mixing bowl, stir together the flour, sugar, cinnamon, and salt until well blended, then blend in 1½ cups of the cream. Pour this batter over the berries.

3. Bake the pie for about 40 minutes, or until the filling is set and the crust is golden brown. Remove the pie from the oven and place on a wire rack to cool for about half an hour.

4. To glaze, heat the raspberry jam over low heat in a small heavy saucepan until syrupy. Brush the surface of the pie with a very thin layer of warm jam. Allow the pie to cool thoroughly, then chill thoroughly before serving.

5. To garnish the pie, whip the remaining ½ cup cream until stiff and, using a pastry tube fitted with a medium star tip, pipe rosettes around the edges of the pie. Top each rosette with one of the reserved berries.

Raspberry Festival Pie, served in a linen-lined basket.

A big tray of sliced watermelon, garnished with mint.

A
Northwestern
Grilled
Dinner

FOR 8
◆
MENU

Grilled Potato Skins with Salmon Caviar
◆

Grilled Alaskan Salmon Steaks with
Wild Mushrooms and Red Onions

Grilled Corn with Green Onion Butter
(page 85)

Grilled Marinated Zucchini and Baby Eggplant

Wilted Salad of Mustard Greens and
Leaf Lettuce with Hickory Nuts
◆

Coals-Roasted Apples
with Blackberries in Honey

A gift of salmon steaks from Alaska last summer inspired this dinner. The weather was perfect, so I decided that outdoor grilling was the only way to go. Coincidentally, the recipe for the marinade came from another friend who had recently returned from a cruise of the Alas-

Dinner is served on a bluff above the beach,
overlooking a fabulous sunset.

kan coastline. The mushrooms and onions seemed like a natural accompaniment to the salmon, and by the time I added those, I figured the whole dinner ought to be cooked in stages on the grill, allowing me to relax outside with my guests.

Getting Ready: The dinner is easy to cook at a very leisurely pace, and it can be even more leisurely for the chef if a few guests are enlisted for KP duty, paring potatoes and apples, getting the corn ready to roast, and so on.

The things that need to be taken care of ahead are: make the green onion butter and the marinade a day in advance; wash the greens for the salad any time during the day of serving; marinate the zucchini and eggplant for about an hour before grilling; marinate the salmon, mushrooms, and onion for a half hour before grilling. For the dessert, the blackberries and honey should be tossed together at the last minute.

I don't recommend cooking this dinner indoors, since it could get rather hectic, but any of the individual recipes except the corn can be cooked in an indoor broiler (though they won't quite taste or look the same).

Beverages: Before dinner and to go with it, I like a full-bodied dry white, such as a Chardonnay, or a not-too-heavy dry Zinfandel. There are excellent types of both wines produced in Washington and Oregon. With dessert, try a Late Harvest Riesling.

Grilled Potato Skins with Salmon Caviar

SERVES 8

◆

6 Idaho baking potatoes
¼ cup (½ stick) butter, melted
2 tablespoons chopped dill
2 ounces salmon caviar
Sour cream

1. Quarter the potatoes lengthwise and cut out the centers as if coring an apple, leaving potato pieces about ¼ inch thick, with skin intact. Parboil the potatoes for 10 minutes and drain.

2. Combine the butter and dill and brush the potato pieces with the mixture. Place the potatoes cut side down onto a grill an inch over hot coals. Cook the potatoes, brushing occasionally with more dill butter, about 10 minutes, or until tender and lightly charred.

3. Remove the potatoes to a serving platter, skin side down, and spoon a few grains of caviar into each piece and pass a small bowl of sour cream for dipping.

Grilled Alaskan Salmon Steaks with Wild Mushrooms and Red Onions

SERVES 8

◆

Marinade/Basting Sauce
½ cup firmly packed dark brown sugar
¼ cup (½ stick) butter
2 tablespoons lemon juice
¼ cup dry white wine
¼ cup soy sauce

8 1-inch-thick salmon steaks, about ½ pound each
16 shiitake or other large wild mushrooms
6 medium sweet red onions, peeled and cut into ½-inch slices

1. Combine all sauce ingredients in a small heavy saucepan over medium-high heat and stir until butter and sugar are melted and combined with the other ingredients. Simmer the mixture until it is thick enough to coat the spoon. Remove from heat and let the marinade cool to room temperature.

2. Brush the salmon, mushrooms, and onions with the sauce and let them stand, loosely covered, for about 30 minutes.

3. Place the salmon, mushrooms, and onions onto well-oiled grilling racks, close securely, and place the racks about 2 inches above hot coals. Cook about 10 minutes on each side (time will vary depending on the heat of the grill), or until the salmon just begins to flake when pricked with a fork. Brush the salmon and vegetables occasionally with any remaining sauce during cooking.

Grilled Marinated Zucchini and Baby Eggplant

SERVES 8

◆

¼ cup olive oil
2 tablespoons lemon juice
1 tablespoon chopped fresh oregano or 1 teaspoon
    dried oregano
1 large garlic clove, crushed
2 medium zucchini, cut into ¼-inch lengthwise slices
3 baby purple eggplants, cut into ¼-inch lengthwise
    slices

1. Combine the oil, lemon juice, oregano, and garlic in a large bowl and beat with a fork to mix. Add the vegetables and toss to coat well with the marinade. Let stand 1 hour.

2. Place the vegetables on a well-oiled grill about 2 inches above the hot coals. (Do this just before turning the salmon, above). Grill the vegetables, turning occasionally, 10 to 15 minutes, or until lightly charred on both sides.

Wilted Salad of Mustard Greens and Leaf Lettuce with Hickory Nuts

SERVES 8

◆

Why heat up the kitchen? Have the greens and nuts ready and cook the dressing in a skillet right on the grill.

½ cup olive oil
¼ cup cider vinegar
2 tablespoons water
1 teaspoon sugar
½ teaspoon freshly ground black pepper
3 cups washed mustard greens
3 cups washed and torn leaf lettuce
½ cup coarsely chopped toasted hickory nuts

1. In a medium saucepan, heat together the olive oil, vinegar, water, sugar, and pepper. Bring to a simmer and cook 3 minutes.

2. Place the greens in a serving bowl, pour the dressing over them, and toss well. Sprinkle the nuts over the salad and serve.

Coals-Roasted Apples with Blackberries in Honey

SERVES 8

◆

Throw these onto the grill right after finishing the main course.

8 medium baking apples, quartered and cored
    (do not peel)
2 tablespoons lemon juice
2 tablespoons vegetable oil
1 pint blackberries
⅓ cup honey

1. Pare the apples up to a few hours ahead and toss with the lemon juice. Cover tightly and refrigerate. Just before cooking, toss the apples again.

2. Brush the apples with the oil and place them cut side down, on the grill. Cover loosely with foil, and cook 10 to 15 minutes, or until the apples are lightly browned and tender, but not mushy (time will depend on the variety of apples and the heat of the grill).

3. In a small bowl, toss together the blackberries and honey. Arrange four apple quarters in each individual serving dish and spoon a few tablespoons of the berries and honey over each serving.

OPPOSITE: Grilled Alaskan Salmon Steaks are served on a Victorian silver fish platter and Grilled Red Onions on a fish-shaped cutting board.

LEFT: Grilled Potato Skins with Salmon Caviar.

ABOVE: A plate of grilled delicacies: marinated Alaskan salmon steaks, wild mushrooms and red onions, and miniature eggplant and zucchini.

RIGHT: Coals-Roasted Apples with Blackberries in Honey.

A Big Southwestern Barbecue

FOR 18

◆

MENU

Chunky Cold Avocado Soup with Tostados

◆

Barbecued Beef Brisket with Tomato, Corn, and Green Chili Salsa

Roasted Bell Pepper Strips in Oil

Black Bean Salad with Coriander

Sage and Cheese Corn Bread with Sweet Butter

◆

Chocolate-Cinnamon Crisps

Lime and Honeydew Sherbet Splashed with Tequila

I became acquainted with southwestern cooking years ago while visiting my father at his winter home in Tucson, and many new flavors were introduced to this midwestern farmboy. Needless to say, I was hooked. Since then, I've experimented with quite a bit of southwestern cooking, and this menu is composed of some of the dishes I'm most partial to. With a big brisket as a centerpiece and hardly any last-minute preparation, this is a great menu to serve when a crowd's coming over. As far as I know, the dessert has absolutely no base in authen-

ticity, but it seems like a perfect refreshing ending to this highly flavored dinner, and to me it's southwestern in spirit, if not in fact.

Getting Ready: There's no last-minute work here, except minding the meat as it's barbecued, but I'd hardly call that work.

Make the cookies and store them, tightly wrapped, in a cool place, up to two weeks in advance; or they can be made well ahead and frozen. Make the sherbet up to a week in advance.

The day before the barbecue, roast the peppers and make the salsa; make the black bean salad; marinate the brisket overnight.

On the day of the barbecue, bake the corn bread (or, less preferably, make it well ahead and freeze it). About eight hours before dinnertime, start the charcoal fire; put the brisket on to cook about six hours before you want to serve it. Make the soup no more than a few hours before serving.

Beverages: I'd skip wine with the soup, but the main course can be served with a full-bodied dry red, such as a Pinot Noir or a Barbera from California. Good strong coffee should be served afterward.

Chunky Cold Avocado Soup with Tostados

SERVES 18 AS A FIRST COURSE

◆

This refreshing cold soup should be made no sooner than early on the day you are serving it, but it only takes a few minutes. As far as the tostados go, I suppose you could make your own tostados by deep-frying strips of soft corn tortillas, but I find it a lot easier to just buy them.

8 ripe medium avocados
3 large garlic cloves
Juice of 2 limes
1 quart well-seasoned chicken stock
½ cup (1 stick) butter, melted and cooled
1 quart half-and-half
Salt
A few dashes of Tabasco sauce

Tostados
2 limes, thinly sliced
2 cups sour cream
½ cup chopped black olives

1. Slice the avocados in half (cutting around the pit), remove the pit, and scoop out the pulp in large chunks. Place half the avocado chunks in the bowl of a food processor fitted with the steel chopping blade, along with the garlic, half the lime juice, and half the chicken stock. Process until smooth.

2. Remove the mixture to a large nonmetallic bowl. Stir the remaining chicken stock, the butter, and the half-and-half into the mixture until all the ingredients are well blended and smooth.

3. Place the remaining avocado chunks and lime juice in the food processor bowl and pulse until the avocado is just coarsely chopped. Stir the chopped avocados into the pureed mixture and season with salt and Tabasco to taste (the soup should not be spicy hot, but have just a touch of piquancy).

4. To store, press a piece of plastic wrap directly onto the surface of the soup (this prevents the avocado from darkening), cover the bowl, and refrigerate.

5. Serve the chilled soup in small bowls and garnish each serving with tostados, a slice of lime, and a dollop of sour cream sprinkled with chopped olives.

Barbecued Beef Brisket

SERVES 18 TO 20

◆

Marinade/Basting Sauce
>   1 cup well-seasoned beef stock
>   1 cup olive oil
>   ½ cup cider vinegar
>   4 large garlic cloves, finely chopped
>   1 tablespoon dried oregano
>   1 teaspoon Tabasco sauce
>   2 teaspoons mild ground chili
>   2 teaspoons ground cumin seed
>   1 teaspoon paprika
>   1 teaspoon freshly ground black pepper
>
>   1 10-pound beef brisket, well trimmed

1. Combine the marinade ingredients in a jar, cover tightly, and shake well to mix. Place the brisket in a plastic bag, pour in the marinade, and tightly close the bag. Press the marinade around in the bag to coat all surfaces of the meat. Refrigerate overnight, turning occasionally.

2. About 8 hours before serving, soak hardwood chips (mesquite, hickory, or a fruitwood) in water. Arrange a single layer of charcoal around a shallow aluminum foil roasting pan in the bottom of a deep grill, preferably one with a cover. Light the fire, and when the charcoal is covered with white ash, arrange a few handfuls of wet wood chips in a single layer over the hot coals and pour water into the pan to a depth of 1 inch.

3. Remove the brisket from the plastic bag and carefully pour the marinade into a small bowl or jar. Place the brisket on the grill, which should be positioned about four inches above the coals. Close the cover of the grill or cover the grill loosely with heavy-duty aluminum foil.

4. Cook the brisket, brushing frequently with the marinade and adding charcoal and soaked wood chips to the fire as necessary, for 6 to 7 hours, until the brisket is very tender. Turn the brisket about once an hour during cooking. Replenish the water in the roasting pan as needed and keep a spray can filled with water handy to spray the fire if there are any flare-ups.

5. Place the brisket on a board and cut it diagonally into ⅛-inch-thick slices. Serve with Tomato, Corn, and Green Chili Salsa.

Oven-Barbecued Brisket After step 1 above, remove the brisket from the bag, put it in a shallow roasting pan, and place it under a preheated broiler to brown on both sides. Brush the meat liberally with marinade, cover it loosely with aluminum foil, and turn the oven to 275°F. Cook the meat, brushing occasionally with the remaining marinade, for about 6 hours, or until the meat is very tender.

Harlequin dishes, an old printed tablecloth from the Fifties, and many-colored napkins create a colorful setting for a colorful dinner, served after sunset by a candle-rimmed pool.

A glass of Lime and Honeydew Sherbet splashed with Tequila and a plate of Chocolate-Cinnamon Crisps.

I love this vibrant combination of colors and flavors: thin slices of Barbecued Beef Brisket with Tomato, Corn, and Green Chili Salsa, Black Bean Salad with Coriander, Sage and Cheese Corn Bread, and Roasted Bell Pepper Strips.

Tomato, Corn, and Green Chili Salsa

MAKES ABOUT 6 CUPS

◆

3 tablespoons olive oil
3 large garlic cloves, finely chopped
½ teaspoon salt
3 pounds very ripe plum tomatoes, peeled and seeded
3 cups freshly scraped cooked corn kernels
1 small jalapeño or serrano chili pepper, finely chopped
6 small mild green chili peppers, finely chopped
1 medium onion, finely chopped

1. Combine the olive oil, garlic, salt, and half the tomatoes in the bowl of a food processor and process until the tomatoes are coarsely pureed. Transfer this mixture to a mixing bowl.

2. Add the remaining tomatoes to the processor bowl and pulse until just coarsely chopped. Add these tomatoes to the mixing bowl.

3. Add the remaining ingredients (the peppers and onion may also be chopped in the processor) to the mixing bowl and toss to combine. Cover the bowl and refrigerate the salsa for at least 4 hours, or overnight, to allow flavors to blend. Bring to room temperature before serving.

Note: If using frozen corn kernels rather than fresh ones, chop them very coarsely in the food processor to release their juices.

Roasted Bell Pepper Strips in Oil

◆

The simple roasting of mild bell peppers, allowing their delicate flavor to shine, is a nice contrast in flavor and texture to the rest of the meal.

4 large green bell peppers
2 large red bell peppers
2 large yellow bell peppers
3 tablespoons extra-virgin olive oil

1. Preheat the broiler. Cut the peppers in half vertically and seed them. Place the peppers on a pan, skin side up, and broil them about 5 minutes, or until the skin blackens, shrivels, and puckers. (Or skewer the pepper halves and grill them, skin side down.)

2. Peel the peppers and cut them into ¼-inch strips. Toss the pepper strips with the olive oil. Serve at room temperature.

Black Bean Salad with Coriander

SERVES 18 TO 20

◆

2 pounds dried black beans
2 large garlic cloves, crushed
Juice of 3 lemons
¼ cup red wine vinegar
⅔ cup olive oil
½ teaspoon salt
1 teaspoon freshly ground black pepper
1 large red pepper, coarsely chopped
4 scallions, white and green parts, thinly sliced
2 tablespoons chopped fresh coriander
Coriander sprigs, for garnish

1. Wash and pick over the beans, then place them in a kettle with water to cover. Place over high heat, bring to a boil, and boil for 2 minutes. Remove from heat and let stand 1 hour. (Or cover the beans with water and soak overnight at room temperature.)

2. Drain and rinse the beans, cover again with water, and add the garlic. Simmer the beans until tender, about 1 hour. Drain and rinse the beans and transfer them to a large bowl. Discard the garlic.

3. In a separate small bowl, combine the lemon juice, vinegar, oil, salt, and black pepper and whisk to blend. Pour this dressing over the beans, add the chopped pepper, scallions, and coriander to the bowl, and toss the salad lightly. Cover and allow to stand in the refrigerator for at least 3 hours before serving, or overnight.

4. Serve in a glass bowl, garnished with coriander sprigs.

Sage and Cheese Corn Bread

MAKES ONE 10-INCH ROUND LOAF

◆

Double or triple this recipe for this menu, but mix the batter and bake in separate batches.

¾ cup all-purpose flour
2½ teaspoons baking powder
2 teaspoons sugar
½ teaspoon salt
1¼ cups stone-ground yellow cornmeal
1 tablespoon chopped sage leaves or 1 teaspoon dried rubbed sage
1 large egg, lightly beaten
1 cup milk
3 tablespoons melted bacon fat or butter
½ cup finely grated Monterey Jack cheese

1. Preheat the oven to 425°F. Using bacon fat or vegetable shortening, generously grease a heavy 10-inch cast-iron skillet and place it in the oven to preheat.

2. In a large mixing bowl, sift together the flour, baking powder, sugar, and salt, then stir in the cornmeal and sage.

3. In a separate bowl, beat together the egg, milk, and melted fat, then pour this mixture over the dry ingredients. Add the grated cheese and, using a fork, quickly stir until the dry ingredients are just moistened (the batter should be slightly lumpy).

4. Pour the batter into the preheated skillet, return it to the oven, and bake for about 25 minutes, or until the surface is nicely browned and a cake tester inserted in the center comes out clean.

5. Cut the corn bread into wedges and serve hot or at room temperature with soft sweet butter.

Chocolate-Cinnamon Crisps

MAKES ABOUT 5 DOZEN COOKIES

◆

⅜ cup (¾ stick) butter
½ cup sugar
½ cup dark corn syrup
½ teaspoon vanilla extract
2 tablespoons unsweetened cocoa powder
1½ cups all-purpose flour
1 teaspoon ground cinnamon

1. Preheat the oven to 375°F. Grease baking sheets.

2. Melt the butter in a large heavy saucepan, then stir in the sugar and corn syrup. Bring the mixture to a simmer, remove from heat, and stir in the vanilla.

3. In a mixing bowl, sift the cocoa powder, flour, and cinnamon together until thoroughly blended. Add this mixture to the contents of the saucepan and mix thoroughly to make a thick batter.

4. Drop the batter by scant teaspoonfuls about 2 inches apart onto the prepared baking sheets. Bake about 5 minutes, or until the cookies have spread and the edges are browned. Do not overbake.

5. Remove the cookies from the oven and allow them to cool for several minutes on the baking sheets before removing them to wire racks to cool completely.

Lime and Honeydew Sherbet

SERVES 18

◆

¾ cup sugar
1 cup water
2 ripe medium honeydew melons
  Grated rind of 2 limes
  Juice of 4 limes
2 large egg whites
¾ cup tequila, approximately
  Mint sprigs, for garnish

1. Combine the sugar and water in a small saucepan over medium-high heat. Bring the mixture to the simmering point, stirring just until the sugar is dissolved. Reduce heat and simmer uncovered for 5 minutes without stirring. Remove the pan from the heat and allow the syrup to cool.

2. Quarter and seed the melons and cut the pulp into chunks. Puree the melon in batches in the bowl of a food processor fitted with the steel chopping blade.

3. Transfer the melon puree to a 9 x 13-inch metal baking pan and add the cooled syrup and the lime rind and juice. Stir until the mixture is well blended, cover the pan with plastic wrap or aluminum foil, and place it in the freezer. Freeze until the mixture is almost frozen through, about 3 hours, stirring every half hour or so to ensure even freezing.

4. Remove the pan from the freezer to allow the frozen mixture to soften slightly. Meanwhile, beat the egg whites until soft peaks form. In batches, place the softened ice in the food processor and process until it becomes light and smooth, then return it to the pan. Gently fold in the beaten egg whites, cover the pan, and return it to the freezer.

5. About a half hour before serving, transfer the pan to the refrigerator to allow the sherbet to soften. Immediately before serving, spoon the sherbet into serving dishes and splash each serving with about a tablespoon of tequila and garnish with a mint sprig.

The towers of lower Manhattan and a sailboat race in New York Harbor provide a spectacular backdrop for our floating picnic.

A Manhattan Melting Pot Picnic

FOR 6 TO 8

◆

MENU

*Cold Grilled Chicken Breasts with
Lemon and Oregano*

Smoked Sausage and New Potato Salad

Red Salad with Basil-Mint Dressing

Radicchio, Parsley, and Blue Cheese Salad

Sesame-Peanut Macaroni

Calico Corn and Bean Salad

◆

Nancy's Old Glory Tart

Lady Liberty Lemon Cookies

On special occasions New York City becomes the biggest small town in America. New Yorkers really know how to celebrate the Fourth with style, and it certainly seems appropriate, since so many of our forebears first set foot on American soil in New York. I've celebrated the Fourth in the city in many ways—from a picnic in Central Park along with a few hundred thousand other celebrants, to a party of six on a sailboat in the harbor, followed by some of the most fabulous fireworks ever.

To celebrate the Statue of Liberty Centennial, a group of friends contributed different dishes to the meal, and our potluck was truly a melting pot, with dishes influenced by cuisines from all over the world.

This may seem like a lot of food for six or eight people, but just about everything in this picnic holds well, and everyone can snack on this menu throughout a lazy afternoon and into the evening.

Getting Ready: This is all do-ahead food, so there's plenty of time to put it all together; and most of the recipes require very little preparation time (the tart is the most complicated, but it requires more patience than skill).

The chicken can be made a day or two ahead, or even made far in advance and frozen; thaw to room temperature to serve.

The sausage and potato salad, corn and bean salad, Sesame-Peanut Macaroni, and the red salad can be made a day in advance, but no sooner. For the radicchio salad, wash, dry, and wrap the greens and make the dressing early the same day; transport the greens and dressing separately and dress and toss the salad just before serving.

The cookies can be made up to a few weeks ahead and stored in tightly covered containers in a cool place. The tart should be assembled no earlier than on the day it is served, though the shell and the filling can each be prepared a day in advance.

A Note on Picnicking Afloat (or for putting together any moveable feast): Make sure you pack everything in sturdy dishes that are low and untippable, and pack everything as compactly as possible so it can't slip and slide about. For our sailing excursion, we packed salads in heavy ceramic soufflé dishes, covered them with plastic wrap, then arranged them in a large shallow basket lined with sturdy leaves of kale to hold the dishes in place. Chicken was wrapped in a linen towel and packed in another shallow basket. Plastic plates are a good idea if you're dining on deck, but use real flatware and napkins. Delicate and tippable stemware is impractical on board; we used sturdy, squat French confiture glasses, which are perfect for serving everything from wine to coffee.

Cold Grilled Chicken Breasts with Lemon and Oregano

MAKES 10 BREAST HALVES

◆

I like to cook this Italian-inspired chicken on the grill on Sunday at my weekend house, bring it back to the city, and have it as a midweek treat. It freezes well, too; just warm it in the oven and allow it to return to room temperature before serving. Outdoor grilling is the best way to cook this chicken, but it's good cooked indoors under the broiler, too. No matter how you cook the chicken, do try to use fresh oregano for this recipe—that's what makes it special.

10   skinless chicken breast halves
2   lemons, quartered
⅓   cup olive oil
¼   cup chopped fresh oregano
½   teaspoon salt
1½   teaspoons freshly ground black pepper
1   lemon, thinly sliced, for garnish
Oregano sprigs, for garnish

1. Place the chicken breasts, skinned side up and in one layer if possible, in a large, shallow nonmetallic pan or bowl. Squeeze the juice from the lemon quarters into a separate small bowl, then whisk in the oil, oregano, salt, and pepper.

2. Pour this marinade over the chicken. Turn the chicken skinned side down, tuck the lemon quarters between the chicken pieces, and cover the bowl tightly. Refrigerate 6 hours or overnight.

3. About an hour before you're ready to cook the chicken, prepare a charcoal fire and allow it to burn down to gray hot coals. Place the grill about 2 inches above the coals.

4. Place the chicken breasts, skinned side down, onto the grill. Cook them, occasionally turning and brushing with any remaining marinade, until they are slightly charred and the juice runs clear when they are pricked with a fork (the timing will depend on the heat of your fire). Remove the chicken to a serving platter and garnish each breast with a lemon slice and a sprig of oregano.

Smoked Sausage and New Potato Salad

SERVES 8

◆

Sort of German- or French-inspired, this salad is perfect picnic fare; there's no mayonnaise to spoil in hot weather, and the salad tastes its best either slightly warm or at room temperature.

> 2 *pounds new potatoes*
> 1 *pounds smoked summer sausage or kielbasa*
> 2 *tablespoons olive oil*
> 2 *tablespoons vegetable oil*
> 1 *medium red onion, coarsely chopped*
> ¼ *cup thinly sliced celery*
> ¼ *cup cider vinegar*
> 1 *teaspoon Dijon mustard*
> 2 *tablespoons chopped fresh chervil or 2 teaspoons dried chervil*
> 1 *tablespoon chopped fresh tarragon or 1 teaspoon dried tarragon*
> ½ *teaspoon salt*
> ½ *teaspoon freshly ground black pepper*
> 4 *large red radishes, thinly sliced*

1. Put the potatoes in a large kettle with water to cover and place over high heat. Bring to a boil, reduce heat, and simmer about 20 minutes, or until the potatoes are just tender. Drain the potatoes and cool them until they can be easily handled.

2. Preheat the broiler. Cut the sausage diagonally into ½-inch slices. Place the slices on a rack in a shallow pan, place the pan under the broiler, and cook the sausage until lightly browned. Turn the sausage and brown the other side. Remove the sausages to paper towels to absorb excess fat.

3. Place the oils in a skillet over medium heat. Add the onion and celery to the skillet and sauté until crisp-tender, about 10 minutes. Remove skillet from heat.

4. To make the dressing, add the remaining ingredients, except radishes, to the skillet and blend well with a fork.

5. Cut the potatoes into quarters and place them in a large serving bowl. Add the sausage, radishes, and dressing and toss gently to mix. Serve the salad warm or at room temperature.

Red Salad with Basil-Mint Dressing

SERVES 6

◆

On the Glorious Fourth, I like to serve this vibrant Mediterranean-style salad of red tomatoes, red peppers, and red onions on a blue and white spongeware platter.

> 2 *large red peppers*
> 1 *medium red onion, peeled and vertically sliced*
> 6 *large, ripe tomatoes*
> ¼ *cup olive oil*
> 1 *tablespoon red wine vinegar*
> 1 *tablespoon lemon juice*
> 1 *teaspoon capers*
> 1 *tablespoon chopped fresh basil*
> 1 *tablespoon chopped fresh mint*

1. Preheat the broiler. Cut red peppers in half vertically and seed them. Place the pepper halves, cut side down, along with the onion strips, in a shallow pan. Broil the vegetables until the pepper skins start to shrivel and pucker, about 5 minutes. Remove from the heat.

2. Peel and seed the tomatoes and peel the peppers and cut them into ¼-inch-wide strips. Place them, along with the onions, in a large mixing bowl.

3. Combine the oil, vinegar, and lemon juice in a small mixing bowl and whisk to blend. Stir in the capers, basil, and mint and pour this dressing over the vegetables. Gently toss the salad, cover, and refrigerate for at least 2 hours before serving. Serve chilled or at room temperature.

A potluck assortment of salads: Sesame-Peanut Macaroni; Red Salad with Basil-Mint Dressing; Calico Corn and Bean Salad; Radicchio, Parsley, and Blue Cheese Salad.

Rows of seasonal berries and whipped crème fraîche form the stars and stripes on Nancy Kenmore's Old Glory Tart. The tart is transported in and served from a shallow tray.

Lady Liberty Lemon Cookies.

A vibrant salad of tomatoes, red peppers, and red onions looks wonderful on a blue and white spongeware platter.

The moment we've been waiting for: after sunset, the fireworks begin!

Radicchio, Parsley, and Blue Cheese Salad

SERVES 6

◆

Using parsley as a salad green is an idea I picked up on a visit to California's Napa Valley, where innovation in the use of fresh produce never ends.

  ½ cup extra-virgin olive oil
  ¼ cup balsamic vinegar
  ¼ teaspoon cracked black pepper
  2 medium heads radicchio, torn into bite-size pieces
  1 cup loosely packed flat Italian parsley, stems removed
  ½ cup crumbled blue cheese

Combine the oil, vinegar, and pepper in a small screwtop jar and shake to blend. In a separate bowl, combine the radicchio, parsley, and blue cheese. Just before serving, shake the dressing again, pour it over the salad, and toss lightly.

Sesame-Peanut Macaroni

SERVES 6 TO 8

◆

An oriental-inspired salad, this is always a favorite.

  1 pound rotelle or other pasta
  ½ cup oriental sesame oil
  ½ cup chunky peanut butter
  ½ teaspoon hot Szechwan oil or ⅛ teaspoon cayenne pepper
  4 scallions, white and green parts, cut into ½-inch slices
  1 medium cucumber, seeded and cut into julienne

1. Cook the pasta in boiling salted water until *al dente*. Drain, toss with a few tablespoons of the sesame oil, and allow it to cool.

2. In large mixing bowl, whisk together the peanut butter, remaining sesame oil, and hot oil. Pour this mixture over the pasta, add the scallions and cucumber, and toss well. Cover and store in the refrigerator up to 8 hours before serving. Serve at room temperature.

Calico Corn and Bean Salad

SERVES 8

◆

This one's all-American—kind of a New England succotash salad with southwestern overtones.

Dressing
  ¼ cup olive oil
  2 tablespoons red wine vinegar
  ½ teaspoon ground cumin
  2 tablespoons chopped parsley
    Pinch of cayenne pepper, or more to taste

  3 cups cooked corn kernels
  1 small green pepper, seeded and chopped
1½ cups cooked kidney beans
  2 scallions, white and green parts, thinly sliced
  ½ pound green beans, cut into 1-inch lengths and steamed

1. Combine all the dressing ingredients in a screwtop jar, cover, and shake well to blend.

2. Combine all the salad ingredients, pour the dressing over them, and toss well. Cover and chill for at least 3 hours to allow the flavors to blend. Serve at room temperature.

Nancy's Old Glory Tart

MAKES ONE 11 X 15-INCH TART

◆

If you can decorate a birthday cake, you can make this spectacular and delicious tart, the creation of Nancy Kenmore. The recipe is long, but it isn't difficult, as long as you have a little patience. And the results (and applause) are worth it.

  1 pound frozen puff pastry, defrosted in the refrigerator
  1 large egg yolk, mixed with 2 teaspoons water
1½ pounds (3 8-ounce containers) crème fraîche
    Grated rind of 1 large orange
  4 tablespoons confectioners' sugar
  4 tablespoons orange liqueur
  1 cup black raspberries or blueberries
  1 pint red raspberries
  ⅔ cup raspberry jelly

1. Roll out the puff pastry into a ⅛-inch-thick rectangle measuring not less than 12 x 16 inches. Cut an 11 x 15-inch rectangle in the center of the pastry, leaving ½-inch-wide strips all around. Place the rectangle on a foil-lined baking sheet. Use the strips to create a vertical lip all around the rectangle, brushing the edges with ice water to make them adhere; trim away any excess pastry. Chill the pastry shell until firm, about half an hour.

2. Preheat the oven to 400°F. Prick the bottom of the pastry shell all over with a fork and brush the top of the outside lip with the egg yolk mixture. Line the bottom of the shell with aluminum foil weighted with dry beans, keeping the foil away from the lip. Bake the pastry shell until the edges begin to brown, 12 to 15 minutes. Remove the beans and foil and continue baking until the shell is golden brown, about 7 minutes longer.

3. In a small bowl, beat the crème fraîche and orange rind until the cream begins to form soft peaks (crème fraîche will whip more quickly than regular heavy cream). Beat in the confectioners' sugar and 2 tablespoons of the liqueur and continue beating until stiff peaks form.

4. Transfer a third of the mixture to a pastry bag fitted with a medium star tip. Spread the remaining mixture over the bottom of the cooled tart shell.

5. Arrange the largest unblemished black raspberries or blueberries checkerboard-style in the upper left corner of the tart to simulate the dark blue background and the stars (use the photograph on page 102 as a reference). Select the largest unblemished red raspberries and arrange them in alternating rows about ½ half inch apart to simulate the stripes. Using the crème fraîche mixture in the pastry bag, pipe in the white stars and white stripes.

6. Melt the raspberry jelly in a small heavy saucepan over very low heat and stir in the remaining 2 tablespoons liqueur. Using a small pastry brush or a clean artist's paint brush, glaze the tops of the berries. Play a John Philip Sousa march to salute your accomplishment.

Lady Liberty Lemon Cookies

MAKES ABOUT 3 DOZEN,
DEPENDING ON COOKIE CUTTERS

◆

When my friend Nancy Kenmore made these cookies I asked for the recipe as soon as I bit into one. Was I surprised to learn that it was the recipe for my grandmother's butter cookies from my first book, with just a bit of lemon rind added! So here's Nancy's version of Grandma Stapleton's Bohemian Butter Cookies.

Lacking Statue of Liberty cookie cutters, use star-shaped ones instead and decorate the cookies with a sprinkling of red-colored sugar before baking.

> 1 cup sugar
> 2 cups (4 sticks) butter
> 4 large eggs
> ½ teaspoon vanilla extract
> 1 teaspoon grated lemon rind
> 4 cups all-purpose flour
>   Green- and yellow-colored sugars

1. In a large mixing bowl, cream the sugar and butter together until light and smooth. Separate 3 of the eggs. Beat the egg yolks and the remaining whole egg into the butter-sugar mixture. Reserve the egg whites.

2. Beat in the vanilla and lemon rind, then gradually add the flour and mix well. Gather the dough into a ball, wrap in plastic wrap, and chill in the refrigerator for 3 hours or overnight.

3. Preheat the oven to 350°F. Grease baking sheets.

4. On a floured surface, roll out the dough to a thickness of ⅛ inch (or roll out the dough between two sheets of wax paper). Cut out shapes with floured cookie cutters. Transfer the cookies to baking sheets.

5. Lightly beat the egg whites. Using a pastry brush, glaze the surfaces of the cookies with the egg whites. Sprinkle green-colored sugar over the cookies, except for the torch, which can be sprinkled with yellow sugar. Bake for 8 to 10 minutes, or until the edges of the cookies are lightly browned. Remove to wire racks to cool.

Orange Cookie Stars Substitute the grated rind of a large orange for the lemon rind; lightly sprinkle the cookies with yellow- or pale orange-colored sugar after brushing with egg white.

THE DOG DAYS OF AUGUST

An Ohio Family Reunion Picnic

FOR 50 OR MORE
◆

I n the Midwest, there is, and has long been, an annual event of grand proportions called the family reunion. Within the various branches of my family, there are four such yearly gatherings, and I try to get back to Ohio for at least one of them. It's that once-a-year time when all the scattered members of the entire family get together, from great-grandaunts to great-grandchildren (in fact, one of our reunions now numbers close to three hundred and fifty relations). Each reunion is always a full day of activities—horseshoe tournaments, softball games, egg, spoon, and three-legged races, and (especially) tongue-wagging. And, of course, there are always tables and tables laden with a potluck assortment of food, since everyone brings a favorite dish. Nothing fancy, mind you, just simple, honest, down-home fare, washed down with gallons of homemade lemon-

MENU

Mom's Summer Meat Loaf
with Uncooked Tomato Sauce

Great-Aunt Susie's Molasses-Glazed
Smokehouse Ham

Aunt Doris's Famous Fried Chicken

Homemade Pickles and Relishes

Aunt Mary's Ohio Potato Salad

Great-Aunt Amelia's American Chop Suey

Aunt Etta's Tomato and Vegetable Aspic

Aunt Frances's Macaroni and Tuna Salad

Aunt Florence's Deviled Eggs with Bacon

Aunt Margaret's Vegetable Patch Slaw
with Boiled Dressing

Great-Aunt Nina's Mansfield Baked Beans

Great-Aunt Elverda's Pickled Beets with Eggs

Lettuce Salad with The Grill's Salad Dressing
(page 128)

Joyce's Whole Wheat-Walnut Bread

Dot's Carrot-Zucchini Bread

◆

Iva Mae's Plum Cake

Harriet's Chocolate Chip Cake

Betty's Peach and Raspberry Cobbler

Grandma Stapleton's Mayonnaise Cake

Aunt Edna's Blueberry Carry Cake

Mom's Chocolate Banana Cream Pie

My Upside-Down Cake

Grandma Wynn's Coconut Custard Pie

Dad's Vanilla Custard Ice Cream

Aunt Minnie's Apricot-Peanut Jumbles

On a hazy afternoon, my family's favorite picnic foods are set out on a red gingham-clothed table under the trees, creating a colorful and bountiful display.

ade. Needless to say, the food is always delicious. For one thing, come August everyone's farm or garden is bursting, so the ingredients are always at their best. For another, there seems to be an unspoken competition among the various family cooks to see who can collect the most praise.

The recipes included here are some favorites I've been collecting over the years from various and sundry relations, dishes that I look forward to having each time. I'm not suggesting that anyone make this entire menu, since that's never how it's really done, but a few fairly efficient cooks could easily throw it together when there's an occasion to feed a big crowd.

Mom's Summer Meat Loaf

MAKES 2 LOAVES

◆

Meat loaf always tasted better in the summer because my mother would add fresh herbs and vegetables from the garden. The Uncooked Tomato Sauce as an accompaniment is my own contribution.

    3 pounds lean ground beef
    1 pound bulk pork sausage
    4 large eggs, lightly beaten
    1 cup fine dry bread crumbs
    4 large ripe tomatoes, seeded and chopped
    1 large green pepper, finely chopped
    6 scallions, white and green parts, finely chopped
    2 large garlic cloves, finely chopped
    ½ cup chopped parsley
    ¼ cup chopped fresh basil
    2 tablespoons fresh thyme leaves
    2 tablespoons chopped summer savory
    1 teaspoon salt
    1 teaspoon freshly ground black pepper
    8 slices bacon
      Fresh herb sprigs, for garnish

1. Preheat the oven to 350°F. Lightly grease two shallow rectangular roasting pans or one large shallow roasting pan.

2. Place all the ingredients except the bacon in a large mixing bowl and mix with your hands until they are just blended together. Divide the mixture in half and shape each portion into a long rectangular loaf. Place the loaves in the prepared pans.

3. Lay 4 slices of bacon diagonally across and down the sides of each of the loaves, and tuck the bacon ends under the loaves. Bake for 1½ hours, or until the loaves are well browned. Remove the loaves from the oven and allow them to cool completely before

wrapping well and storing in the refrigerator. If meat loaves are to be served hot from the oven, allow them to cool about 20 minutes for easier slicing.

Note: If fresh herbs are unavailable, substitute 2 teaspoons each of dried basil, savory, and thyme and increase the chopped fresh parsley to 1 cup.

Uncooked Tomato Sauce

MAKES ABOUT 3 CUPS

◆

    3 pounds ripe tomatoes, peeled, seeded, and chopped
    ¼ cup olive oil
    1 large garlic clove, finely chopped
    4 scallions, white and green parts, thinly sliced
    2 tablespoons chopped fresh basil
    ¼ teaspoon salt
    1 teaspoon freshly ground black pepper

Combine all the ingredients in a nonmetallic bowl, cover tightly, and refrigerate for 3 hours before serving.

Great-Aunt Susie's Molasses-Glazed Smokehouse Ham

SERVES 30

◆

My father's Aunt Susie lived on a farm outside Cleveland, and like most farm people at that time, she and her family smoked their own meats in the smokehouse out back. Whenever Aunt Susie opened her cellar doors, the most wonderful smoky smells would come wafting up from the cool stone-lined cellar, where rows of hams and bacons were hung to age. If you've never tasted a real smokehouse ham, you're really missing something.

    1 smoked ham, 12 to 14 pounds
      Whole cloves
    1 cup light molasses, approximately

1. Using a stiff brush, scrub the ham, then place it in a large pot with enough cold water to cover. Cover the pot and soak overnight at room temperature.

2. Drain the ham well and rinse, then return it to the pot and cover with cold water again. Place on the stove and bring the water to a simmer. Simmer, loosely covered, for 20 minutes a pound, or until the ham reaches an internal temperature of 150°F. Add water as needed to keep the ham covered during cooking.

3. When the ham is cooked, allow to cool enough to handle easily. Remove it from the water and with a sharp knife, remove the tough rind and carve away almost all the outer fat, leaving only a ⅛-inch layer. (*The ham can be prepared ahead up to this point. When fully cool, wrap the ham in foil or plastic wrap and refrigerate.*)

4. To bake and glaze the ham, preheat the oven to 350°F. Remove the ham from the refrigerator, unwrap it, and place it on a rack in a shallow roasting pan, flatter side down. Diagonally score the layer of fat, being careful not to cut into the meat itself; stud the ham with cloves, then brush a thin layer of molasses over the surface.

5. Bake the ham, brushing with additional molasses as needed, for about 15 minutes a pound, or until heated through and well glazed and browned. Serve the ham warm or at room temperature, thinly sliced. To transport, wrap the ham with heavy-duty aluminum foil and carry it in a corrugated cardboard box. Bring along a large cutting board or platter.

Aunt Doris's Famous Fried Chicken

MAKES 24 PIECES

◆

One "secret" of my Aunt Doris's best-you-ever-ate fried chicken is the garlic she puts in the buttermilk when the chicken is marinating. Aunt Doris offers the following advice: make sure the oil is the right temperature so the chicken begins to cook as soon as it hits the pan; don't overcrowd the chicken pieces in the skillet; and use tongs to turn the chicken during cooking, so you don't pierce the skin.

We most often had this chicken at room temperature, picnic style, but if you want to serve it hot with corn fritters or mashed potatoes, make the old-fashioned cream gravy at the end of the recipe.

8 *chicken breast halves*
8 *chicken thighs*
8 *chicken drumsticks*
3 *cups buttermilk, approximately*
3 *large garlic cloves, peeled, halved, and crushed*
3 *cups vegetable shortening or lard, approximately*
2 *cups all-purpose flour*
1 *teaspoon salt*
2 *teaspoons rubbed sage*
2 *teaspoons paprika*
2 *teaspoons freshly ground black pepper*
1 *teaspoon cayenne pepper*

1. Trim the chicken pieces of excess skin and fat. Pack them fairly tightly into a deep, nonmetallic bowl and pour buttermilk over them to cover. Tuck the garlic pieces down among the chicken pieces, cover the bowl, and refrigerate overnight or at least 6 hours. Using tongs, turn the chicken once or twice during the marinating time.

2. Just before frying, melt the shortening or lard in a large, deep skillet or chicken frying pan over medium-high heat, and bring it to 370°F. The shortening should be about 1½ inches deep. Combine the remaining ingredients in a small brown paper bag. Place 2 or 3 chicken pieces in the bag at a time and shake to coat them well with the flour mixture.

3. Loosely arrange one layer of chicken skin side down (dark meat first) in the pan and fry, turning occasionally, until the chicken is well browned on all sides. The dark meat should cook in about 12 minutes, the breasts in about 10 minutes, depending on their size.

4. Drain the chicken on wire racks lined with paper towels. If it's to be served hot, keep it warm in a low oven while you finish frying the remaining pieces and make the cream gravy. If the chicken is being made ahead to serve cold, allow it to cool completely at room temperature before wrapping and refrigerating so the coating remains crisp. Bring the chicken back to room temperature before serving.

Cream Gravy

¼ *cup all-purpose flour*
3 *cups half-and-half*
Salt and freshly ground black pepper

1. Remove all but ¼ cup of fat from the frying pan and add the flour (or use flour coating mix if any is left over) to the pan. Over medium heat, cook the flour about 3 minutes, stirring constantly and scraping any browned bits from the bottom of the pan.

2. Slowly add the half-and-half and continue cooking, stirring constantly until the gravy is smooth and thick. Season with salt and pepper. Serve immediately with the hot fried chicken.

Aunt Mary's Ohio Potato Salad

SERVES 12

◆

3 pounds russet potatoes
1 medium green pepper, coarsely chopped
1 medium onion, coarsely chopped
¾ cup sliced red radishes
½ cup diced celery
¼ cup diced dill pickles
2 hard-boiled eggs, coarsely chopped
1 cup mayonnaise
1 tablespoon grainy mustard
2 teaspoons cider vinegar
2 tablespoons chopped fresh dill
  Salt and freshly ground black pepper
  Whole radishes, for garnish

1. Prick the unpeeled potatoes with a fork, boil them until just tender, and drain. Coarsely cut the potatoes into ¾-inch chunks and place them in a large serving bowl. Add the green pepper, onion, radishes, celery, pickles, and eggs.

2. In a separate bowl, combine the mayonnaise, mustard, vinegar, and dill, along with salt and plenty of freshly ground pepper to taste. Add this dressing to the large mixing bowl and toss the mixture gently to coat all the vegetables. Serve the potato salad at room temperature, garnished with whole radishes with their leaves.

Great-Aunt Amelia's American Chop Suey

SERVES 8

◆

Why is it called chop suey? No one in the family seems to know where this recipe or its name originally came from, but my guess is that, since macaroni first came from China and tomatoes originated in America, this sort of Italian dish of pasta in a tomato-based sauce became known as American Chop Suey.

This is not a recipe for food snobs, since, yes, that *is* canned tomato soup you see listed in the ingredients. But what could be more American than the familiar red and white can that's lurking somewhere in all our closets. (I did try adapting this recipe using only fresh, unadulterated ingredients, but it never tasted right, so here's the old-fashioned original recipe, just as Aunt Amelia made it for all those church suppers and reunions for so many years.)

12 thin slices smoked bacon, diced
4 large green peppers, chopped
4 medium onions, chopped
¾ cup chopped celery
2 large garlic cloves, finely chopped
1 pound elbow macaroni
2 cans condensed tomato soup
1 can water

1. Place bacon in the bottom of a Dutch oven and sauté over medium heat until well browned. Add the green peppers, onions, celery, and garlic and sauté them until very soft, about 20 minutes.

2. While the vegetables are cooking, cook the macaroni in salted boiling water. Drain the macaroni and add it to the Dutch oven, along with the tomato soup and water. Toss well to combine.

3. Remove the chop suey from the heat, cover, and allow it to cool and stand for several hours before gently reheating and serving it, or pack the chop suey in an insulated jug to keep it warm for several hours while transporting it.

Aunt Etta's Tomato and Vegetable Aspic

MAKES ONE 6-CUP MOLDED SALAD

◆

1 envelope unflavored gelatin
1 cup chicken stock
½ cup tomato juice
1 tablespoon lemon juice
1 tablespoon chopped fresh basil or parsley
¼ teaspoon Tabasco sauce
1 cup peeled, seeded, and coarsely chopped cucumbers
1 cup seeded and coarsely chopped tomatoes
½ cup diced celery
1 small green pepper, coarsely chopped
2 scallions, white and green parts, thinly sliced

1. In a small saucepan, soften the gelatin in the chicken stock. Place the pan over medium heat and stir until the gelatin is dissolved. Remove from the heat and stir in the tomato juice, lemon juice, basil, and Tabasco. Cover and chill the mixture until syrupy, 15 to 20 minutes.

2. Combine the vegetables and the gelatin mixture and transfer the aspic to a well-oiled 6-cup mold. Cover and chill until firm, at least 3 hours. Unmold the aspic onto a serving plate and garnish with basil leaves, parsley, or cucumber slices.

Aunt Frances's Macaroni and Tuna Salad

SERVES 18

◆

2 pounds elbow or bowtie macaroni, cooked al dente
2 15-ounce cans white tuna in oil, drained and flaked
2 cups broccoli flowerets, steamed and chilled
2 cups cooked peas
½ cup coarsely chopped walnuts
⅔ cup Red Wine Vinaigrette (page 188)

Place all ingredients in a large bowl and toss well to combine. Chill for 3 hours before serving.

Aunt Florence's Deviled Eggs with Bacon

MAKES 2 DOZEN

◆

1 dozen large eggs, hard-boiled and peeled
8 slices bacon, cut into ½-inch pieces and cooked crisp
2 tablespoons mayonnaise
2 tablespoons butter, melted and cooled
1 teaspoon cider vinegar
4 teaspoons prepared horseradish
1 teaspoon dry mustard
⅛ teaspoon salt
⅛ teaspoon cayenne pepper
¼ cup finely chopped pimiento

1. Cut the eggs in half lengthwise. Scoop out the yolks into a mixing bowl and mash the yolks with a fork. Crumble half of the bacon and add it to the bowl with the remaining ingredients. Mix well to form a smooth paste.

2. Spoon the yolk mixture into the halved egg whites, mounding the filling. Top each filled half with a piece of the remaining bacon. Place the stuffed eggs on a platter and chill for an hour before covering with aluminum foil or plastic wrap. Store in the refrigerator for up to 24 hours before serving.

TOP TO BOTTOM:
Clockwise from left: Ohio Potato Salad, Sweet-and-Hot Corn Relish, Macaroni and Tuna Salad, Summer Meat Loaf and Uncooked Tomato Sauce, and American Chop Suey.

Tomato and Vegetable Aspic, served on a green majolica plate and garnished with cucumber slices and parsley, and Aunt Doris's Famous Fried Chicken.

Deviled Eggs with Bacon surround a glass chicken dish.

Aunt Margaret's Vegetable Patch Slaw with Boiled Dressing

MAKES ABOUT 2 QUARTS

◆

Mayonnaise as the basis for slaw dressing is a fairly recent innovation; my Aunt Margaret always fixed this tasty old-fashioned dressing, which isn't really boiled at all, for her slaw. Since mayonnaise and hot weather can be unhappy companions, her recipe is perfect picnic fare.

Dressing

- ½ teaspoon salt
- ½ teaspoon dry mustard
- ½ cup sugar
- 2 tablespoons butter
- 6 tablespoons heavy cream
- 4 tablespoons cider vinegar
- 2 tablespoons lemon juice
- 1 teaspoon celery seeds

- 1 medium head green cabbage, shredded
- 1 large green pepper, grated
- 1 medium onion, grated
- 2 carrots, peeled and grated
- 2 celery ribs, thinly sliced

1. To make the dressing, combine the salt, mustard, sugar, butter, and cream in the top of a double boiler over simmering water and stir until smooth. Gradually stir in the vinegar, lemon juice, and celery seeds and cook, stirring constantly, until the dressing thickens. Remove the dressing from the heat and allow it to cool.

2. Toss the vegetables together in a large serving bowl. Pour the dressing over them and toss again. Cover and refrigerate the slaw at least 3 hours. Toss the slaw again just before serving.

Great-Aunt Nina's Mansfield Baked Beans

MAKES 3 QUARTS

◆

Aunt Nina always added apples to her baked beans; she said the fruit helped keep the beans moist. The complex flavor of these beans comes from the use of smoked bacon rather than the more traditional salt pork along with the addition of garlic and ginger.

- 2 pounds dried navy (pea) beans
- ¼ cup chopped parsley
- 8 slices thick smoked bacon, cut into 1-inch pieces
- 2 Granny Smith apples, peeled, cored, and diced
- 2 medium onions, coarsely chopped
- 3 large garlic cloves, chopped
- 2 tablespoons finely chopped fresh gingerroot or 1 teaspoon ground ginger
- 1½ cups dark molasses
- ½ cup firmly packed dark brown sugar
- 2 tablespoons dry mustard

1. Place the beans in a large pot with water to cover and soak overnight. Drain the beans, cover with fresh water, add the parsley and bacon, and place over medium heat. Bring to a boil, reduce the heat, and simmer the beans for about 40 minutes, or until tender. Drain the beans, reserving the cooking liquid.

2. Preheat the oven to 250°F. Grease a large bean pot or heavy 3-quart casserole. Mix the apples, onions, garlic, and ginger with the beans and transfer the mixture to the bean pot. Combine the remaining ingredients in a small bowl and pour the mixture over the beans. Add enough reserved bean liquid to barely cover the beans.

3. Cover the bean pot with the lid (or tightly cover with a double layer of aluminum foil) and bake the beans for about 8 hours, adding a bit of bean liquid if needed during baking to keep the beans moist. Uncover the pot for the last half hour of baking to brown the top. Serve warm or at room temperature.

Great-Aunt Elverda's Pickled Beets with Eggs

MAKES ABOUT 1 GALLON

◆

- 1 cup sugar
- 2 cups cider vinegar
- 2 cups water
- ½ teaspoon salt
- ½ teaspoon whole cloves
- 1 tablespoon whole allspice
- 2 cinnamon sticks
- 15 medium beets, untrimmed and unpeeled
- 3 medium onions, sliced ¼ inch thick
- 18 large eggs, hard-boiled and peeled

1. Combine the sugar, vinegar, water, salt, and spices in a saucepan and place over medium heat. Bring to a boil, reduce the heat, and simmer for 10 minutes. Remove from the heat and reserve.

2. Wash the beets and trim the stems, leaving about 1 inch of stem. Place in a pot, cover with water, and boil for 15 to 20 minutes, or until the beets are just tender. Drain, cool, and peel them.

3. Place the beets, onions, and eggs in a large jar and pour the sugar-vinegar mixture over them. Cover tightly, allow to cool, and store in the refrigerator up to two weeks.

Joyce's Whole Wheat-Walnut Bread

MAKES TWO 9 X 5-INCH LOAVES

◆

I love to make cheese sandwiches on this richly flavored bread; the recipe is from my sister-in-law Joyce.

1¼ cups coarsely chopped walnuts
2¼ cups scalded milk
1 teaspoon salt
3 tablespoons brown sugar
3 tablespoons soft butter
2 envelopes active dry yeast
3 cups all-purpose flour
3 to 3½ cups whole wheat flour

1. Spread the walnuts in an even layer on a baking sheet and toast in a 400°F. oven for about 10 minutes, or until lightly browned. Remove from the oven and reserve.

2. Mix together the milk, salt, brown sugar, and butter in a large bowl. Allow to cool to lukewarm and stir in the yeast. Stir in the white flour and then add the whole wheat flour, mixing well with your hands. Place the dough on a lightly floured surface and knead it until it is satiny and elastic, adding more whole wheat flour if necessary.

3. Place the dough in a lightly oiled bowl, cover with a cloth, and allow to rise in a warm place until doubled in bulk, about 1 hour.

4. Lightly grease two 9 x 5 x 3-inch loaf pans. Punch down the dough, knead in the reserved walnuts, and shape the dough into two loaves. Place the loaves in the pans and let rise until doubled in bulk, about 50 minutes.

5. Preheat the oven to 400°F. Bake the loaves for 20 minutes, reduce heat to 350°F., and bake an additional 45 minutes, or until the bread is well browned and sounds hollow when tapped with a finger. Remove the loaves from the pans and cool on wire racks.

Dot's Carrot-Zucchini Bread

MAKES THREE 8½ X 4½ X 2½-INCH LOAVES OR TWO 9 X 5 X 3-INCH LOAVES

◆

My sister-in-law Dot gets requests to make this recipe for every reunion (from me!). The oil in this bread keeps it moist for several days, if it lasts that long.

2½ cups sugar
6 large eggs
2½ cups vegetable oil
1½ teaspoons vanilla extract
4 cups all-purpose flour
4 teaspoons baking powder
1 teaspoon salt
1½ teaspoons ground cinnamon
1½ teaspoons ground cloves
½ teaspoon grated nutmeg
2 cups grated raw carrots
2 cups grated raw and unpeeled zucchini
2 cups chopped walnuts
1 teaspoon grated orange rind

1. Preheat the oven to 350°F. Lightly grease three 8½ x 4½ x 2½-inch loaf pans or two 9 x 5 x 3-inch loaf pans.

2. In a large mixing bowl, beat together the sugar, eggs, oil, and vanilla. In a separate bowl, sift together the flour, baking powder, salt, and spices. Stir the dry mixture into the wet mixture until just blended in, then fold in the carrots, zucchini, nuts, and orange rind all at once.

3. Pour the batter into the prepared pans, place pans in the oven, and bake for about 50 minutes (60 minutes for larger loaves), or until a toothpick or cake tester inserted in the center of a loaf comes out clean.

4. Remove the pans to wire racks, cool 15 minutes, then remove the loaves from the pan. Place the loaves on their sides and cool completely before serving. This bread will keep well, tightly wrapped and stored at room temperature, for 3 or 4 days.

Iva Mae's Plum Cake

MAKES ONE 10-INCH CAKE

◆

1¼ cups unsifted all-purpose flour
½ cup plus 2 tablespoons sugar
1¾ teaspoons baking powder
½ teaspoon salt
¼ cup (½ stick) butter
1 large egg
½ cup milk
1 teaspoon vanilla extract
10 ripe Italian prune plums, pitted and quartered
1 tablespoon brown sugar
½ teaspoon ground cinnamon

Topping

6 ripe purple plums, pitted and coarsely chopped
1 cup sugar
½ teaspoon almond extract

1. Preheat the oven to 350°F. Lightly grease an oven-proof glass or ceramic 10-inch pie pan.

2. Combine the flour, ½ cup sugar, baking powder, and salt in a mixing bowl, then cut in the butter with a pastry blender or two knives. In a separate bowl beat together the egg, milk, and vanilla, then stir into the dry mixture until just moistened.

3. Pour the batter into the prepared pan and arrange the plum quarters, cut side up, in a circular pattern on the batter. In a small bowl, combine the brown sugar, the remaining 2 tablespoons sugar, and the cinnamon; sprinkle this mixture over the plums and batter.

4. Bake for 30 to 35 minutes, or until the surface is lightly browned and a toothpick or cake tester inserted into the center of the cake comes out clean. Remove the cake from the oven and cool, in the pan, on a wire rack.

5. When the cake is completely cool, make the topping: Combine the chopped plums and sugar in a small heavy saucepan and place over medium heat. Cook, stirring constantly, until the sugar is dissolved and the mixture is syrupy, about 7 minutes. Remove from the heat and stir in the almond extract.

6. Spread the topping over the cake and allow it to cool completely before serving. Serve the cake at room temperature, cut into wedges.

Clockwise from bottom: Chocolate Chip Cake, Mayonnaise Cake with Chocolate-Orange Frosting, Peach and Raspberry Cobbler, and Plum Cake.

In the evening, desserts are set out on the kitchen porch.

Harriet's Chocolate Chip Cake

MAKES ONE 9-INCH ROUND CAKE

◆

3 cups all-purpose flour
3 teaspoons baking powder
¼ teaspoon salt
4 large eggs
1 cup (2 sticks) butter
2 cups sugar
1½ teaspoons vanilla extract
1 cup milk
1 cup chopped walnuts or pecans
1 12-ounce package chocolate chips

1. Preheat the oven to 350°. Butter and flour a 9-inch springform pan.

2. Sift the flour, baking powder, and salt together twice and set aside. Beat the eggs until light and fluffy. Set aside.

3. In a large bowl, cream together the butter and sugar until smooth. Add the eggs and vanilla and beat well.

4. Add the dry ingredients alternately with the milk. Beat very well at full speed.

5. Pour one third of the batter into the prepared pan and smooth out. Sprinkle on one third of the nuts and chips. Repeat two more times.

6. Bake for 1 hour and 15 minutes to 1½ hours, or until a cake tester inserted into the center comes out clean. Allow to cool in the pan for 30 minutes, then release springform. Cool cake completely before serving.

Betty's Peach and Raspberry Cobbler

MAKES ONE 9-INCH COBBLER

◆

Happily, peaches and raspberries are both at their best at the same time of year, and the combination is one of those rare cases where the sum is greater than its parts.

Orange Pastry for a 10-inch pie (page 188)
1 cup sugar
1 teaspoon ground ginger
2 tablespoons cornstarch
8 large, ripe peaches, peeled, pitted, and sliced
1½ pints red raspberries
¼ cup (½ stick) butter
Milk
Sugar

1. Preheat the oven to 425°. Roll out the pastry crust into a large circle ⅛ inch thick. Line a 10-inch deep-dish pie pan with the crust, letting the wide edges overhang.

2. In a large mixing bowl, combine the sugar, ginger, and cornstarch. Add the peaches and toss well to coat them. Add the raspberries and toss them gently to combine.

3. Mound the fruit mixture in the pie pan and dot the fruit with the butter. Turn the edges of the crust over the fruit, making overlapping folds every few inches or so, and leaving the center of the fruit uncovered. Brush the surface of the dough with milk and sprinkle it with coarse sugar.

4. Bake for 40 to 45 minutes, or until crust is well browned and the peaches are tender. If, during baking, the crust begins to get too brown, cover the cobbler with foil vented in the center to allow steam to escape. Serve the cobbler warm or at room temperature with whipped cream or ice cream.

Grandma Stapleton's Mayonnaise Cake

MAKES ONE 8-INCH 2-LAYER CAKE

◆

This quick and simple chocolate cake, which apparently originated in the years of rationing during World War II, was an after-school favorite in our house. The frosting is a postwar indulgence added by my grandmother.

2 cups all-purpose flour
4 tablespoons unsweetened cocoa powder
2 teaspoons baking soda
1 cup sugar
1 cup store-bought mayonnaise
1 cup cold water
2 teaspoons vanilla extract

1. Preheat the oven to 350°F. Grease two 8-inch round cake pans and dust them very lightly with flour.

2. Sift together the flour, cocoa, and baking soda in a small bowl. In a separate bowl, mix together the sugar and mayonnaise, then beat in the water and vanilla. Gradually beat in the dry mixture.

3. Pour the batter into the prepared pans and bake for 20 to 25 minutes, or until a toothpick inserted in the center of the cake comes out clean. (Make the frosting while the cake is baking.) Remove the cake from the oven, remove the layers from the pans, and place them on wire racks to cool before frosting.

Chocolate-Orange Frosting

Grated rind of 1 large orange
½ cup (1 stick) butter, softened
3 cups confectioners' sugar
2 squares unsweetened chocolate, melted and cooled
Pinch of salt
¼ cup orange juice

In a mixing bowl, blend together the orange rind and butter. Gradually beat in about half of the sugar until well blended. Beat in the chocolate and salt, then gradually beat in the remaining sugar alternately with the orange juice to a smooth, spreadable consistency.

Quick Chocolate Sheet Cake Bake the cake in a single 10 x 13-inch pan for 30 to 35 minutes. Remove the cake from the oven and immediately break three 1.65-ounce milk chocolate bars into squares and distribute them evenly over the cake's surface. When the chocolate is melted, spread it evenly over the cake to frost it. Allow the cake to cool completely in the pan before cutting it into squares.

Aunt Edna's Blueberry Carry Cake

SERVES 16 TO 20

◆

As the name implies, this old-fashioned cake was meant to be carried, since it has no gooey icing and it's baked and served from the same pan. Whether it's going next door for morning coffee or across town to a potluck supper or picnic, or whether it's just going from the oven to the table, I'd carry myself anywhere to have some.

      3 cups all-purpose flour
      1 tablespoon baking powder
      1 teaspoon salt
      ¾ cup sugar
      1 teaspoon grated nutmeg
    1½ teaspoons ground cinnamon
      ½ cup vegetable shortening
      3 large eggs, lightly beaten
      1 cup milk
      1 teaspoon vanilla extract
      3 cups blueberries

Topping
      ⅔ cup all-purpose flour
      ⅔ cup quick-cooking (not instant) oatmeal
      ⅔ cup firmly packed light brown sugar
      ½ cup (1 stick) cold butter, cut into pieces

1. Preheat the oven to 350°F. Lightly grease a shallow 9 x 13-inch cake pan, preferably one that has a cover.

2. In a mixing bowl, stir together the flour, baking powder, salt, sugar, and spices. Cut in the shortening until the mixture resembles coarse meal. Beat in the eggs, milk, and vanilla and continue beating until the batter is smooth and thick. Stir in 1 cup of blueberries.

3. Spread the batter into the prepared baking pan and sprinkle the remaining blueberries evenly over the top of the batter.

4. To make the topping, stir together the flour, oatmeal, and brown sugar in a small bowl. Using a pastry blender, or two knives, cut in the butter until coarse crumbs are formed. Sprinkle the crumbs evenly over the blueberries.

5. Place the pan in the oven and bake the cake for 40 to 45 minutes, or until a cake tester or toothpick inserted in the center comes out clean. Remove the cake from the oven, place on a wire rack, and cool completely in the pan before covering. Cut into squares to serve.

Mom's Chocolate Banana Cream Pie

MAKES ONE 9-INCH PIE

◆

      Basic Pastry for a 9-inch pie (page 188)
    1¼ cups sugar
      ¼ teaspoon ground cinnamon
      ½ cup all-purpose flour
      ¼ teaspoon salt
      2 cups half-and-half
      2 ounces unsweetened chocolate, coarsely chopped
      4 large eggs, separated
    1½ teaspoons vanilla extract
      2 large ripe bananas
      ¼ teaspoon cream of tartar

1. Preheat the oven to 450°F. Line a 9-inch pie pan with the pastry crust, prick with a fork, and line the crust with aluminum foil weighted with dry beans. Bake the crust until it begins to brown, about 10 minutes. Remove the foil and beans, lower the oven temperature to 400°F., and continue baking until the crust turns a rich golden brown, about 10 minutes longer. Remove the crust to a wire rack to cool.

2. In the top of a double boiler, combine 1 cup of the sugar, the cinnamon, flour, and salt. Place over simmering water and gradually whisk in the half-and-half and the chocolate. Continue stirring with the whisk until the chocolate is melted and combined and the mixture thickens, about 10 minutes. Remove from the heat.

3. Whisk the egg yolks lightly in a small bowl. Gradually whisk about a third of the chocolate mixture into the egg yolks and then whisk this mixture into the original chocolate mixture. Stir in the vanilla and allow to cool.

4. Line the bottom of the cooled pastry shell with the sliced bananas. Spoon the chocolate mixture over the bananas.

5. Preheat the oven to 325°F. In a small bowl, beat the egg whites until soft peaks form, then beat in the cream of tartar. Beat until stiff peaks form, then beat in the remaining ¼ cup sugar. Mound the mixture over the chocolate filling and touching the edges of the pastry shell and bake until the meringue is lightly browned, about 12 minutes. Cool completely and chill until serving time.

My Upside-Down Cake

MAKES ONE 9 X 13-INCH CAKE

◆

6 tablespoons (¾ stick) butter
1 cup firmly packed dark brown sugar
2 tablespoons dark rum
2 8-ounce cans pineapple chunks with juice
15 to 20 seedless red grapes, halved
¼ cup chopped pecans
¼ cup coconut

½ cup (1 stick) butter
¾ cup sugar
2 large eggs
2 tablespoons rum
2 cups flour
1½ teaspoons baking soda
¼ teaspoon salt

1. Preheat the oven to 350°F. Melt the butter and pour into the bottom of a 9 x 13-inch cake pan. Press the brown sugar evenly over the butter and sprinkle with the rum. Drain the pineapple chunks, reserving the juice, and cut the chunks in half. Arrange pineapple and grapes (cut side up) in diagonal rows on top of the brown sugar. Sprinkle the pecans and coconut between the fruit.

2. In a mixing bowl, cream together the butter and sugar. Beat in the eggs and the rum. In a separate bowl, sift together the flour, baking soda, and salt and beat this into the butter and sugar mixture alternately with ½ cup of the reserved pineapple juice. Carefully spoon the batter into the pan, so as not to disturb the fruit and nuts.

3. Bake for 30 to 35 minutes, or until a cake tester inserted in the center of the cake comes out clean. While the cake is still warm, turn it out onto a serving platter and allow it to cool before serving.

TOP TO BOTTOM:
Clockwise from top left: Mayonnaise Cake with Chocolate-Orange Frosting, Plum Cake, Peach and Raspberry Cobbler, Upside-Down Cake, Blueberry Carry Cake, Apricot-Peanut Jumbles, Chocolate Banana Cream Pie, Chocolate Chip Cake.

An upside-down cake topped with pineapple and red grapes.

A big galvanized tub helps to keep watermelon icy cold.

Grandma Wynn's Coconut Custard Pie

MAKES ONE 10-INCH PIE

◆

There's nothing terribly unusual about this pie, but it's one of those old-fashioned recipes that we tend to forget. Try to use fresh coconut if you can—it involves a little work, but the rest of the recipe is "easy as pie."

> Basic Pastry for a 10-inch pie (see page 188)
> 4 large eggs
> ½ teaspoon salt
> 1½ teaspoons vanilla extract
> ⅔ cup sugar
> 1 cup light cream or half-and-half
> 1½ cups milk
> 1 cup shredded coconut
> Nutmeg, for dusting

1. Preheat the oven to 425°F. Line the pastry shell with aluminum foil weighted with dry beans or other weights and bake the shell for 10 minutes. Remove the shell from the oven and set it on a wire rack; remove the weights.

2. Combine the eggs, salt, vanilla, sugar, cream or half-and-half, and milk in a mixing bowl, then fold in the coconut. Pour this mixture into the pie shell and dust the surface of the filling with nutmeg.

3. Place the pie in the oven and bake for 15 minutes. Turn the oven down to 350°F. and bake an additional 30 minutes, or until a knife inserted in the center of the pie comes out clean and the surface is lightly browned. Cool the pie on a wire rack and store in the refrigerator until an hour before serving.

Dad's Vanilla Custard Ice Cream

MAKES ABOUT 2 QUARTS

◆

Nobody loves ice cream more than my father does, and he loves vanilla ice cream best of all. This is the perfect topper for almost any dessert.

> 1 cup sugar
> ½ cup water
> 7 large egg yolks
> Pinch of salt
> 1 teaspoon vanilla extract
> 2 pints heavy cream

1. Combine the sugar and water in a small heavy saucepan and place over medium heat. Cook, stirring, until the sugar is dissolved, and continue cooking until the syrup forms a thin thread.

2. Beat the egg yolks until light and frothy. Very gradually pour in the syrup, beating constantly, until all the syrup is incorporated and the mixture is cool. Beat in the salt and vanilla, then stir in the cream.

3. Pour the mixture into an ice cream maker and freeze according to the manufacturer's directions.

Aunt Minnie's Apricot-Peanut Jumbles

MAKES 3½ DOZEN COOKIES

◆

This may sound like a crazy combination of ingredients, but the results are delicious. Almost any kind of jam could be substituted for the apricot jam—this is just my favorite.

> 2 cups all-purpose flour
> 2 tablespoons sugar
> ¾ teaspoon baking soda
> ¾ cup (1½ sticks) butter
> 2 large eggs, separated
> 1 cup apricot jam
> ½ cup sugar
> 1 tablespoon unsweetened cocoa powder
> ⅔ cup grated coconut
> 2 cups roasted unsalted peanuts, coarsely chopped

1. Preheat the oven to 350°. Grease a jelly roll pan (approximately 10½ x 15 inches).

2. In a mixing bowl, sift together the flour, sugar, and baking soda. Cut in the butter, then beat in the egg yolks, forming a stiff dough. Press the dough into the pan in an even layer. Bake for 10 minutes and remove the pan from the oven (do not turn off oven).

3. Spread the surface of the baked layer evenly with the jam. In a small mixing bowl, beat the egg whites lightly with a fork, then beat in the sugar and cocoa. Stir in the coconut and peanuts and spread this mixture evenly over the jam. Brush the top very lightly with water.

4. Bake an additional 20 minutes, or until the surface is well browned. Cool in the pan on a wire rack, then cut into 1½-inch squares.

Pickling and Preserving

FOR STORING AND GIVING

◆

Horseradish Jelly

Carrot Marmalade

Pear and Apple Butter

Cinnamon-Blueberry Jam

Gingered Peach Chutney

Pennsylvania Chow Chow

Carolyn's Bread-and-Butter Zucchini Pickles

Pickled Crabapples

Mom's Piccalilli

Green Tomato Mincemeat

Cranberry-Walnut Ketchup

Sweet-and-Hot Corn Relish

The Grill's Salad Dressing

Herb Vinegar   Berry Vinegar

Many people think of traditional American meals as being very simple, and they often were, but what we tend to forget is that most meals were served with a variety of condiments—relishes, pickles, chutneys, fruit butters, ketchups, and so on. In our house there was always a cellarful of foods that my mother and grandmothers had "put up," from simple canned fruits and vegetables to a wide assortment of jellies, pickles, relishes, and preserves, that were always ready to make their appearance on the dinner table, and at the end of the summer, at the Ohio State Fair.

Every August, my brothers and sister and I would start counting the days until we would be packed up, along with the best from Dad's farm and Mom's vegetable garden and kitchen, and go off to Columbus to the Fair. There was so much excitement, so much to see and do—appearances by such Ohioans as Bob Hope, Roy Rogers, and the McGuire Sisters. There were tests of skill, such as the ox pull and the hog chase, and we would always be there when one of my grandfather's horses ran a race. The thing we kids hated most of all, and that my father dragged us to every year, was the endless display of new farm equipment. And the thing we loved best was the mountainous carved butter display at the dairy pavilion, depicting a major event of the year. Now I look back most fondly on the food competitions—the largest squash, the most perfect tomato, the reddest and most delicious strawberry jam, and the best apple pie.

Some of the recipes here are ones from our farmhouse kitchen, others have been picked up over the years, and there are a few I've developed myself when inspiration and the right fresh ingredients found their way into my kitchen. Some of these recipes are used within the menus throughout the book and others are here just because I like them.

A Few Notes on Canning: Inspect all produce very carefully—fruits and vegetables should be at their peak of ripeness, not beyond it. If any signs of spoilage or bruising exist, cut them away completely.

Always wash canning jars well and sterilize them by boiling them for 15 minutes just before using.

To be absolutely certain that no spoilage will occur after canning, process all pickles and relishes in a hot water bath. To do this, place sealed jars at least an inch apart on a rack in a large kettle. Pour water into the kettle to cover the jars by two inches and gradually bring the water to a boil. Boil pint jars for fifteen minutes and quart jars for twenty minutes. Remove the jars immediately with tongs and allow to cool gradually in a warm place before labeling and storing.

When opening a home-canned jar, if there is any reason to think that spoilage has occured, discard the contents.

Packing Home-Canned Goods for Gifts: Use the prettiest jars or bottles you can find, either saved from store-bought goods or found at kitchenware shops or flea markets. I like to cover jar lids with pinked circles of fabric tied on with ribbon, with tags attached that offer serving suggestions.

Horseradish Jelly

MAKES ABOUT 2 HALF-PINTS

◆

3 pounds tart apples
3 cups water
2 cups sugar
½ cup prepared horseradish, drained

1. Cut the apples into chunks (do not core or peel). Put the apples and water in a heavy pot and place over high heat. Bring to a boil, reduce the heat, and simmer for 30 minutes.

2. Strain the apple juice through a colander into another saucepan; discard the fruit. Line the colander with a double layer of damp cheesecloth and strain the juice again. It will take about an hour for the juice to drip through.

3. Place the pan over medium-high heat and bring the juice to a boil. Add the sugar and boil the juice gently until it reaches 220°F. on a candy thermometer (or place a few drops on a small plate in the freezer to cool; it is done if the juice jells). Stir in the horseradish and simmer for 1 minute.

4. Skim any foam from the jelly and pour into sterilized half-pint jars. Seal with the lids or melted paraffin and store in a dark, cool place.

Carrot Marmalade

MAKES 4 HALF-PINTS

◆

I suspect this recipe came about during those times when carrots were in plentiful supply and oranges weren't. Now, when oranges are available almost all year, there's no reason to make it other than the fact that it's just plain good. Try this vividly colored marmalade with soft cream cheese or with cold sliced turkey or ham on sandwiches.

2 pounds carrots, peeled and grated
4 cups sugar
  Juice and grated rind of 3 lemons or 1 large orange
  and 1 lemon
1 tablespoon finely chopped fresh ginger

1. Place the carrots in a heavy saucepan with just enough water to cover. Simmer the carrots for 20 minutes and then drain them.

2. Return the carrots to the pan, add the remaining ingredients, and stir well to combine. Return the pan to the heat and bring to a boil, stirring until all the sugar is dissolved. Reduce the heat and simmer gently, stirring occasionally to prevent sticking, until the mixture is quite thick, about 45 minutes.

3. Ladle the marmalade into 4 sterilized half-pint jars and seal. Store the jars in a cool, dark place.

Pear and Apple Butter

MAKES ABOUT 4 PINTS

◆

Delicious with roasted duck, goose, and pork, this butter is easy to make, and a jar of it is a perfect holiday gift. To make for spreading onto breads rather than as a condiment for meat, substitute additional cider for the brandy.

2 pounds firm ripe pears
1 pound apples
1 cup cider
½ cup brandy
1 cup dark brown sugar
2 teaspoons ground cinnamon
1 teaspoon ground cloves
1 teaspoon ground ginger
½ teaspoon ground allspice

1. Core and quarter the fruit; do not peel. Place the fruit, cider, and brandy in a heavy saucepan over medium heat. Bring the mixture to the simmering point, reduce the heat, and simmer the apples and pears until they soften, about 20 minutes.

2. Remove the pan from the heat and stir in the brown sugar and spices. Puree the mixture very well in batches in the bowl of a food processor fitted with the steel chopping blade (or puree in a food mill). Taste and add more brown sugar, if necessary.

3. Return the mixture to the saucepan and place over low heat. Bring to a simmer and cook, stirring frequently, for about 30 minutes, or until a spoonful placed onto a small plate does not separate.

4. Pour the mixture into sterilized jars and seal. Or allow to cool and pour into jars or plastic containers, cover tightly, and refrigerate.

Cinnamon-Blueberry Jam

MAKES ABOUT 2 PINTS

◆

4 pints blueberries, washed and picked over
3 cups sugar
2 tablespoons water
4 cinnamon sticks

1. Place the blueberries, sugar, and water in a heavy saucepan over low heat. Cook, stirring constantly, until the berries begin to release their juice (add a bit more water if necessary to prevent sticking). Raise the heat slightly and add the cinnamon sticks. Boil the mixture gently, stirring frequently, until thick and syrupy, approximately 20 minutes.

2. Transfer to sterilized pint jars, seal with the lids or melted paraffin, and store in a cool, dark place.

Gingered Peach Chutney

MAKES ABOUT 4 HALF-PINTS

◆

One of my Grandma Stapleton's specialties, which she made from the fruit of the tree she had started years before from a peach pit. This tangy, sweet condiment goes well with slices of country ham, grilled duck, or simple grilled or roasted chicken, and it's the perfect accompaniment to a spicy curry.

10 firm ripe peaches
Grated rind of 2 lemons
Juice of 1 lemon
2 cups sugar
1½ cups cider vinegar
½ teaspoon salt
1 teaspoon mustard seeds
3 tablespoons finely chopped fresh gingerroot
1 medium onion, coarsely chopped
1 small garlic clove, finely chopped
1 cup golden raisins
⅛ teaspoon cayenne pepper

1. Peel the peaches and cut them into ¼-inch dice. There should be about 4 cups. Place the peaches in a nonmetallic bowl and add the grated lemon rind and juice. Toss well and set aside.

2. Combine the sugar, vinegar, salt, mustard seeds, ginger, onion, and garlic in a large heavy saucepan over high heat. Bring to a boil, reduce the heat, and simmer for 10 minutes.

3. Add the peaches and their liquid and the raisins to the saucepan. Bring the mixture to the simmer again and cook, stirring frequently, until the syrup is thick, about 45 minutes. Remove from the heat and stir in the cayenne pepper.

4. Transfer the chutney to sterilized half-pint jars and seal. Process in a boiling-water bath (page 120) for 15 minutes. Cool and label the jars and store in a cool, dark place.

Pennsylvania Chow Chow

MAKES 4 PINTS

◆

1 10-ounce container Brussels sprouts, trimmed and halved
3 cups cauliflower flowerets
2 cups pearl onions, peeled
2 cups coarsely chopped green tomatoes
1 large green pepper, coarsely chopped
1 large red pepper, coarsely chopped
2 medium carrots, cut into ¼-inch slices
4 small cucumbers, cut into ¼-inch slices
3 tablespoons salt
2½ cups cider vinegar
1½ cups sugar
2 teaspoons dry mustard
1 teaspoon turmeric
½ teaspoon ground ginger
1 teaspoon mustard seeds
1 teaspoon celery seeds

1. Combine the vegetables in a large heavy pot, sprinkle with the salt, and let stand for 4 hours in a cool place. Drain well and rinse the pot.

2. Combine the vinegar, sugar, mustard and spices in the pot and place over medium-high heat. Simmer the mixture for 10 minutes. Add the vegetables and simmer for 10 minutes longer. Turn up the heat and bring the mixture to a rolling boil.

3. Immediately pack into 4 sterilized pint jars, leaving ¼ inch of space at the top of each jar, and seal the lids. Process the jars in a boiling-water bath (page 120) for 15 minutes. Cool and label the jars and store in a cool, dark place.

OPPOSITE: *At the end of the summer, the pick of the garden is brought into the kitchen to become home-canned pickles and relishes. On the cutting board are the raw ingredients for Pennsylvania Chow Chow.*

Carolyn's Bread-and-Butter Zucchini Pickles

MAKES 4 QUARTS

◆

While visiting the Spainhour family in Winston-Salem, North Carolina, some years ago, I happened to mention to Carolyn Spainhour that I always had a surplus of zucchini in my garden (who doesn't?). Since then she's sent me quite a few zucchini recipes. This is one of the best.

  1 quart white vinegar
  1 cup sugar
  ¼ cup salt
  1 tablespoon celery seeds
  1 tablespoon dill seeds
  2 teaspoons mustard seeds
  4 quarts small zucchini, cut into ⅛-inch slices
  2 pounds medium onions, peeled and thinly sliced

1. Put the vinegar, sugar, salt, and seeds in a large heavy pot over high heat and bring to a boil. Add the zucchini and onions to the pot and cover. Remove from the heat and let stand 1 hour.

2. Return the pot to the stove over high heat. Bring the mixture to a boil again, reduce the heat, and simmer for 3 minutes. Pack the pickles loosely in four sterilized 1-quart jars (or eight 1-pint jars), pour the pickling liquid over to cover, and seal.

3. Process the jars in a boiling-water bath (page 120) for 20 minutes (15 minutes for 1-pint jars). Cool and label the jars and store in a cool, dark place.

Pickled Crabapples

MAKES 5 PINTS

◆

  1 quart cider vinegar
  1 cup water
  3 cups sugar
  3 cinnamon sticks
  2 tablespoons whole cloves
  1 tablespoon whole allspice
  7 pounds small crabapples (or lady apples)

1. Combine all ingredients except apples in a large heavy pot over high heat. Bring the mixture to a boil, remove from the heat, and allow the syrup to stand for 2 hours.

2. Place the pot over medium-low heat, add the apples, and bring the mixture to a boil slowly, to prevent the apple skins from splitting. When the mixture has reached the boiling point, reduce heat and simmer 5 minutes. Remove the pot from the heat, cover tightly, and allow to stand overnight.

3. Pack the apples into sterilized 1-pint jars, pour the syrup over them to cover, and seal. Process the jars in a boiling-water bath (page 120) for 15 minutes. Cool and label the jars and store in a cool, dark place. Allow the apples to stand for at least 3 weeks before using.

Mom's Piccalilli

MAKES 4 PINTS

◆

My mother made jars and jars of this relish when green tomatoes and sweet peppers were in abundance. All winter long she served the piccalilli as a condiment, a pleasant cold-weather reminder of the bounty of summer. I've pared her recipe down to less Herculean proportions.

  2 quarts green tomatoes, chopped
  4 large green peppers, chopped
  ¼ cup salt
  2 cups cider vinegar
  ½ teaspoon freshly ground black pepper
  ½ teaspoon dry mustard
  1½ teaspoons ground cinnamon
  1½ teaspoons ground allspice
  1½ teaspoons ground cloves
  1 teaspoon mustard seeds
  1 teaspoon celery seeds
  2 large onions, chopped
  3 cups sugar

1. Combine the tomatoes and green pepper in a large bowl, sprinkle the salt over them, and cover. Let stand 8 hours or overnight. Drain well.

2. Combine the vinegar and spices in a large heavy pot and bring to a boil. Add the remaining ingredients, including the tomatoes and green pepper, and bring to a boil again. Reduce the heat and simmer for 30 minutes, stirring occasionally.

3. Transfer the piccalilli to sterilized 1-pint jars and seal. Process the jars in a boiling-water bath (page 120) for 15 minutes. Cool and label the jars and store in a cool, dark place.

Green Tomato Mincemeat

MAKES ABOUT 4 PINTS,
ENOUGH FOR FOUR 9-INCH PIES

◆

Grandma Wynn, who cooked in a restaurant in Mansfield, Ohio, at one point in her life, had two favorite ways of using up the last green tomatoes left on the vines just before the first freeze: she would fry them up or she would make Green Tomato Mincemeat, which would later be baked in fragrant and rich pies.

My old friend June Huffman recently reminded me of this method we used on the farm for ripening up the season's last tomatoes that had to be picked green so they wouldn't freeze: Wrap each tomato loosely in a sheet of newspaper. Pack them into a brown paper bag and store them in a cool, dry place. This method allows the tomatoes to ripen slowly and keep for weeks.

   1 *dozen small green tomatoes, about 2 inches in diameter*
1½ *teaspoons salt*
   4 *cups diced tart apples*
   1 *large orange, seeded and finely chopped (including rind)*
   1 *cup dark raisins*
  ¾ *cup chopped beef suet*
   2 *cups firmly packed brown sugar*
     Juice of 1 large lemon
  ¼ *cup cider vinegar*
  ½ *cup apple juice or water*
   2 *teaspoons ground cinnamon*
   1 *teaspoon ground cloves*
  ½ *teaspoon grated nutmeg*
   1 *tablespoon finely chopped fresh gingerroot or 1 teaspoon ground ginger*
1½ *cups brandy or rum, approximately*

1. Core the tomatoes and cut them into ¼-inch dice. Sprinkle the salt over them, cover, and let stand for 30 minutes.

2. Drain the tomatoes in a colander and rinse them well under hot running water. Place the tomatoes in a large heavy pot, add the remaining ingredients except the brandy, and stir well to combine with a large heavy spoon. Place the pot over medium heat and, stirring frequently, bring the mixture to a simmer. Reduce the heat and simmer slowly, stirring constantly, for 10 minutes, or until all liquid evaporates and the mixture is very thick. Remove the pot from the heat and stir in 1 cup of the brandy or rum.

3. Ladle the mincemeat into sterilized 1-pint jars, leaving about ½ inch unfilled in each. Pour brandy or rum into each jar just to cover the mincemeat. Seal the jars.

4. Process the jars in a boiling-water bath (page 120) for 15 minutes. Cool and label the jars and store in a cool, dark place. Before using the mincemeat, stir it well.

Cranberry-Walnut Ketchup

MAKES ABOUT 3 PINTS

◆

What could be better with turkey than this zesty alternative to cranberry relish? Try it on turkey or ham sandwiches, too, or with pork and poultry based pâtés. This has become a favorite of photographer Randy O'Rourke, who ate it on almost everything during our photography sessions.

   2 *large onions, coarsely chopped*
   1 *large tart apple, peeled, cored, and coarsely chopped*
   1 *large garlic clove, finely chopped*
   1 *tablespoon finely chopped gingerroot (see note)*
   1 *teaspoon grated orange rind*
   1 *cup water*
   6 *cups (2 12-ounce bags) cranberries*
   2 *cups firmly packed light brown sugar*
1½ *cups finely chopped walnuts*
   1 *cup cider vinegar*
   1 *teaspoon ground cinnamon*
   1 *teaspoon ground cloves*
  ½ *teaspoon salt*
  ½ *teaspoon freshly ground black pepper*

1. Put the onions, apple, garlic, ginger, orange rind, and water in a large heavy saucepan, place the pan over medium heat, and bring the mixture to a boil. Lower heat and simmer for 10 minutes. Add the cranberries to the pan, bring to a simmer again, and cook, stirring frequently, until all the cranberries pop.

2. Puree the mixture in a food processor fitted with the steel chopping blade (or use a food mill) and return the puree to the pan. Stir in the remaining ingredients. Place the pan over high heat and bring the mixture to a rolling boil, stirring constantly.

3. Ladle the ketchup into 3 sterilized 1-pint jars and seal. Process the jars in a boiling-water bath (page 120) for 15 minutes. Cool and label the jars and store in a cool, dark place.

Note: If fresh gingerroot is absolutely unavailable, substitute 1 teaspoon ground ginger and add it in step 2.

Pickled Crabapples and Bread-and-Butter Zucchini Pickles to be served as condiments with Thanksgiving dinner.

This sweet, sour, and oniony salad dressing from the Brunswick Grill is a hometown favorite.

Pungent Horseradish Jelly is delicious with barbecued meats.

A bottle of herb vinegar and jars of Carrot Marmalade and Cranberry-Walnut Ketchup.

Jars of Mom's Piccalilli and Sweet-and-Hot
Corn Relish cool on the windowsill.

Pennsylvania Chow Chow is made from a mixture of
vegetables in a sweet-and-sour mustard sauce.

Sweet-and-Hot Corn Relish

MAKES ABOUT 6 PINTS

♦

4 medium onions, coarsely chopped
4 large ripe tomatoes, skinned, seeded, and chopped
3 large cucumbers, peeled, seeded, and chopped
2 large green peppers, chopped
4 cups coarsely chopped cabbage
8 cups corn kernels (about 10 ears)
3 cups sugar
2 teaspoons salt
1 tablespoon celery seeds
1 teaspoon turmeric
1 teaspoon crushed red pepper
4 cups cider vinegar

1. Combine all the ingredients in a large saucepan, place over medium-high heat, and bring to a boil. Reduce the heat and simmer uncovered, stirring occasionally, for 20 minutes.

2. Transfer the relish to sterilized 1-pint jars and seal. Process the jars in a boiling-water bath (page 120) for 15 minutes. Cool and label the jars and store in a cool, dark place.

The Grill's Salad Dressing

MAKES ABOUT 3 PINTS

♦

Years ago, the Brunswick Grill in my hometown was the only restaurant around for miles, and it was known for its delicious sweet-and-sour salad dressing. Someone managed to get a copy of the recipe, and soon "The Grill's" dressing was being served in houses all over the county.

2 cups corn oil
1 cup cider vinegar
1 cup sugar
3½ cups tomato ketchup
1 teaspoon salt
3 medium onions, finely chopped
3 large garlic cloves, finely chopped

Mix all ingredients and let stand for about 10 days in the refrigerator, stirring each day. Pack into small jars and store in the refrigerator. The dressing keeps for 3 or 4 weeks.

Herb Vinegar

MAKES 2 PINTS

♦

Use fresh herbs, such as rosemary, oregano, marjoram, thyme, parsley, and basil, alone or in combinations. Or combine them with strong-flavored vegetables such as garlic, hot peppers, or shallots. Use decorative 1-quart bottles, available at kitchenware shops, for storing the vinegar and for gift-giving.

1 quart white wine vinegar or red wine vinegar
2 or 3 sprigs of fresh herbs
2 or 3 large garlic cloves or shallots
1 small hot red or green pepper

1. Pour the vinegar into a small nonaluminum saucepan over medium heat. Heat the vinegar to just below simmering and remove the pan from the heat.

2. Place herbs and/or vegetables into two sterilized 1-pint bottles that have tight-fitting caps or corks and fit the neck with a funnel. Ladle the warm vinegar into the bottles and seal. Place the jars in a cool, dark place to age for at least a month before using.

Berry Vinegar

MAKES 2 PINTS

♦

Raspberry vinegar was one of the darling ingredients of nouvelle cuisine, but country cooks have been making berry vinegars for generations.

1 pint raspberries, strawberries, or blueberries, crushed slightly
1 quart white wine vinegar

1. Place the fruit in a sterilized 2-quart jar with a tight-fitting lid and pour the vinegar over it. Close the lid tightly, shake well, and place the jar in a cool, dark place for 3 weeks. Shake the jar daily.

2. Strain the contents of the jar through a colander lined with cheesecloth to strain out the fruit. Pour the vinegar into sterilized 1-pint jars, seal, and store in a cool, dark place.

A Lazy-Day Lunch

FOR 4–6

◆

MENU

Iced Sun Tea with Lemon and Spearmint

*Tomato Sandwiches
with Basil and Chive Butter*

Quick Squash and Radish Slaw

◆

*Nectarine-Buttermilk Ice Cream
with Fresh Raspberry Sauce*

Store-Bought Cookies

Even though sun and warm weather don't end abruptly on Labor Day, the long weekend always signals the last few lazy days of summer, just before reality sets in, and the last thing I want to do is be cooped up in the kitchen. Now is the time for a bit of noncooking. The tomatoes and squash are literally bursting on the vine with flavor and color, the herbs are lush and fragrant, and I usually have some homemade ice cream stashed in the freezer. Who needs to cook?

Getting Ready: Make the ice cream up to a week in advance. When you do your marketing, buy loaves of thinly sliced pumpernickel or rye bread and your favorite store-bought cookies.

Set out the sun tea 4 to 6 hours before you want to drink it; have ice, lemon, and mint ready at serving time. In the kitchen, mix up the basil and chive butter, puree the raspberries, and make the slaw any time before lunch. With a food processor, this will all take about 15 minutes. The tomato sandwiches should be assembled at the table.

Iced Sun Tea with Lemon and Spearmint

Here's the laziest way of making iced tea I know; you don't even have to boil water. Combine 1 gallon of water, ½ cup loose tea leaves, and a large sprig of fresh mint in a large jar. Cover the jar and set it in the sun for 4 to 6 hours. Strain the tea and chill. Serve over ice with lemon slices, superfine sugar, and extra sprigs of mint.

Tomato Sandwiches with Basil and Chive Butter

◆

I can't think of too many things I'd rather eat than a simple open-faced tomato sandwich. To my eye, there's nothing prettier than a freshly sliced *real* summer tomato, and the tomato's vivid color somehow makes its flavor even more intense.

Basil and Chive Butter
  ½ cup (1 stick) butter, softened
  ¼ cup basil leaves, coarsely chopped
  2 tablespoons snipped chives
  ⅛ teaspoon salt

  Whole ripe tomatoes
  Thinly sliced pumpernickel or rye bread

1. Combine all ingredients for the basil and chive butter in a small bowl and mix well. Cover and refrigerate, but return to room temperature before serving.

2. To make the sandwiches, spread thinly sliced light or dark pumpernickel bread with a thin layer of Basil and Chive Butter, layer thick slices of tomatoes onto the bread and serve open-faced.

ABOVE: *On a hot and lazy day, I like to serve lunch in a tree-shaded spot in the yard, next to the pond.*

LEFT: *On a day like this one, I let the sun make the tea.*

BELOW: *Nectarine-Buttermilk Ice Cream and Fresh Raspberry Sauce meld together in a green Depression glass sherbet on the railing of the deck.*

A simple lunch that celebrates the best from the vegetable garden: Quick Squash and Radish Slaw, and open-faced tomato sandwiches with Basil and Chive Butter.

Quick Squash and Radish Slaw

SERVES 6

◆

The food processor makes this ready in just a few minutes.

  ½ cup loosely packed parsley sprigs
  2 tablespoons Homemade Mayonnaise (page 188)
  3 tablespoons olive oil
  3 tablespoons cider vinegar
  1 teaspoon grainy mustard
  ½ teaspoon sugar
    Salt and freshly ground black pepper to taste
  1 medium zucchini
  1 medium yellow summer squash
  12 large red radishes, washed and trimmed

1. Place the parsley in the bowl of a food processor fitted with the steel chopping blade and process to chop the parsley coarsely. Add the mayonnaise, oil, vinegar, mustard, sugar, and salt and pepper; process to blend.

2. Replace the processor's chopping blade with the grating blade and grate the squash and radishes into the processor bowl. Transfer the mixture to a serving bowl and toss the vegetables with the dressing to coat.

Nectarine-Buttermilk Ice Cream with Fresh Raspberry Sauce

MAKES ABOUT 2½ QUARTS

◆

This recipe makes more than you need for lunch, but everyone can usually be talked into having some more during the course of the afternoon.

  6 large, ripe nectarines, peeled and finely chopped
  ½ cup honey
  1 tablespoon lemon juice
  ¼ teaspoon ground ginger
  ⅛ teaspoon ground cloves
  ⅛ teaspoon ground cinnamon
  ½ cup sugar
  ¼ teaspoon salt
  1 quart buttermilk
  4 large egg yolks, lightly beaten
  2 pints heavy cream
  4 teaspoons vanilla extract

1. Combine the nectarines, honey, lemon juice, and spices in a small heavy saucepan and place over medium heat. Bring the mixture to a simmer, remove from heat, and cool.

2. In a separate pan, combine the sugar, salt, and buttermilk and bring to the scalding point, stirring to dissolve the sugar. Remove from heat and slowly stir this mixture into a bowl containing the beaten egg yolks, stirring constantly until blended.

3. Pour the mixture back into the pan and return to the heat. Cook, stirring constantly until the mixture thickens slightly, but *do not allow the custard to boil.* Remove from heat, stir in the cream and vanilla, and cool. Cover and chill thoroughly.

4. Stir the nectarine mixture into the custard mixture. Pour into an ice cream maker and freeze according to the manufacturer's instructions. Serve the ice cream slightly softened with fresh raspberry sauce.

Fresh Raspberry Sauce

Combine 1 pint raspberries, ⅓ cup sugar (or more to taste), and 1 tablespoon lemon juice in the bowl of a food processor fitted with the steel chopping blade and process to a coarse puree. Store the sauce in a covered jar in the refrigerator.

A Soup and Sandwich Supper

FOR 10 TO 12

◆

MENU

Mom's Potato and Celery Chowder

◆

*Grilled Chicken Breasts
with Cranberry, Pear, and Thyme Relish
on Rye and Indian Bread*

*Hot Dogs with Hot Onion and Mustard Relish
on Store-Bought Sourdough Rolls*

*Sliced Grilled Flank Steak
with Spicy Guacamole Salsa
on Peppered Batter Bread*

◆

Apple-Oatmeal Squares with Apple Snow

I must admit that I have always been a diehard Cleveland Indians fan, and every spring I make the optimistic prediction that this could be the year. Well, maybe someday. . . .

While I don't watch much baseball on TV during the season, I never miss a World Series game, and I always assume my friends feel the same way, so I have a group over to watch the first game of the series, before things get too emotionally charged.

Getting Ready: Assuming that the chowder and Apple-Oatmeal Squares have been made a day in advance, the Cranberry, Pear, and Thyme Relish has been made ahead, and that the breads have been made ahead and frozen, there's little to do on the night of the party except cook the chicken, hot dogs, and steak. These can all be done in quick succession while you make the Hot Onion and Mustard Relish. The chicken and steak can be served warm or at room temperature, but the hot dogs are best served hot. Make the Apple Snow and start the salsa anytime up to three hours before serving; add the avocado to the salsa at the last minute.

Beverages: I serve an assortment of local beers and hearty red and white jug wines.

Mom's Potato and Celery Chowder

SERVES 12

◆

¼ pound lean thick-sliced bacon, coarsely chopped
3 cups thinly sliced celery
1 large onion, chopped
3 scallions, white and green parts, chopped
1 medium green pepper, chopped
4 cups hot chicken stock
3 cups diced boiling potatoes
2 tablespoons chopped fresh dill
¼ cup chopped parsley
2 cups half-and-half
   Salt and freshly ground black pepper
   Leafy celery sticks, for garnish

1. In a large Dutch oven over medium heat, sauté the bacon until some of the fat is rendered. Add the celery, onion, scallions, and green pepper and sauté for about 15 minutes, or until the celery is crisp-tender.

2. Add the chicken stock, potatoes, and herbs to the Dutch oven and simmer about 12 minutes, or until the potatoes are just tender. (*May be prepared ahead up to this point, cooled, covered, and refrigerated. Reheat slowly before proceeding with step 3.*)

3. Stir in the half-and-half and simmer the soup gently over low heat for about 10 minutes. Season to taste with salt and plenty of fresh pepper and serve immediately in mugs. Garnish each serving with a leafy celery stick.

ABOVE: *The buffet is set up on the desk in the den, not far from the television. The mugs commemorate my old "home team," the Cleveland Indians.*

RIGHT: *Apple-Oatmeal Squares with Apple Snow, a satisfying fall dessert.*

Cranberry, Pear, and Thyme Relish

MAKES 4 CUPS

◆

3 cups (1 12-ounce bag) cranberries
4 large ripe pears, peeled, cored, and cut into chunks
1 small onion, very finely chopped
¼ cup sugar
1 tablespoon lemon juice
1 heaping teaspoon fresh thyme leaves or ½ teaspoon dried thyme

Put all ingredients in the bowl of a food processor fitted with the steel chopping blade and pulse several times until berries and pears are coarsely chopped. Transfer to a bowl, cover, and refrigerate overnight. Will keep several weeks in the refrigerator.

Mugs of Mom's Potato and Celery Chowder with (clockwise) Grilled Flank Steak with Spicy Guacamole Salsa on Peppered Batter Bread; Grilled Chicken Breast with Cranberry, Pear, and Thyme Relish on Rye and Indian Bread; and a hot dog with Hot Onion and Mustard Relish on store-bought sourdough rolls.

Grilled Chicken Breasts

◆

1. Allow 1 large boneless and skinless chicken breast half for each sandwich. Flatten each breast half slightly with a mallet and arrange the breasts in a shallow bowl. Sprinkle the meat generously with ground black pepper, lemon juice, and olive oil. Cover and refrigerate for an hour or two.

2. Preheat the broiler. Season the breasts lightly with salt, if desired, and arrange them on a broiling pan with a rack. Broil until lightly browned on both sides and firm to the touch, about 5 minutes on each side; do not overcook. (Or cook on a grill about 4 inches above hot white coals, about 5 minutes on each side.)

Rye and Indian Bread

MAKES 2 LOAVES

◆

My theory on breadmaking is that if you're going to do all the work, you might as well have something to show for it, so make two loaves. And since this earthy, wonderfully textured bread freezes well, use one for this menu and save one for another time.

- 2 cups milk
- 1 cup water
- 1/3 cup molasses
- 1 teaspoon salt
- 4 cups all-purpose flour
- 1 1/2 cups stone-ground yellow cornmeal
- 2 packages active dry yeast
- 1 1/2 cups rye flour

1. In a heavy saucepan, combine the milk, water, molasses, and salt. Place over low heat and heat until just warm. Remove from heat.

2. In a large mixing bowl, stir together 3 cups of the flour, the cornmeal, and the yeast. Gradually stir the milk mixture into the flour mixture and beat with an electric mixer for about 3 minutes. Beat in the remaining cup of flour and the rye flour. (This step may also be done in a food processor fitted with the steel chopping blade if the bowl is large enough to accommodate the mixture.)

3. Remove the dough to a floured board and knead until the dough is elastic and satiny. Form the dough into a ball and remove to a lightly oiled bowl, cover with a damp cloth, and allow to rest in a warm, draft-free place until doubled in bulk, about 1 hour.

4. Punch down the dough, divide it in half, and shape it into two 8-inch loaf pans. Cover with the cloth, and allow to double in bulk again, about 45 minutes.

5. Preheat the oven to 325°F. Bake for 50 to 55 minutes, or until the loaves are well-browned and sound hollow when tapped with a finger.

Hot Onion and Mustard Relish

MAKES 2 CUPS

◆

This zesty condiment can be made well in advance and stored for up to a week in the refrigerator. Try it, too, with ham or any smoked sausage.

- 1/4 cup (1/2 stick) butter
- 8 medium onions, sliced
- 1 cup dark beer
- 2 tablespoons dark brown sugar
- 1/4 cup prepared grainy mustard
- 1/4 cup prepared yellow mustard
  Dash of cayenne pepper

Melt the butter in a skillet over medium heat, add the onions, and sauté until golden brown, about 20 minutes. Stir in the remaining ingredients and cook, stirring frequently, until thick, about 10 minutes. Serve hot.

Spicy Guacamole Salsa

MAKES ABOUT 3 CUPS

◆

- 3 large ripe tomatoes, seeded and chopped
- 3 scallions, white and green parts, chopped
- 1 large garlic clove, finely chopped
- 3/4 cup olive oil
- 2 tablespoons lemon juice
- 1 tablespoon chopped fresh coriander
- 1 small hot green chili pepper, finely chopped
  Salt and freshly ground black pepper to taste
- 2 ripe avocados, peeled and coarsely chopped

Combine all ingredients except the avocado, cover, and refrigerate. Add the avocado no more than an hour before serving and toss well.

Peppered Batter Bread

MAKES ONE 9 X 5 X 3-INCH LOAF

◆

An easy white bread with a wonderful texture and a surprising flavor due to the pepper. It requires no kneading, but no one will suspect you weren't slaving away for hours. If you're making more than one loaf, it's best to make batches of batter separately, measuring and mixing simultaneously. The loaves can be baked all at once.

    4 to 4½ cups all-purpose flour
    3 tablespoons sugar
    2 teaspoons salt
    2 teaspoons coarsely ground black pepper
    2 packages active dry yeast
    1 cup milk
    ½ cup water
    3 tablespoons butter
    2 large eggs, lightly beaten

1. In a large mixing bowl, sift together 1 cup of the flour, the sugar, salt, pepper, and yeast. Combine the milk, water, and butter in a small heavy saucepan over low heat and heat until butter is melted. Gradually beat the liquid mixture into the dry mixture, beat 2 minutes, then beat in the eggs.

2. Beat in 1 more cup of flour and beat at high speed for 2 minutes; repeat until a total of 4 cups of flour have been used. Beat in just enough additional flour to form a very stiff batter.

3. Cover the bowl with a towel, place in a warm place, and allow the batter to rise till doubled in bulk, about 1 hour.

4. Preheat the oven to 375°F. and butter a 9 x 5 x 3-inch loaf pan very well. With a heavy spoon, punch down the batter and beat it for half a minute. Transfer the batter to the pan and let it rise again until it just reaches the top of the pan, about 20 minutes.

5. Bake the bread until the crust is well browned and the loaf sounds hollow when tapped with a finger, about 45 minutes. Turn out onto a wire rack to cool.

Apple-Oatmeal Squares

MAKES 1 DOZEN 3-INCH SQUARES

◆

    2 large tart apples, peeled, cored, and diced
    ½ teaspoon baking soda
    ½ cup sugar
    ½ cup firmly packed dark brown sugar
    ½ cup (1 stick) butter
    1 large egg
    1½ cups flour
    1 teaspoon ground cinnamon
    1 teaspoon ground ginger
    ½ cup quick-cooking (not instant) oats
    ½ cup chopped walnuts

1. Preheat the oven to 350°F. and lightly grease a shallow 9 x 12-inch baking pan. Combine the apples and baking soda in a nonmetallic bowl and let stand while proceeding with step 2.

2. Cream the sugars, butter, and egg in a mixing bowl. Beat in the flour and spices, then stir in the oatmeal, apples, and nuts. Pour the batter into the prepared pan.

3. Bake for 30 to 35 minutes, or until the cake begins to shrink from the edges of the pan and a cake tester inserted into the center comes out clean. Cool in the pan about 20 minutes, then cut into squares.

Apple Snow

MAKES ABOUT 6 CUPS

◆

    2 cups unsweetened applesauce, chilled
    ¾ cup confectioners' sugar
    ½ teaspoon ground cinnamon
    1 teaspoon lemon juice
    ½ teaspoon salt
    2 large egg whites
    1 cup heavy cream

1. Combine the applesauce, confectioners' sugar, cinnamon, lemon juice, and salt in a large mixing bowl. In a separate bowl beat the egg whites until soft peaks form and fold them into the applesauce mixture.

2. In a separate chilled bowl, beat the cream until stiff peaks form. Fold the whipped cream into the apple mixture and serve spooned over Apple-Oatmeal Squares. Apple Snow may be stored, tightly covered, in the refrigerator up to 3 hours before serving.

*A brigade of glowing Jack O' Lanterns
on my front stoop welcomes all the
witches, werewolves, and hobgoblins.*

An Old Salem Pumpkin Supper

FOR 12 TO 16

◆

ABOVE: *A buffet supper is laid out on an old homespun bedspread. Clockwise from left: Harvest Vegetable Soup served in a pumpkin, Corned Beef and Cheddar Sandwiches on Whole Wheat-Walnut Bread, Cabbage-Pepper Slaw, Cider and Ginger Punch, and Pecan-Popcorn Balls.*

LEFT: *Hallowe'en sweets: A Pumpkin-Spice Donut and a Pecan-Popcorn Ball with Cider and Ginger Punch.*

Cider and Ginger Punch   Witches' Brew

◆

Harvest Vegetable Soup in a Pumpkin
Corned Beef and Cheddar Sandwiches
on Whole Wheat-Walnut Bread
with Cabbage Pepper Slaw

◆

Pecan-Popcorn Balls
Pumpkin-Spice Doughnuts   Apples

Hallowe'en may be for children, but I don't suppose I'll ever really grow up. The sight of a glowing jack-o'-lantern still makes me smile.

I used to live along the route of the annual parade that winds its way through the narrow streets of Greenwich Village, so every year I would have a group of friends over to watch the parade pass by. I live in a different neighborhood now, and the Village Hallowe'en parade has become a huge affair attended by hundreds of thousands rather than the small neighborhood celebration it was, but my Hallowe'en party continues.

The group tends to evolve during the evening, since some of the guests are usually on their way to or from some other party, so I always try to put together a menu that will hold up as trick-or-treaters come and go. Another consideration is that it require a minimum of last-minute work, since Hallowe'en often falls on a week night. I also try to serve food that both kids and grown-ups like. Since I was a kid, Hallowe'en has always meant cider and donuts, so they're always part of my Hallowe'en menu, too.

Getting Ready: The bread can be made well in advance and frozen. The Pecan-Popcorn Balls can be made up to a week ahead and stored in tins. The doughnuts and slaw should be made a day ahead. The soup can be made up to a day ahead and gently reheated at serving time. No more than a few hours ahead, assemble the sandwiches; add the slaw at the last minute. The punch can be put together just before serving.

Cider and Ginger Punch and Witches' Brew

◆

Mix equal amounts of chilled apple cider and ginger ale in a punch bowl and garnish with cinnamon sticks and clove-studded lady apples. For Witches' Brew, pour a shot of applejack or rum into each serving cup and fill the glass with punch.

Harvest Vegetable Soup

SERVES 16

◆

I always hollow out a big pumpkin to use as a tureen when serving this colorful soup

- ¼ cup (½ stick) butter
- 2 medium onions, coarsely chopped
- 4 scallions, white and green parts, thinly sliced
- 2 large garlic cloves, finely chopped
- 6 carrots, thinly sliced
- 1½ cups diced celery
- 3 quarts chicken broth
- 6 medium potatoes, peeled and quartered
- 4 parsnips, peeled and sliced
- 4 cups cubed pumpkin or butternut squash
- 4 white turnips, peeled and quartered
- 3 large tart apples, peeled and coarsely chopped
- 2 bay leaves
- 1 teaspoon dried basil
- ½ teaspoon dried thyme
  Salt and freshly ground black pepper

1. Melt the butter in a large heavy pot over medium heat. Add the onion, scallions, garlic, carrots, and celery and sauté for 10 minutes.

2. Add the chicken broth, vegetables, apple, and bay leaves and bring the mixture to a boil. Lower the heat and simmer the soup for 20 minutes. Add the basil, thyme, and salt and pepper to taste and simmer for about 15 minutes longer, or until the vegetables are tender. Serve. (*The soup can be made a day in advance and reheated over low heat before serving.*)

Corned Beef and Cheddar Sandwiches on Whole Wheat-Walnut Bread with Cabbage-Pepper Slaw

SERVES 12 TO 16

◆

Cabbage-Pepper Slaw

    1 small head cabbage, coarsely grated
    2 large green peppers, coarsely grated
    ⅔ cup mayonnaise
    2 tablespoons milk
    1 tablespoon prepared mustard

    3 pounds thinly sliced corned beef
    2 pounds sliced sharp Cheddar cheese
    2 loaves Whole Wheat-Walnut Bread (page 113),
       sliced

1. To make the slaw, combine the cabbage and green pepper in a large bowl. Mix together the mayonnaise, milk, and mustard in a small bowl, pour this dressing over the vegetables, and toss well to coat. Refrigerate until ready to use.

2. Assemble the sandwiches a few hours ahead, in the usual manner, and store tightly wrapped, at room temperature. Add a half-inch layer of slaw just before cutting and serving.

Pecan-Popcorn Balls

MAKES 2 DOZEN 3-INCH BALLS

◆

    1 cup sugar
    1 cup firmly packed light brown sugar
    1 cup light corn syrup
    ⅔ cup water
    1 pound butter
    4 cups pecans
    8 cups popcorn

1. Combine the sugars, corn syrup, and water in a heavy pan fitted with a candy thermometer over high heat. Bring the mixture to a boil. Add the butter, stirring until it has melted. Continue cooking for 20 to 30 minutes, until the mixture reaches 300°F.

2. Meanwhile, preheat the oven to 350°F. Spread the pecans in an even layer on a baking sheet and bake them for about 10 minutes, or until lightly browned. Remove the nuts from the oven and toss them with the popcorn in a large, lightly oiled bowl.

3. Carefully pour the hot syrup over the popcorn-nut mixture. Carefully but quickly toss the mixture with a long-handled wooden spoon to coat the popcorn and nuts completely with syrup.

4. As soon as the mixture is cool enough to handle, quickly shape into 3-inch balls and place the balls on a lightly oiled baking sheet to cool. Or spread the mixture in a thin layer on two lightly oiled baking sheets to cool completely before breaking into bite-size pieces. Store in tightly covered tins up to a week.

Pumpkin-Spice Doughnuts

MAKES ABOUT 2 DOZEN

◆

It seems that hardly anyone makes doughnuts anymore, and it's a shame, since they're really quite easy. Make the doughnuts no earlier than a day ahead.

    6 cups sifted all-purpose flour
    2 tablespoons baking powder
    ½ teaspoon salt
    2 teaspoons ground cinnamon
    2 teaspoons ground ginger
    1 teaspoon grated nutmeg
    ¼ cup vegetable shortening
    1 cup firmly packed light brown sugar
    2 large eggs
    2 cups pumpkin puree
       Vegetable shortening or lard, for frying
       Sugar, for coating

1. In a large bowl, sift together the flour, baking powder, salt, and spices. In a separate bowl, cream together the shortening and sugar, then add the egg and pumpkin puree and beat well to blend. Gradually stir the dry mixture into the wet one until just blended together.

2. Heat about 4 inches of vegetable oil or lard in a large heavy pot to 360°F. (use a frying or candy thermometer to determine temperature).

3. Roll dough out on a floured board to a thickness of ⅜ inch. Cut the dough with a floured 2½-inch doughnut cutter and let stand about 10 minutes.

4. A few at a time, fry the doughnuts in the hot fat until nicely browned on both sides, turning once during frying. Transfer the doughnuts to absorbent paper to drain. Dust with confectioners' or granulated sugar while still slightly warm.

A Tailgate Picnic

FOR 6
◆
MENU
Mulled Cider with Brandy
Deviled Nuts (page 84)
◆

Veal, Mushroom, and Barley Soup
Ham-and-Cheese-on-Rye Bread
Chicken, Pear, and Pecan Salad
Carrot Salad with Cumin Dressing
◆

Buckeye Maple Cake
A Basket of Apples

Our picnic is laid out on a plaid blanket in the back of the car. Left to right: Mulled Cider, served in crystal tumblers, and a flask of brandy; Chicken, Pear, and Pecan Salad; Carrot Salad with Cumin Dressing; and Ham-and-Cheese-on-Rye Bread on an old breadboard.

Come fall, I'm still not willing to give up the outdoors. I look forward to those Saturdays that involve an outing through the cool, crisp, autumn-colored countryside to a college football game. The parking fields around the stadium start filling up in the late morning and pretty soon they look like one huge picnic ground, with elaborate meals spread out on tailgates, hoods, and trunks of cars.

Part of the fun is making the picnic as elaborate as possible. The food itself may be simple, but great care should be taken in its presentation. I always drag along things that are ordinarily not found at picnics, such as crystal glasses, silver flatware, and cotton napkins. This is utter simplicity compared to some tailgaters who, it seems, have brought everything from their dining rooms except the walls.

Getting Ready: Since this meal is traveling, everything should be ready to be packed in the morning.

The bread can be made well in advance and frozen. Take it out of the freezer just before leaving home and it should be thawed by lunchtime. (Or bake the bread no sooner than a day in advance.)

The soup can be made a day or two in advance and reheated before packing it into an insulated jug for traveling. The Carrot Salad should be made a day in advance, and the Chicken, Pear, and Pecan Salad can be too. Prepare the cider just before leaving home, pack it in an insulated jug, and take along a flask of brandy.

The layers for the Buckeye Maple Cake can be baked a day in advance, or well ahead and frozen. The cake is best if assembled and frosted early on the day of the picnic.

Mulled Cider with Brandy

MAKES 12 SERVINGS

◆

3 *quarts freshly pressed apple cider*
2 *teaspoons whole cloves*
2 *teaspoons whole allspice*
  Brandy
  Cinnamon sticks

Combine the cider, cloves, allspice, and 6 cinnamon sticks in a saucepan, place over low heat, and bring to just below the simmering point. Transfer to an insulated jug to keep the mixture warm. To serve, pour into glasses, stir in brandy to individual tastes, and add a cinnamon stick to each glass.

Veal, Mushroom, and Barley Soup

SERVES 6

◆

A hearty, rib-sticking soup for a chilly fall day.

¼ *cup (½ stick) butter*
1 *pound lean stewing veal, trimmed and cubed*
1 *large onion, finely chopped*
1 *carrot, finely chopped*
1 *celery rib, finely diced*
8 *large mushrooms, sliced*
2 *quarts veal or chicken stock*
¾ *cup pearl barley*
2 *tablespoons chopped fresh dill or 2 teaspoons dried dill*
  Salt and plenty of freshly ground black pepper

1. Melt the butter in the bottom of a Dutch oven or large heavy kettle over medium heat. Add the veal and brown it on all sides; remove the veal and reserve. Add the onion, carrot, celery, and mushrooms and sauté 10 minutes.

2. Add the stock and the veal to the kettle and bring to a boil. Rinse the barley under warm running water, drain well, and add it to the kettle. Bring to a boil, cover loosely, and simmer 45 minutes. Add the dill and salt and pepper to taste and continue simmering until the barley is tender, another 10 or 15 minutes.

3. Pack the hot soup into an insulated jug and bring along heavy mugs to keep the soup hot once it's served.

Ham-and-Cheese-on-Rye Bread

MAKES 2 LOAVES

◆

My friend Renie Ladden always makes a stuffed bread for tailgate parties, and with good reason. This travels well and has all the elements of a sandwich rolled (literally) into one compact package.

2 *packages active dry yeast*
2 *tablespoons dark brown sugar*
1 *tablespoon salt*
2 *cups hot water*
2 *tablespoons vegetable shortening*
2 *tablespoons caraway seeds*
1 *small onion, grated*
3 *cups rye flour*
3 *to 4 cups all-purpose flour*

Filling
- ⅓ cup prepared brown mustard, approximately
- ¾ cup coarsely shredded smoked ham
- ¾ cup coarsely grated sharp Cheddar cheese

- 1 large egg yolk, lightly beaten, for glaze
  Caraway seeds

1. Stir together the yeast, sugar, and salt in a large bowl. Stir in the hot water and shortening and allow the mixture to cool to lukewarm.

2. Add the caraway seeds, grated onion, rye flour, and 3 cups of all-purpose flour to the dissolved mixture and mix well with your hands. Add more white flour as necessary to make the dough easy to handle (the rye flour will cause the dough to remain slightly sticky). Transfer the dough to a lightly floured surface and knead it until it is satiny and elastic, adding additional white flour if needed.

3. Transfer the dough to a lightly oiled bowl, cover it with a cloth, and allow it to rest in a warm place until doubled in bulk. Punch down the dough and allow it to rise again, about 1 hour. Punch down the dough again and remove it to a floured surface.

4. Divide the dough in half. Roll out the first half into a circle about ½ inch thick. Liberally brush the surface with the mustard and spread half of the ham and cheese over the mustard.

5. Roll the dough, jelly roll fashion, give the roll a slight twist to hold it together, and place it, seam side down, on a lightly greased baking sheet. Repeat the process with the other half and cut diagonal slashes into the tops of the loaves. Cover the loaves, and allow to rise again until almost doubled in bulk, about 45 minutes.

6. Preheat the oven to 375°F. Brush the surface of the loaves with beaten egg yolk and sprinkle the loaves lightly with caraway seeds. Place the pan in the oven and bake until the loaves are well browned, about 45 minutes. Cool the loaves on a wire rack. Cut into ½-inch slices to serve.

Chicken, Pear, and Pecan Salad

SERVES 6

◆

- 4 unpeeled firm ripe pears, diced
- 2 tablespoons lemon juice
- 1 cup coarsely chopped pecans
- 2 cups cubed cooked chicken breast
- 1½ cups diced celery
- ¾ cup Homemade Mayonnaise (page 188)

Toss the pears with the lemon juice. Add the remaining ingredients, toss to coat well with the mayonnaise, cover, and chill up to 4 hours before serving.

Note: If the weather is cool and the salad is to travel in an unheated part of the car, put it into a serving dish and cover tightly. If the weather is warm, transport the salad in an insulated jug or in a covered container packed in a cooler.

Carrot Salad with Cumin Dressing

SERVES 6

◆

Dressing
- 1 large garlic clove, crushed
- 3 tablespoons olive oil
- 3 tablespoons vegetable oil
- 3 tablespoons red wine vinegar
- ¾ teaspoon ground cumin
- ½ teaspoon paprika
  Pinch of cayenne pepper
  Pinch of salt

- 1½ pounds carrots, peeled and grated or julienned
- ½ cup chopped parsley

1. Combine the dressing ingredients in a jar, cover, and shake well to mix. Place the carrots in a bowl, pour the dressing over them, and toss well. Cover and refrigerate for at least 6 hours, or preferably overnight.

2. Remove the garlic clove, and no more than a few hours before serving, add the parsley and toss well. Serve chilled or at room temperature.

Buckeye Maple Cake

MAKES ONE 8-INCH SQUARE
2-LAYER CAKE

◆

When I was growing up I never heard of *Vermont* maple syrup—as far as we were concerned, Ohio was prime maple country. The Bauer family was the biggest producer around my hometown of Willard, and this recipe for a classic Ohio cake that always reminds me of home was given to my mother years ago by Pearl Bauer. The cake is square, so it can easily be packed for traveling.

   3 *cups cake flour*
   4 *teaspoons baking powder*
 ¼ *teaspoon salt*
 ½ *cup (1 stick) butter*
   1 *cup maple syrup*
 ⅔ *cup milk*
   1 *cup chopped walnuts*
   1 *cup chopped apples*
   4 *large egg whites*

Frosting

   3 *cups confectioners' sugar*
   2 *tablespoons soft butter*
 ¼ *teaspoon salt*
 ¼ *teaspoon vanilla extract*
 ¼ *cup maple syrup*
 ½ *cup coarsely chopped walnuts*

1. Preheat the oven to 350°F. Grease two 8-inch square cake pans, line them with wax paper, and grease the paper.

2. In a mixing bowl, sift together the flour, baking powder, and salt. In a separate bowl, beat the butter until fluffy. Beat in the syrup and then the milk. Gradually beat the dry mixture into the wet mixture, then stir in the walnuts and apples.

3. In a separate small bowl, beat the egg whites until stiff but not dry. Gently fold the egg whites into the batter, then pour the batter into the prepared cake pans. Bake 35 to 40 minutes, or until a cake tester inserted in the center comes out clean. Transfer the cake layers to wire racks to cool.

4. To make the frosting, beat together all ingredients except walnuts, adding a bit more maple syrup if necessary to achieve a soft, spreadable consistency. Spread half the frosting over one layer, top with the other layer, and frost with the remaining frosting. Sprinkle the walnuts over the frosting.

Note: For transport, place the cake on a board and pack it in a deep basket or box so it won't slide around while traveling. Cover the basket or box with its lid or a cloth napkin or dish towel.

OPPOSITE: *Ham-and-Cheese-on-Rye Bread is a compact, spiral-shaped sandwich.*

ABOVE: *Buckeye Maple Cake, sprinkled with chopped walnuts and decorated with autumn maple leaves.*

An Old New England Grateful Dinner

FOR 10 TO 12

◆

Thanksgiving, the oldest American celebration, is the one holiday throughout the year that is based on food itself. And our Thanksgiving dinners are the most steeped in tradition. Even though I vary my menu somewhat from year to year, I go only so far. It just wouldn't be Thanksgiving without turkey as the centerpiece, surrounded by the best of the fall harvest. This menu is deeply rooted in New England tradition, even going back to succotash, a dish the colonists learned how to make from the Indians.

Getting Ready: This is a big dinner, but a good deal of work can be done ahead. The Cranberry-Walnut Ketchup can be made well in advance. The Horseradish Butter for the red cabbage can be made

MENU

Wellfleet Oyster Chowder

◆

Maple-Glazed Turkey with Roasted Apples and Pears

Applejack Gravy   Apple-Chestnut Stuffing

Skillet Squash with Red Onions

Cranberry-Walnut Ketchup (page 125)

Oven-Stewed Succotash

Steamed Red Cabbage Wedges with Horseradish Butter

◆

Brandied Green Tomato Mincemeat Pie

Pumpkin-Black Walnut Pie

Gingered Indian Pudding with Iced Sweet Cream

up to a week ahead and stored in the refrigerator. The desserts can be made a day ahead; reheat the Indian pudding in a low oven after the turkey comes out. The succotash, too, can be made a day in advance and reheated. Also prepare the base for the chowder.

On Thanksgiving day, the stuffing can be made early in the morning, but do not stuff the turkey until just before roasting. The roasting time of the turkey depends on the size—check the recipe and plan accordingly.

About half an hour before serving, finish the chowder, make the Skillet Squash with Red Onions, and steam the cabbage; these can happen simultaneously on top of the stove. Make the gravy as soon as the turkey comes out of the oven.

Beverages: I like fresh or hard cider with this one. Alternatively, a good wine choice would be a fruity, dry white, such as Gewürztraminer or Sauvignon Blanc.

Wellfleet Oyster Chowder

SERVES 12 AS A FIRST COURSE,
6 TO 8 AS A MAIN COURSE

◆

The most delicious oyster chowder I ever had was served on a rainy fall afternoon in an oyster bar in Wellfleet, near the tip of Cape Cod. This recipe is a reconstruction of that memorable soup. Almost any kind of oysters will do—buy the freshest and plumpest ones available no more than a day ahead and have them shucked at the market.

¼ cup (½ stick) butter
1 cup finely diced celery
1 medium onion, finely chopped
4 cups diced cooked potatoes
1½ cups diced cooked carrots
2 quarts oysters, with their liquor
4 cups milk
2 cups light cream or half-and-half
1 tablespoon chopped sage leaves or 1 teaspoon dried sage
Salt and freshly ground black pepper

1. Melt the butter in a large Dutch oven over medium heat. Add the celery and onion and sauté for 10 to 12 minutes, or until the onion is transparent. Add the potatoes and carrots and toss. (*Can be prepared up to this point and stored overnight in the refrigerator.*)

2. Add the oysters and their liquor, bring to a simmer, and cook until the edges of the oysters curl. Add the remaining ingredients, stir well, and bring the chowder to just below the simmering point. Season with salt and plenty of fresh pepper to taste and serve immediately.

Maple-Glazed Turkey with Roasted Apples and Pears and Applejack Gravy

SERVES 12, WITH PLENTY OF LEFTOVERS

◆

1 18- to 20-pound turkey
Salt and freshly ground black pepper
Apple-Chestnut Stuffing (recipe follows)
¼ cup (½ stick) butter, softened
⅔ cup maple syrup
2 red baking apples, quartered and cored
2 Comice pears, quartered and cored
Sage leaves, for garnish

1. Preheat the oven to 325°F. Rinse the turkey well, inside and out, and pat dry with paper towels. Rub salt and pepper into both the neck and body cavities.

2. Stuff both cavities loosely with stuffing (see note) and close both ends with trussing skewers and string. Place the turkey breast side up on a rack in a large roasting pan. Rub the skin lightly with softened butter. Insert a meat thermometer into the thickest part of the thigh without touching the bone.

3. Place the turkey in the oven and roast about 12 minutes a pound (15 minutes a pound if the turkey weighs less than 15 pounds), basting every 30 minutes with the pan juices. During the last half hour of roasting, brush the turkey with the maple syrup. Add the apples and pears to the pan and baste them with the pan juices.

4. The turkey is done when the meat thermometer registers 180°F., or when the juices run clear when the thigh is pricked with a meat fork. Remove the turkey to a warm platter and garnish the platter with sage leaves and the roasted apples and pears. Cover the turkey loosely with aluminum foil and let it rest for 20 to 30 minutes before carving while you make the gravy.

Note: Any stuffing that does not fit into the turkey can be packed into a buttered heavy-duty aluminum foil packet and roasted for about 45 minutes.

Applejack Gravy

¼ cup (½ stick) butter
¼ cup all-purpose flour
½ cup applejack or fresh or hard cider
Pan drippings, skimmed of fat
Chicken or turkey stock, or water

1. Melt the butter in a heavy saucepan over medium heat and stir in the flour until absorbed. Gradually stir in the applejack to form a smooth paste and cook 5 minutes, stirring constantly.

2. When the turkey comes out of the roasting pan, skim off the fat from the pan juices and discard. Scrape the bottom of the pan to remove any browned bits, stir them into the juices, and pour the juices into the saucepan.

3. Stir the contents of the saucepan until smooth. Add stock or water to thin the gravy if necessary. Bring to a boil, reduce the heat, and simmer 5 minutes longer. Pour into a gravy boat and serve.

Thanksgiving dinner in the country offers traditional and colorful New England flavors. Clockwise from top: Maple-Glazed Turkey surrounded by Roasted Apples and Pears and stuffed with Apple-Chestnut Stuffing; Steamed Red Cabbage Wedges with Horseradish Butter; Skillet Squash with Red Onions; Oven-Stewed Succotash; and Cranberry-Walnut Ketchup.

During the summer, I gather and dry masses of flowers so that during the winter and fall I can enjoy wonderful bouquets like this one.

A flaky pastry crust with cut-out maple-leaf shapes tops fragrant brandy-laced green tomato mincemeat in this rustic-looking pie.

Apple-Chestnut Stuffing

MAKES ABOUT 8 CUPS

◆

6   slices smoked bacon, chopped
½   cup (1 stick) butter
1   medium onion, chopped
1   cup diced celery
6   cups soft fresh white bread crumbs
4   large red baking apples, unpeeled and chopped
2   cups chopped roasted chestnuts
1½ teaspoons dried sage
1½ teaspoons dried thyme
½   cup chopped parsley
2   large eggs, lightly beaten
½   cup cider or apple juice
1   teaspoon freshly ground black pepper

1. Sauté the bacon in a skillet over medium-high heat for about 10 minutes, or until most of the fat is rendered. Reduce heat to medium-low, add the butter, onion, and celery, and sauté the vegetables until crisp-tender, about 10 minutes.

2. Transfer the contents of the skillet to a large mixing bowl, add the remaining ingredients, and mix well until well blended and bread crumbs are lightly moistened. Add a bit more apple juice if necessary.

Skillet Squash with Red Onions

SERVES 10 TO 12

◆

Any type of winter squash works well here, but my favorites are either Hubbard squash or pumpkin.

¼   cup (½ stick) butter
2   medium red onions, coarsely chopped
6   cups diced winter squash
1   teaspoon sugar
¼   teaspoon ground cloves
    Salt and freshly ground black pepper

1. Melt the butter in a large skillet over medium heat. Add the onions and sauté 5 minutes. Add the squash and stir to blend. Cover the skillet and cook the mixture, stirring occasionally, until the squash is crisp-tender, 6 to 8 minutes.

2. Add the sugar and cloves, toss to coat the squash, and cook an additional 3 or 4 minutes. Season with salt and pepper to taste and serve.

Oven-Stewed Succotash

SERVES 12

◆

6   thin slices bacon, coarsely chopped
2   tablespoons butter
1   small onion, grated
2   cups milk
1   tablespoon brown sugar
½   teaspoon salt
½   teaspoon freshly ground black pepper
5   cups corn kernels (preferably freshly scraped)
4   cups fresh or frozen lima beans

1. Preheat the oven to 350°F.

2. Sauté the bacon in a 3-quart Dutch oven or flame-proof casserole over medium heat until most of the fat is rendered. Remove the bacon with a slotted spoon and reserve. Add the butter and grated onion to the Dutch oven and sauté the onion for 5 minutes. Add half the bacon, milk, brown sugar, salt, and pepper and bring the mixture to the simmering point.

3. Add the corn and lima beans and stir well to combine all ingredients. Sprinkle the reserved bacon over the surface. Loosely cover the Dutch oven, place it in the preheated oven, and bake for about 1 hour, or until the lima beans are very soft and the succotash is quite thick.

Note: If you have no space in the oven, the succotash can be simmered on top of the stove over very low heat; stir frequently to prevent sticking. Or it can be made a day ahead and reheated in the oven.

Steamed Red Cabbage Wedges with Horseradish Butter

SERVES 12

◆

Colorful and flavorful, red cabbage steamed until crisp-tender is far more appealing than the sodden cabbage of boiled dinners we all grew up with.

2   cups water
½   cup cider vinegar
2   small heads red cabbage

¼   cup (½ stick) soft butter
2   tablespoons prepared horseradish
1   tablespoon grainy prepared mustard

1. Pour the water and vinegar into a large saucepan fitted with a steamer rack, place over medium-high heat, and bring to a simmer.

2. Meanwhile, cut each cabbage into six wedges (do not core) and secure the coreless end of each wedge with a toothpick. Place the cabbage on the steamer rack, cover, and steam the cabbage for 10 to 12 minutes, or until crisp-tender. Remove the toothpicks and arrange the wedges on a platter.

3. In a small bowl, beat together the butter, horseradish, and mustard until well blended. Pass the horseradish butter separately.

Brandied Green Tomato Mincemeat Pie

MAKES ONE 9-INCH PIE

◆

Basic Pastry for a double-crust 9-inch pie
(page 188)
4 cups Green Tomato Mincemeat (page 125)

1. Preheat the oven to 425°F. Line a 9-inch pan with the bottom crust. Spoon the mincemeat into the crust. Roll out the top crust and cut out 3 or 4 holes with a cookie cutter (I use a maple leaf–shaped cutter). Cover the pie with the top crust and roughly crimp the edges—this pie should look rather rustic.

2. Bake the pie for 30 to 40 minutes, or until the crust is nicely browned. Serve warm or at room temperature.

Pumpkin-Black Walnut Pie

MAKES ONE 9-INCH PIE

◆

Basic Pastry for a 9-inch pie (page 188)
3 large eggs, lightly beaten
¾ cup firmly packed light brown sugar
1½ cups pumpkin puree
1½ cups half-and-half
½ teaspoon ground cinnamon
½ teaspoon grated nutmeg
½ teaspoon ground ginger
¼ teaspoon ground mace
¼ teaspoon ground cloves
⅔ cup coarsely chopped black walnuts, toasted

1. Preheat the oven to 400°F. Line a 9-inch pie pan with the pastry and prick it all over with a fork. Line the pastry with aluminum foil weighted with dry beans. Bake the pastry until very lightly browned, about 7 minutes. Remove the pan to a wire rack to cool and remove the foil and beans.

2. In a mixing bowl, beat together the remaining ingredients except the walnuts until smooth. Stir in ⅓ cup of the walnuts. Pour the mixture into the cooled pastry shell and sprinkle the remaining walnuts over the filling. Bake until the filling has set and a knife inserted in the center of the pie comes out clean, about 40 minutes. Cool on a wire rack.

Gingered Indian Pudding

SERVES 10 TO 12

◆

An ancient dish that the colonists first learned from the Indians, this is one of my favorite comforting desserts all winter long, served warm with a dollop of melting frozen cream.

5 cups scalded milk
⅔ cup dark molasses
2 tablespoons butter
⅔ cup stone-ground yellow cornmeal
¼ teaspoon salt
1 teaspoon ground cinnamon
¼ teaspoon grated nutmeg
2 tablespoons finely chopped preserved ginger
1 large egg, lightly beaten

1. Preheat the oven to 250°F. Butter a shallow, non-metallic 2-quart baking dish.

2. Place the scalded milk in the top of a double boiler over simmering water. Stir in the molasses and butter until well blended, then gradually stir in the cornmeal until completely blended in. Cook, stirring constantly, until the mixture is smooth and thick, about 15 minutes. Remove from heat and beat in the salt, cinnamon, nutmeg, and ginger until well blended. Beat in the egg.

3. Transfer the mixture to the prepared baking dish, place in the oven, and bake until the pudding is set and lightly browned, about 4 hours. Serve the pudding warm, spooned into individual serving dishes and topped with Iced Sweet Cream and a sprinkling of chopped preserved ginger.

Iced Sweet Cream

◆

Place 2 cups of heavy cream, ½ teaspoon vanilla extract, and ¼ cup confectioners' sugar in a small metal bowl and stir to blend. Place in the freezer for 3 hours, stirring to break up ice crystals about every 30 minutes. Cover tightly and store in the freezer. Transfer to the refrigerator about half an hour before serving.

A Bountiful Southern Feast

FOR 12 TO 16

◆

MENU

Cream of Peanut Soup

Beaten Biscuits with Sweet Butter

◆

Roasted Herbed Turkey

Giblet Gravy

Corn Bread, Pecan, and Oyster Dressing

Gingered Peach Chutney (page 122)

Pickled Crabapples (page 124)

*Carolyn's Bread-and-Butter Zucchini Pickles
(page 124)*

*Oven-Braised Parsnips and Carrots
with Rosemary*

Vinegar Green Beans

◆

Alma Folkes's Wine Jelly with Custard Sauce

Brandied Pear Tart   Lane Cake

*Cream of Peanut Soup, garnished with chives
and chopped peanuts.*

*Slices of roasted turkey are served with Gingered Peach
Chutney and Giblet Gravy, a corn bread dressing with
oysters and pecans, herbed carrots and parsnips, and green
beans with a sweet-and-sour bacon-flavored sauce.*

OPPOSITE: *My city dining room is the candle-lit setting
for this Thanksgiving dinner, with a huge bouquet
of fall-colored flowers by the window and a centerpiece
of autumn fruits, nuts, and leaves on the table.*

There has long been a quiet controversy about the origins of our oldest celebration: Virginians maintain that theirs was the first, since the earliest officially proclaimed American feast of thanksgiving took place at Berkeley Plantation on the James River in December 1619, a year before the Pilgrims landed in Massachusetts.

155

Since my sister Betty has lived in Georgia, I've spent a few Thanksgiving weekends down south. This Thanksgiving menu, though far different from the one that those early colonists probably had, is based on traditional southern recipes I've collected over the years that make good use of the fall's harvest.

After the recipes for the menu, I've included a recipe for Turkey and Sausage Gumbo, a good way to finish off the Thanksgiving bird.

Getting Ready: Plenty of the preparation can be taken care of ahead of time. The Gingered Peach Chutney, Pickled Crabapples, and Zucchini Pickles can be made far in advance. The Lane Cake can be made a few days ahead, covered, and stored in a cool place. The wine jelly, too, can be made a few days ahead, covered tightly and refrigerated.

On the day before Thanksgiving, make the soup and the custard sauce, which is best made no more than a day in advance.

Early on Thanksgiving day, bake the Brandied Pear Tart and make the stuffing, but do not stuff the turkey until just before it goes into the oven.

About an hour and a half before serving, start the parsnips and carrots and get them into the oven. About an hour before serving, make the dough for the biscuits; as soon as the turkey comes out of the oven, turn up the heat and bake them. Half an hour before serving, start reheating the soup over low heat. Next, make the green beans. Make the gravy when the turkey comes out of the oven.

Beverages: With the main course, I like a not-too-heavy red wine, such as Merlot, but a full-bodied dry white wine, such as a California Chardonnay or a white Burgundy, would be fine, too.

Cream of Peanut Soup

SERVES 12 TO 16 AS A FIRST COURSE

◆

1 cup (2 sticks) butter
2 cups finely chopped celery
4 medium onions, finely chopped
½ cup all-purpose flour
6 cups milk
1½ cups smooth peanut butter
3 quarts hot chicken stock
1 cup unsalted roasted peanuts, coarsely chopped
½ cup snipped chives

1. Melt the butter in the bottom of a large heavy pot over medium heat; add the celery and onions and sauté until the onion is transparent, about 15 minutes. Stir in the flour until well blended. Reduce the heat and slowly stir in the milk. Cook, stirring occasionally to prevent sticking, until the mixture is smooth and slightly thickened, about 5 minutes (do not allow the mixture to boil).

2. Add the peanut butter and chicken stock and stir until smooth. (*The soup may be made up to two days ahead, covered, and refrigerated; bring to room temperature before reheating.*) Serve the soup hot and garnish each serving with chopped peanuts and snipped chives.

Beaten Biscuits

MAKES 1½ TO 2 DOZEN

◆

When many southern households had large kitchen staffs, beaten biscuits were the daily bread, but they've almost disappeared today, since they require about half an hour of heavy beating with a strong arm. Now that the food processor can do all the work, beaten biscuits are among the quickest of quick breads. Lard is the traditional shortening, but butter, while giving a slightly different end result, will work equally well.

2 cups all-purpose flour
1 teaspoon salt
½ cup chilled lard or butter (or a mixture),
    cut into chunks
½ cup very cold milk

1. Preheat the oven to 350°F. Lightly grease two baking sheets.

2. In the bowl of a food processor fitted with the steel chopping blade, combine the flour and salt and process to blend. Add the lard or butter and pulse 5 or 6 times, until the mixture resembles coarse meal. Pour the milk over this mixture and process until the dough forms a ball. Process for 2 minutes more. The dough should be shiny and elastic, resembling a yeast bread dough.

3. Remove the dough to a floured surface and roll it into a rectangle about ¼ inch thick. Lightly flour the surface of the dough and fold it over on itself. Using a 1½-inch cutter, cut the dough into biscuits, prick them with a fork (traditionally a silver one), and place them on the prepared baking sheets.

4. Bake the biscuits for about 30 minutes, or until they are golden brown. Serve the biscuits hot or at room temperature with soft sweet butter.

Roasted Herbed Turkey with Giblet Gravy

SERVES 16, WITH LEFTOVERS

◆

1 20- to 24-pound fresh turkey
Salt and freshly ground black pepper
Corn Bread, Pecan, and Oyster Dressing (recipe follows)
1 tablespoon chopped sage leaves or 1 teaspoon dried rubbed sage
1 tablespoon fresh thyme leaves or 1 teaspoon dried thyme
½ cup (1 stick) butter, softened

1. Remove the giblets from the turkey and reserve for gravy. Rinse the turkey well, inside and out, and pat dry with paper towels.

2. Preheat the oven to 325°F. Stuff both cavities loosely with stuffing (see note) and close both ends with trussing skewers and string. Place the turkey breast side up on a rack in a large roasting pan. Insert a meat thermometer into the thickest part of the thigh without touching the bone.

3. Sprinkle the chopped sage and thyme over the breast. Melt the butter in a small saucepan and soak a 12-inch-square double layer of cheesecloth in it. Gently lay the cheesecloth over the breast.

4. Place the turkey in the oven and roast about 12 minutes a pound, basting every 30 minutes with the pan juices. Remove the cheesecloth after 3 hours of roasting. The turkey is done when the meat thermometer registers 180°F., or when the juices run clear when the thigh is pricked with a meat fork. (If any part of the turkey begins to get too brown during roasting, cover loosely with aluminum foil.)

5. Remove the turkey to a warm platter, cover the turkey loosely with aluminum foil, and let it rest for 20 to 30 minutes before carving while making the gravy.

Note: Any stuffing that does not fit into the turkey can be packed into a buttered heavy-duty aluminum foil packet and roasted for about half an hour.

Giblet Gravy

Giblets from turkey
1 large garlic clove, crushed
¼ teaspoon salt
¼ cup fat skimmed from roasting pan
¼ cup flour
Pan drippings and enough chicken or turkey stock to make 2 cups

1. While the turkey is roasting, place the giblets, garlic, and salt in a small saucepan with water to cover and place over medium heat. Simmer the giblets for 20 minutes, until cooked through. Remove the giblets, discard the garlic and cooking liquid, and finely chop the giblets. Cover and store in the refrigerator until the turkey is done.

2. When the turkey is done, skim off the fat from the roasting pan. Place ¼ cup fat in a medium saucepan over medium heat (discard any remaining fat) and whisk in the flour. Cook, whisking constantly, until the flour is absorbed and a thick paste forms.

3. Scrape the bottom of the roasting pan to remove any browned bits and stir them into the pan juices. Pour the juices into a measuring cup and add chicken or turkey stock to measure 2 cups. Whisk the juices into the flour-fat mixture until smooth. Add the reserved giblets and simmer the gravy until thickened and the flour is cooked, about 7 minutes.

Corn Bread, Pecan, and Oyster Dressing

◆

1 cup (2 sticks) butter
2 medium onions, finely chopped
1 cup finely chopped celery
12 cups crumbled dry corn bread
1 quart shucked oysters, with their liquor
1½ cups coarsely chopped pecans
¼ cup chopped parsley
1 teaspoon salt
1 teaspoon freshly ground black pepper
2 large eggs, lightly beaten
1 tablespoon thyme leaves or 1 teaspoon dried thyme
1 tablespoon chopped sage or 1 teaspoon dried sage

1. Melt the butter in a skillet over medium heat; add the onion and celery and sauté about 7 minutes. Transfer the mixture to a large mixing bowl, add the corn bread, and toss to mix. Set aside.

2. Place the oysters and their liquor in a medium saucepan over medium heat. Bring to a boil, reduce heat, and simmer until the edges of the oysters curl, 2 or 3 minutes. Remove from the heat and transfer the oysters with a slotted spoon to a cutting board. Reserve the oyster liquor. Cut the oysters in half (in quarters if they're very large).

3. Add the oysters to the mixing bowl. Add the remaining ingredients and mix with your hands until all ingredients are evenly distributed. Add about 1 cup of the reserved oyster liquor to moisten the dressing.

Oven-Braised Parsnips and Carrots with Rosemary

SERVES 12

◆

An easy and flavorful way to prepare vegetables, these can even be fully cooked a day in advance and reheated; the flavor only improves.

    8 medium parsnips, peeled
1½ pounds baby carrots, peeled
    1 heaping teaspoon fresh rosemary leaves or
      ½ teaspoon dried rosemary
    ¼ cup (½ stick) butter, softened
    1 cup chicken stock

1. Preheat the oven to 325°F. Cut the parsnips into ¼-inch by 2-inch strips. Place them and the carrots in a shallow baking dish and sprinkle the rosemary leaves over them. Dot with the butter and pour the chicken stock over all. (*May be prepared ahead up to this point, and tightly covered*).

2. Loosely cover the baking dish with the lid or aluminum foil and bake for 1 hour, or until the vegetables are very tender. Stir once or twice during cooking.

Vinegar Green Beans

SERVES 12

◆

    2 pounds green beans
    1 small onion, thinly sliced vertically
    6 thin slices bacon, coarsely chopped
    2 large eggs
    ½ cup cider vinegar
    ¼ cup sugar

1. Trim the beans and cut them in half lengthwise. Cook them in boiling salted water until crisp-tender, about 8 minutes, then drain the beans and place them in a warm serving dish.

2. Place the onion and bacon in a small skillet and sauté until the bacon is crisp. Whisk together the eggs, vinegar, and sugar in a small mixing bowl and whisk this mixture into the skillet. When the sauce is hot, pour it over the beans, toss, and serve immediately.

Alma Folkes's Wine Jelly with Custard Sauce

MAKES 12 SERVINGS

◆

This simple, classic southern dessert was a great holiday favorite of Lindsay Miller's grandfather Dr. Clifford Folkes. Lindsay's grandmother Alma Folkes always served it in *her* grandmother's wineglasses.

Wine Jelly
1½ cups cold water
   3 envelopes unflavored gelatin
   1 cup sugar
   ¼ teaspoon salt
   3 cups boiling water
   ¾ cup lemon juice
   ¾ cup dry red wine

Custard Sauce
   3 cups milk
   3 large eggs
   6 tablespoons sugar
   ½ teaspoon salt
1½ teaspoons vanilla extract
   ¼ cup sliced almonds, toasted

1. For the jelly, pour the water into a large mixing bowl and sprinkle the gelatin over it to soften. Add the sugar, salt, and boiling water, and stir until sugar and gelatin are dissolved. Stir in the lemon juice and wine and strain the mixture through a double layer of cheesecloth.

2. Allow the mixture to cool and spoon it into 12 footed sherbet dishes or wineglasses. Refrigerate until set and well chilled, about 3 hours.

3. For the custard sauce, heat the milk in the top of a double boiler over simmering water until it is just below the simmering point. In a small bowl, beat the eggs, sugar, and salt together, then stir a few tablespoons of the hot milk into the mixture.

4. Pour this mixture slowly into the milk in the double boiler, stirring constantly. Cook, continuing to stir constantly, until the mixture is thick. Remove from the heat and stir in the vanilla. Pour the sauce into a pitcher, cover, and chill.

5. To serve, pour custard sauce over each serving of wine jelly and sprinkle each serving with a few toasted sliced almonds.

OPPOSITE: Dessert and coffee are served in the den: Wine Jelly with Custard Sauce, Brandied Pear Tart, and, on the cakestand, a beautiful Lane Cake.

*The main course, ready to be
served from the sideboard.*

Brandied Pear Tart

MAKES ONE 10-INCH TART

◆

This is a nice alternative to the more usual Thanksgiving apple pie, but it's not so different that it will cause an uproar among traditionalists.

Cream Cheese Pastry Crust
- ½ cup (1 stick) butter, softened
- 1 3-ounce package cream cheese, softened
- 1 cup all-purpose flour
- ⅛ teaspoon salt

Filling
- 9 cups sliced firm ripe pears
- 1 tablespoon lemon juice
- ¼ cup brandy
- ½ cup sugar
- ⅓ cup flour
- 1 teaspoon ground cinnamon
- ¼ teaspoon grated nutmeg
- ¼ cup (½ stick) butter, softened

1. In the bowl of a food processor fitted with the steel chopping blade, cream the butter and cream cheese together until thoroughly blended and smooth. Add the flour and salt and process to form a stiff dough. Shape the dough into a ball, cover with plastic wrap or wax paper, and chill until firm, about 2 hours.

2. On a lightly floured surface, roll the dough into a circle about ⅛ inch thick. Line a 10-inch tart tin with the dough. Trim off excess dough and roll it out again. Cut it into decorative shapes with small cookie cutters and place on a small baking sheet.

3. Preheat the oven to 350°F. In a large mixing bowl, toss the pears with the lemon juice and brandy. Sift together the sugar, flour, and spices in a small mixing bowl, add to the pear mixture, and toss well to mix.

4. Transfer the filling to the pastry shell and dot with the butter. Place the tart and the baking sheet with the decorative pastry shapes in the oven. Bake the tart until the fruit is tender and the edges of the pastry are nicely browned, about 1 hour. Bake the decorative pastry until golden brown, about 20 minutes.

5. Transfer decorative pastry and the tart to a wire rack to cool and arrange the decorative shapes on the fruit. Serve alone or with whipped cream.

Lane Cake

MAKES ONE 4-LAYER 9-INCH CAKE

◆

Here's a spectacular holiday cake that comes from a southern friend who made me promise not to divulge her name, since she never gives out her "secret" recipe.

- 1 cup (2 sticks) butter, softened
- 2 cups sugar
- ½ teaspoon vanilla extract
- ½ teaspoon almond extract
- 3¼ cups all-purpose flour
- 1 tablespoon baking powder
- ¼ teaspoon salt
- 1 cup milk
- 8 large egg whites (reserve yolks for frosting)

Frosting
- 12 large egg yolks
- 1½ cups sugar
- 2 cups (4 sticks) butter
- ½ cup bourbon
- 1 teaspoon vanilla extract
- 1 teaspoon almond extract
- 1 cup chopped candied orange peel
- 1 cup muscat raisins
- 1 cup chopped pecans
- ¾ cup shredded coconut

1. Preheat the oven to 375°F. Grease four 9-inch round cake pans, line the bottoms with wax paper, and grease the wax paper.

2. In a large mixing bowl, cream the butter and sugar together until light and fluffy, then beat in the vanilla and almond extracts. In a separate bowl, sift together the flour, baking powder, and salt. Gradually beat this dry mixture into the butter-sugar mixture, alternating with the milk, until smooth.

3. In another small bowl, beat the egg whites until stiff but not dry, then gently fold them into the batter. Divide the batter evenly among the four prepared pans.

4. Bake for 15 to 20 minutes, or until a cake tester or toothpick inserted in the center of a layer comes out clean. Cool the cake layers in the pans for 10 minutes, then turn them out onto wire racks to cool completely.

5. To make the frosting, stir the egg yolks and sugar together in the top of a double boiler over simmering water and cook, stirring constantly, until the mixture is smooth and pale in color. Gradually add the butter, a few tablespoons at a time, and cook, continuing to stir constantly, until the mixture is thick and translucent.

6. Remove the pan from the heat and stir in the bourbon and vanilla and almond extracts. Stir in the fruit, nuts, and coconut and cool slightly to a spreadable consistency before using, about 10 minutes.

7. Place one cake layer on a cakestand or cake plate and spread the top with a thin layer of frosting; repeat with each layer, and then frost the sides. After the frosting sets, about half an hour, the cake can be stored for several weeks in the refrigerator, tightly wrapped.

Turkey and Sausage Gumbo

MAKES ABOUT 4 QUARTS

◆

Here's a great way to use up the last of the turkey. This recipe makes quite a bit, but the soup freezes well (add the filé powder after reheating and just before serving).

Stock
- 1 meaty turkey carcass
- 2 quarts water
- 2 celery stalks with leaves, coarsely chopped
- 1 large onion, coarsely chopped
- 3 carrots, coarsely chopped
- 1 teaspoon crushed peppercorns
- 2 bay leaves, crushed

Soup
- 3 slices bacon, diced
- 1 large green pepper, chopped
- 1 large onion, chopped
- 2 large garlic cloves, finely chopped
- ½ cup diced celery
- 3 cups chopped canned tomatoes
- 1½ cups sliced okra
- 1 cup corn kernels
- 1 pound smoked sausage, cut into ¼-inch slices
- 1 teaspoon dried thyme
- ¼ cup chopped parsley
- 1 teaspoon Tabasco sauce
- Salt
- 1 tablespoon filé powder

1. To make the stock, combine all ingredients in a kettle over medium heat and bring to a boil. Reduce the heat and simmer, loosely covered, for about 2 hours, or until the meat falls from the bones. Strain the stock and discard the vegetables. Cut the meat from the bones in chunks, and reserve stock and meat separately.

2. In the bottom of a Dutch oven or heavy kettle, sauté the bacon, green pepper, onion, garlic, and celery until the vegetables are tender, about 10 minutes. Remove any excess bacon fat.

3. Add the reserved stock, tomatoes, okra, corn, sausage, thyme, and parsley and bring to a boil. Reduce the heat and simmer about 20 minutes, or until the okra is tender. Stir in the Tabasco sauce and the reserved turkey meat. Season with salt to taste, remove from the heat, and let stand for 1 hour to allow flavors to blend. (May be made ahead up to this point and refrigerated or frozen.)

4. Reheat the soup to just below simmering and stir in the filé powder (do not allow the soup to boil after the filé is added). Serve the gumbo in large shallow soup plates, surrounding mounds of steamed rice and garnished with a sprinkling of chopped parsley.

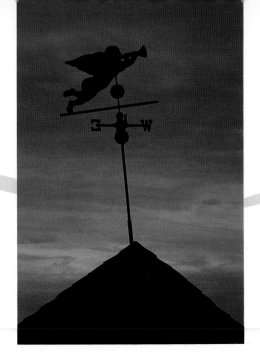

A Boston Tea Party

FOR 20

◆

MENU

"Patriot's Tea" Punch   *Coffee*

◆

Boston Brown Bread

Pumpkin-Orange Tea Muffins

Sweet Butter   *Cream Cheese*

*Smoked Turkey Sandwiches
on Anadama Bread with
Cranberry-Walnut Ketchup (page 125)*

◆

Iva Mae's Apple Cake

Banana-Coconut Custard Tartlets

*RIGHT: The first guest, decked in his holiday finery,
is ready for teatime.*

I've said it before but I'll say it again: Christmastime is my favorite time of the year. I look for any excuse to get the season into full gear and, since I love teatime almost as much as Christmastime, this happy coincidence of the calendar gives me just the excuse I need to ease into it sanely with a relaxed late-afternoon gathering of good friends. The original Boston Tea Party (when the American colonists rebelled against the tea tax imposed on them by George III's government and threw shiploads of tea into Boston Harbor) took place just before Christmas, on December 16, 1773.

The menu combines fine old Yankee fare such as Boston Brown Bread and Anadama Bread with such seasonal New England flavors as those found in Cranberry-Walnut Ketchup, Pumpkin-Orange Tea Muffins, and apple cake. And since this is, after all, a Boston tea party, no tea at all is served.

Getting Ready: The only things that need to be done just before serving are pouring the chilled punch ingredients together and assembling the sandwiches. The rest can be done well ahead of the party.

The muffins and Anadama Bread can be made well in advance and frozen, tightly wrapped; or make them a day ahead. The Cranberry-Walnut Ketchup can be made well in advance and canned or stored in jars in the refrigerator.

Up to two days in advance, make the Boston Brown Bread and store it, tightly wrapped, in the refrigerator.

No more than a day in advance, make the tartlets and store them in the refrigerator, tightly covered. Bake the apple cake, cover it, and store it in a cool place.

"Patriot's Tea" Punch

MAKES ABOUT 3 QUARTS

◆

It may look like tea, but there's not a drop of tea in it. (But it does have a punch!)

2 cups apple cider
1 cup brandy
½ cup dark rum
½ cup Curaçao
    Juice of 2 lemons
1 teaspoon sugar
1 fifth Champagne
1 liter seltzer
    Lemon slices

1. Chill all ingredients thoroughly. Combine the cider, brandy, rum, Curaçao, lemon juice, and sugar and stir until the sugar is dissolved.

2. Just before serving, pour the above mixture over a block of ice in a punch bowl and stir in the Champagne and seltzer. Serve the punch in tea cups with thin slices of lemon.

Boston Brown Bread

MAKES 2 LOAVES

◆

There are lots of recipes for Boston Brown Bread around, but I'm including one here to encourage the making of this simple, near-forgotten treat. I use chopped dates, but if you want to be more traditional, use raisins instead.

1½ cups rye or whole wheat flour
1½ cups graham flour
1½ cups stone-ground yellow cornmeal
1 tablespoon baking soda
1 teaspoon salt
3 cups buttermilk
1 cup dark molasses
¼ cup pure maple syrup
1 cup chopped dates

1. Combine the flours, cornmeal, baking soda, and salt in a mixing bowl. Add the remaining ingredients and mix well.

2. Grease two 1-pound coffee cans very well. Transfer the batter into the greased cans (they should be about two-thirds full) and cover the cans tightly with greased aluminum foil.

3. Place the cans in a large kettle fitted with a rack (or a large steamer) and fill the kettle with hot water about halfway up the sides of the cans. Cover the kettle, place it over medium-high heat, and bring the water to the boil. Reduce the heat so the water is just simmering and steam the bread for 3 hours, replenishing water if necessary.

4. Remove the cans from the kettle, place them on a wire rack, and allow the bread to cool completely before removing it from the cans. Store the bread, tightly wrapped, in a cool, dry place up to 1 week.

Pumpkin-Orange Tea Muffins

MAKES 4 DOZEN MINIATURE MUFFINS,
OR 2 DOZEN REGULAR MUFFINS

◆

4 cups flour
2 tablespoons baking powder
1 teaspoon baking soda
½ teaspoon salt
½ teaspoon ground cinnamon
½ teaspoon ground ginger
¼ teaspoon grated nutmeg
¼ teaspoon ground cloves
3 large eggs
1 cup pumpkin puree
½ cup sugar
2 cups milk
2 tablespoons grated orange rind
½ cup (1 stick) butter, melted
    Sugar

1. Preheat the oven to 425°F. Lightly grease two 12-cup muffin tins or four 12-cup miniature muffin tins.

2. In a mixing bowl, sift together the flour, baking powder, baking soda, salt, and spices. In a separate bowl, beat together the eggs, pumpkin, sugar, milk, and orange rind. Pour the liquid mixture over the dry mixture, pour in the melted butter, and mix well with a spoon until the dry ingredients are just moistened.

3. Fill the muffin pans two thirds full and sprinkle the batter with a little sugar. Place the pans in the oven and bake 20 to 25 minutes (15 minutes for miniature muffins) or until risen and browned. Transfer the muffins to wire racks to cool or serve them hot from the oven.

Smoked Turkey Sandwiches

◆

Smoked turkey breast is available in most grocery store meat departments; slice it thin and layer it onto freshly sliced triangles of Anadama Bread. Spread Cranberry-Walnut Ketchup on top, or use Cranberry Mayonnaise, made by combining equal parts of cranberry relish and Homemade Mayonnaise (page 188).

Anadama Bread

MAKES TWO 9 X 5 X 3-INCH LOAVES

◆

1¾ cups boiling water
¾ cup stone-ground yellow cornmeal
2 tablespoons butter
½ cup dark molasses
2 teaspoons salt
2 packages active dry yeast
½ cup warm water
6 to 7 cups all-purpose flour
2 tablespoons milk

1. Pour the boiling water into a large mixing bowl and gradually add the cornmeal, stirring constantly. Stir in the butter, then the molasses and salt. Allow the mixture to cool to room temperature.

2. In a separate small bowl, soften the yeast in the warm water for 5 minutes, then stir this into the cornmeal mixture. Gradually stir in 6 cups flour, using more if necessary, to form a stiff dough.

3. Remove the dough to a board and knead it until satiny and elastic. Add a bit more flour if necessary. Transfer the dough to a lightly oiled bowl, cover with a damp cloth, and place in a warm spot until the dough is doubled in bulk, about 1 hour.

4. Punch down the dough and knead it again lightly in the bowl. Divide the dough in half, shape it into two loaves and place each in an oiled 9 x 5 x 3-inch loaf pan. Cover the loaves with a damp cloth and allow to double in bulk again, about 45 minutes.

5. Preheat the oven to 400°F. Brush the tops of the loaves with milk, place them in the oven, and bake for 15 minutes. Reduce the oven temperature to 350°F, and bake about 40 minutes longer, or until the loaves are nicely browned and sound hollow when tapped lightly with a finger.

6. Remove the loaves from the pans, place them on wire racks, and allow them to cool completely before slicing and serving.

Iva Mae's Apple Cake

MAKES ONE 9 X 13-INCH CAKE

◆

2 cups flour
4 teaspoons baking powder
½ teaspoon salt
¼ cup sugar
½ cup (1 stick) butter
1 large egg, lightly beaten
1 cup milk

Topping
3 cups peeled and sliced baking apples, approximately
1 cup sugar
1 teaspoon ground cinnamon
2 teaspoons cornstarch
½ cup (1 stick) butter, melted

1. In a large mixing bowl, sift together the flour, baking powder, salt, and sugar, then cut in the butter. Beat in the egg and milk.

2. Preheat the oven to 375°F. Line a 9 x 13-inch baking pan with a single piece of foil, allowing the edges of the foil to hang over the edges of the pan. Lightly butter the foil.

3. Spread the batter evenly in the pan. Arrange the apple slices on the batter in rows, overlapping them slightly and alternating the direction of the rows. Combine the sugar, cinnamon, and cornstarch and sprinkle this mixture over the apples. Drizzle the melted butter over all.

4. Bake for 50 minutes, or until the apples are nicely browned and glazed and a cake tester comes out clean. Remove the cake to a wire rack and cool it in the pan.

5. To serve, hold the foil edges and gently lift the cake from the pan. Transfer the cake to a serving tray and gently peel away the foil. Cut the cake into 4-inch strips between the apple rows.

Variations In season, substitute firm ripe peaches, nectarines, or pears for the apples.

Banana-Coconut Custard Tartlets and a caramel-glazed apple cake.

Banana-Coconut Custard Tartlets

MAKES ABOUT 2 DOZEN

◆

Basic Pastry for a 10-inch pie (page 188), doubled
4 large eggs
²⁄₃ cup sugar
¼ teaspoon salt
1½ cups shredded coconut
2 cups half-and-half
²⁄₃ cup milk
1 teaspoon vanilla extract
2 to 3 large ripe bananas

1. Preheat the oven to 450°F. Line 24 2-inch tartlet tins with the pastry dough.

2. To make the custard, beat the eggs lightly and beat in the sugar, salt, 1 cup of the coconut, the half-and-half, milk, and vanilla.

3. Slice the bananas and divide the slices among the tartlet shells. Pour the custard mixture over the bananas and sprinkle the remaining ½ cup coconut over the custard.

4. Bake for 15 minutes, reduce the oven heat to 350°F., and bake 15 to 20 minutes longer, or until a knife inserted in the filling comes out clean. (The centers may look softer, but will set as the tartlets cool. Overbaking will cause the custard to become watery.) Serve the tartlets slightly warm or well chilled.

An old tavern table is set for a cozy tea party on a cold winter day. Top to bottom: "Patriot's Tea" Punch, Banana-Coconut Custard Tartlets, Smoked Turkey Sandwiches on Anadama Bread with Cranberry-Walnut Ketchup, Boston Brown Bread, and tiny Pumpkin-Orange Tea Muffins with cream cheese.

A Plain and Fancy Dinner

FOR 12 TO 16

◆

My favorite Christmases are when I go home to Ohio and a houseful of family. All the kids are zooming about or getting underfoot with their new toys, the adults are busily catching up on family and local gossip, and wonderful smells of Christmas dinner spread through the house from the kitchen.

This dinner, one I'm especially partial to, is very much like the Christmas Day feasts we enjoyed on the farm when I was growing up. It is also similar to Christmas dinners eaten in Amish farm country, both in my area of Ohio and in Pennsylvania, and since the Amish have so strongly influenced our American Christmas tradition (they gave us Christmas cookies and the hospitable custom of putting candles in our windows at Christmastime), it makes perfect sense. Dinner begins with homemade bread and an array of condiments, similar to the seven sweets and seven sours that traditionally grace an Amish table; at our house, the best from Mom's cellarful of home-canned pickles and relishes were served. At the center of the dinner is a spectacular and succulent roasted fresh ham, surrounded by a colorful assortment of winter vegetables. Dessert offers a pie, Cranberry Gingerbread, and five different kinds of cookies.

MENU

Peppered Batter Bread (page 137)

Sweet-and-Hot Corn Relish (page 128)

Cottage Cheese with Chives

Pear and Apple Butter (page 121)

Pennsylvania Chow Chow (page 122)

Carolyn's Bread-and-Butter Zucchini Pickles (page 124)

Pickled Red Cabbage

Mom's Piccallili (page 124)

◆

Roasted Stuffed Fresh Ham with Sour Cream Pan Gravy

Chicken and Corn Pie

Potato Filling

Brussels Sprouts and Cauliflower with Walnut Butter

Cranberry Carrots

◆

Spice and Vinegar Pie

Cranberry Gingerbread

◆

Christmas Cookies:

Snickerdoodles (page 65)

Fig and Almond Tarts

Mimi's Pecan Tassies

Janet's Jam Shortbread

Molasses-Pepper Cookies

Getting Ready: Another big dinner here, but last-minute preparation is minimal. Most of the condiments to be served before the main course are best made at the end of the summer when all the fresh ingredients are at their peak; make the Pickled Red Cabbage up to a week in advance. The bread can be made well in advance and frozen, or it can be made a day in advance, though it's at its best baked early on the day it is served. Make two or three loaves for this menu, but make batches of batter separately. The pastry for the pies can also be made well ahead and stored in the freezer. The cookies can be made up to a few weeks ahead and stored in tins in a cool place.

The day before Christmas, make the filling for the Chicken and Corn Pie and bake the dessert pie. If you like, make the Potato Filling and store it in the refrigerator; the texture will be a bit denser, however, than if it is made the same day.

On Christmas day, stuff the ham and get it into the oven about four and a half hours before you want to serve it. The carrots should be ready to go into the oven an hour before serving. Have the Chicken and Corn Pie and the Potato Filling ready to go into the oven when the ham comes out to rest. The last thing to do is make the Brussels Sprouts and Cauliflower in Walnut Butter and the gravy.

Pickled Red Cabbage

MAKES ABOUT 4 CUPS

◆

½ teaspoon celery seeds
½ teaspoon mustard seeds
¼ teaspoon ground allspice
1 large garlic clove, finely chopped
1 bay leaf
1 cup water
¾ cup red wine vinegar
2 tablespoons sugar
1 teaspoon salt
1 medium head red cabbage, shredded
1 medium Bermuda onion, thinly sliced

1. Place all ingredients except the cabbage and onion in a small heavy saucepan over high heat. Bring to a boil and remove from the heat.

2. In a large mixing bowl, toss together the cabbage and onion and pour the hot mixture over it. The liquid should cover the cabbage and onion. Allow to cool, cover tightly, and refrigerate for 48 hours before eating. The cabbage will keep in the refrigerator for up to a week.

Roasted Stuffed Fresh Ham with Sour Cream Pan Gravy

SERVES 16, WITH LEFTOVERS

◆

A succulent fresh ham is one of the pig's greatest contributions to the dinner table. This method for stuffing a ham with fragrant seasonings is not only delicious, but beautiful as well.

Stuffing
2 large garlic cloves, peeled
1 small onion, coarsely chopped
1 teaspoon salt
½ teaspoon freshly ground black pepper
1 teaspoon rubbed sage
1 teaspoon dried thyme
1 teaspoon dried marjoram
2 cups coarse soft bread crumbs
¼ cup (½ stick) butter, melted
1 teaspoon fennel seeds
1 teaspoon caraway seeds
1 cup finely chopped kale or spinach
½ cup chopped parsley

1 12-pound fresh ham
1 cup apple juice

1. Place the garlic, onion, salt, pepper, sage, thyme, and marjoram in the bowl of a food processor fitted with the steel chopping blade and process to form a thick paste. Transfer this mixture to a large mixing bowl, add the remaining ingredients, and toss to mix.

2. Preheat the oven to 350°F. Using a very sharp knife, cut the skin from the ham and remove all but a ⅛-inch layer of fat. Diagonally cut 1½-inch-deep gashes into the ham about 2 inches apart.

3. Using your fingers, push the stuffing tightly into the gashes. Place the ham on a rack in a shallow open roasting pan and cover loosely with foil. Put the ham in the oven and roast for 1 hour.

4. Remove the foil and pour the apple juice over the ham. Insert a meat thermometer into the butt end of the ham, being careful not to touch the bone. Continue roasting, basting occasionally with the pan juices, until the thermometer reaches a temperature of 180°F., about 4 hours. If the ham begins to get too brown, replace the foil. Remove the ham to a carving platter and allow to stand for half an hour before carving; make the gravy.

Christmas dinner at my house, with a fire blazing and the tree in a corner by the window, isn't much different from the ones we had years ago on the farm. Some of my favorite Santas line the mantel.

A PLAIN AND FANCY DINNER 171

Sour Cream Pan Gravy

¼ cup flour
¼ cup water
½ cup pan juices, skimmed of fat
1 cup apple juice
2 cups sour cream
Salt and freshly ground black pepper

1. Mix the flour and water together in a small bowl until smooth. Place the pan juices in a saucepan over medium heat and gradually stir in the flour mixture. Stirring constantly, gradually add the apple juice and simmer the gravy for 5 minutes, until thick and smooth.

2. Immediately before serving, stir in the sour cream and heat through, but do not allow to reach the boiling point. If the gravy is too thick, stir in additional skimmed pan juices. Season with salt and freshly ground black pepper to taste.

Chicken and Corn Pie

MAKES ONE 9-INCH PIE, SERVES 8

◆

1 3½-pound chicken, boiled
1½ cups chicken stock
½ cup diced celery
1 carrot, peeled and diced
20 small pearl onions, peeled
¼ cup (½ stick) butter
¼ cup all-purpose flour
1½ cups corn kernels (or 1 10-ounce package frozen corn), coarsely chopped
¼ cup chopped parsley
Basic Pastry for a 9-inch pie (page 188), made without sugar

1. Skin the chicken and cut it into chunks; discard the skin and bones. Place the chicken stock, celery, carrot, and pearl onions in a small heavy saucepan over medium heat and simmer until the vegetables are tender, about 12 minutes.

2. Melt the butter in a small skillet over medium heat and stir in the flour until smooth. Spoon about half a cup of the stock into the butter mixture and stir until smooth. Gradually stir this mixture into the vegetable mixture, and cook, stirring constantly, until thickened.

3. Add the corn, parsley, and the reserved chicken to the sauce and stir to mix. Transfer this mixture to a 9-inch pie pan. (*May be prepared ahead to this point, cooled, covered with plastic wrap, and refrigerated.*)

4. Preheat the oven to 425°F. Roll out the pastry and use a small cookie cutter to cut out 3 or 4 holes. Top the pan with the pastry crust and crimp the edges. Bake the pie until the filling is bubbly and the crust is golden brown, 20 to 30 minutes.

Potato Filling

SERVES 16

◆

I'm not quite sure why it's called filling, but I assume that this was originally used to stuff (fill) turkeys and boned roasts.

4 pounds boiling potatoes
½ cup (1 stick) butter
1 small onion, finely chopped
½ cup chopped parsley
¼ teaspoon grated nutmeg
¼ teaspoon salt
¼ teaspoon white pepper
4 large eggs, separated
1½ cups milk

1. Cook the potatoes in a large pot of boiling salted water until tender, about 25 minutes. While potatoes are cooking, melt the butter in a small skillet, add the onion and ¼ cup of the parsley and sauté until the onion is transparent and tender, about 12 minutes.

2. Drain the potatoes, and peel them; cut into chunks and return to the pot, off the heat. Mash the potatoes with a masher and, using a wooden spoon, beat in the butter-onion mixture and the seasonings.

3. Preheat the oven to 350°F. Beat the egg yolks until light and lemon-colored, then beat in the milk. Beat this mixture into the potatoes. Beat the egg whites until stiff peaks form and gently fold them into the potato mixture.

4. Mound the mixture into a well-buttered 3-quart baking dish and dot the top with butter. (*If necessary, this may be made ahead up to this point, covered tightly with plastic wrap, and refrigerated up to a day in advance; return to room temperature before baking.*) Bake until heated through and the top is nicely browned, about half an hour. Sprinkle the remaining ¼ cup chopped parsley over the top before serving.

Brussels Sprouts and Cauliflower with Walnut Butter

SERVES 12

◆

2 10-ounce cartons Brussels sprouts
1 large head cauliflower
⅓ cup (⅔ stick) butter
½ cup coarsely chopped walnuts

1. Trim the Brussels sprouts, cut an **X** into the stem ends, and rinse well under cold running water. Cut the cauliflower into flowerets. Place the vegetables in a steamer in a pot filled with an inch of simmering water. Cover the pot and steam the vegetables until crisp-tender, about 8 minutes.

2. Meanwhile melt the butter in a large heavy saucepan or Dutch oven over medium heat. Add the walnuts and sauté until the walnuts begin to brown, about 5 minutes. Add the vegetables and toss well to coat them with the butter. Remove to a warmed serving dish and serve.

Cranberry Carrots

SERVES 12 TO 16

◆

This couldn't be easier to make, especially if you grate the carrots in the food processor.

3 pounds carrots, peeled and grated
1½ cups cranberries, coarsely chopped
¼ cup (½ stick) butter, cut into chunks
¼ cup sugar
½ teaspoon salt
Juice of 2 lemons

Preheat the oven to 350°F. and butter a shallow 3-quart baking dish with a lid. Place all the ingredients in the baking dish and toss to mix. Cover the dish and bake until the carrots are tender, about 1 hour. Stir once or twice during baking.

Spice and Vinegar Pie

MAKES ONE 9-INCH PIE

◆

Basic Pastry for a 9-inch pie (page 188)
2 large eggs, separated
2 additional large egg yolks
1 cup sugar
1 cup sour cream
¼ cup (½ stick) butter, softened
¼ cup cider vinegar
⅓ cup flour
1 teaspoon ground cinnamon
½ teaspoon ground cloves
½ teaspoon grated nutmeg
¼ teaspoon salt
1 cup chopped walnuts
1½ cups raisins

1. Preheat the oven to 450°F. Line a 9-inch pie pan with the pastry (see note).

2. In a mixing bowl, beat the 4 egg yolks and the sugar until light and lemon-colored, then beat in the sour cream, butter, and vinegar. In a separate small bowl, sift together the flour, spices, and salt. Beat this dry mixture into the wet mixture, then stir in the walnuts and raisins.

3. In a separate small bowl, beat the egg whites until stiff peaks form. Fold the egg whites into the filling, then transfer the batter to the prepared crust.

4. Bake for 10 minutes. Reduce the heat to 350°F. and bake about 20 minutes longer, or until the filling is set. Cool the pie on a wire rack.

Note: Leftover pastry scraps can be cut out with cookie cutters, baked on a small baking sheet, and used to decorate the cooled pie.

Colorful Cranberry Carrots and crusty Potato Filling.

Chicken and Corn Pie, Brussels Sprouts and Cauliflower in Walnut Butter, and Roasted Stuffed Fresh Ham.

OPPOSITE: *Dessert is served on the sideboard. Spice and Vinegar Pie encircled by a holly and grapevine wreath, Cranberry Gingerbread, and a basket of Pecan Tassies, Snickerdoodles, Fig-and-Almond Tarts, Molasses-Pepper Cookies, and Jam Shortbread.*

Cranberry Gingerbread

MAKES ONE 9 X 13-INCH CAKE

◆

⅓ cup (⅔ stick) butter, melted
⅔ cup milk
1 cup dark molasses
1 large egg, lightly beaten
3 cups sifted all-purpose flour
2 teaspoons baking powder
½ teaspoon baking soda
½ teaspoon salt
1 tablespoon ground ginger
1 teaspoon ground cinnamon
½ teaspoon ground cloves
1 cup very coarsely chopped cranberries
1 tablespoon grated orange rind
¼ cup sugar

1. Preheat the oven to 350°F. Grease a 9 x 13-inch baking pan.

2. In a large mixing bowl, stir together the melted butter, milk, molasses, and beaten egg until well mixed. In a separate bowl, sift together the flour, baking powder, baking soda, salt, and spices. Gradually add this mixture to the liquid mixture, stirring until completely blended.

3. In a small bowl, stir together the cranberries, orange rind, and sugar, then stir half this mixture into the batter. Pour the batter into the prepared pan and spoon the remaining cranberry mixture on top.

4. Bake about 50 minutes, or until a knife inserted in the center comes out clean. Cool in the pan and cut into 2-inch squares to serve.

Fig and Almond Tarts

MAKES ABOUT 3 DOZEN COOKIES

◆

1½ cups firmly packed light brown sugar
1 cup (2 sticks) butter, softened
3 large eggs
1 teaspoon almond extract
4 cups all-purpose flour
2 teaspoons baking soda
2½ cups chopped dried figs
½ cup chopped almonds
1 cup sugar
1 cup water

1. Cream the brown sugar and butter together in a large bowl. Gradually beat in the eggs and then the almond extract. In a separate bowl, sift together the flour and baking soda, then beat them into the wet mixture, forming a stiff dough. Cover the bowl and chill until the dough is firm, about 1½ hours.

2. Combine the remaining ingredients in a medium saucepan over medium-high heat and bring the mixture to a boil. Reduce the heat and simmer for 10 minutes, stirring occasionally to prevent sticking. Remove from the heat and cool.

3. Preheat the oven to 375°F. On a well-floured surface, roll out half the dough to a thickness of ⅛ inch. Cut into circles with a floured 2½-inch biscuit cutter and place them on ungreased baking sheets. Roll out the remaining dough, cut into circles, and using floured 1½-inch cookie cutters, cut stars, hearts, or diamonds out of the center of each circle.

4. Spoon a teaspoonful of the fig mixture onto the center of the dough circles on the baking sheets and top with the cutout circles. Moisten the edges with water and, with the tines of a fork, press the edges together to seal. Bake until golden brown, 8 to 10 minutes. Remove to wire racks to cool. Store in tightly covered containers in a cool place.

Mimi's Pecan Tassies

MAKES ABOUT 3½ DOZEN COOKIES

◆

These chewy treats are simple to make and a specialty of Mimi Benowitz, who has a way with desserts.

2 3-ounce packages cream cheese, softened
1 cup (2 sticks) butter, softened
2 cups all-purpose flour
2 large eggs
2 cups firmly packed dark brown sugar
1 tablespoon butter
2 teaspoons vanilla extract
1 cup chopped pecans
½ cup raisins

1. Beat together the cream cheese and butter until smooth, then gradually beat in the flour until smooth (the step can be done easily in the bowl of a food processor fitted with the steel chopping blade). Roll the dough into a ball, wrap in plastic wrap, and chill 1 hour.

2. Preheat the oven to 350°F. To make the filling, beat the eggs lightly with a fork in a bowl, then beat in the sugar, butter, and vanilla. Stir in the pecans and raisins.

3. Pinch off pieces of dough the size of a small walnut and press lightly into miniature muffin tins. Place a

teaspoon of the filling inside the dough. Bake until the crust is lightly browned, about 25 minutes. Remove to a wire rack to cool and store in tightly covered containers at room temperature.

Janet's Jam Shortbread

MAKES ABOUT 4 DOZEN COOKIES

◆

My friend Janet Sutherland, a professed noncook, is not so bad as she thinks. This recipe is proof.

- 1 cup sugar
- 1 cup (2 sticks) butter, softened
- 1 large egg
- ½ teaspoon almond extract
- 2 cups all-purpose flour
- 1 cup finely chopped almonds
- ¾ cup tart cherry or raspberry preserves

1. Preheat the oven to 325°F. Grease a 9 x 12-inch cake pan. In a large mixing bowl, cream together the sugar and butter. Add the egg and almond extract and beat until the mixture is light and fluffy. Gradually stir in the flour and the almonds, forming a stiff dough.

2. Divide the dough in half; wrap one half in plastic wrap and chill. Press the remaining dough into the bottom of the prepared pan in an even layer. Spread the preserves in an even layer on the dough, keeping it ¼ inch from the sides of the pan. Roll out the chilled dough half between two sheets of wax paper to a 9 x 12-inch rectangle and press this dough into the pan.

3. Bake the shortbread until golden brown, about 1 hour. Place the pan on a wire rack and cut the shortbread into 1 x 1½-inch bars, leaving them in the pan to cool completely. Remove to tightly covered containers and store in a cool place.

Molasses-Pepper Cookies

MAKES ABOUT 5 DOZEN, DEPENDING ON THE SIZE OF CUTTERS

◆

I tasted the original version of these incredibly flavored cookies at my friend Nolan Drummond's house and they reminded me of Amish molasses cookies I had eaten long ago. When I asked about the recipe, he admitted the cookies had been sent from Ohio by his sister-in-law. Nolan did get me the recipe, which was first brought to this country from Latvia years ago by Velta Ozolins, but when I made the cookies I discovered that the dough required *hours* of kneading. Well, the cookies were delicious, but I have to admit that I don't have the patience for all that kneading. So here's my almost-as-good, but much lazier, adaptation.

- 1 cup dark molasses
- ½ cup (1 stick) butter, at room temperature
- 1 teaspoon baking soda
- 2¼ cups sifted all-purpose flour
- 1¾ teaspoons baking powder
- 1 teaspoon salt
- 2 teaspoons ground ginger
- ½ teaspoon ground cloves
- 1½ teaspoons ground cardamom
- 1 tablespoon ground coriander
- 1 tablespoon grated nutmeg
- 1½ teaspoons ground cinnamon
- ¼ teaspoon ground black pepper

1. Place the molasses in a medium heavy saucepan over medium-high heat and bring it to a boil. Remove the pan from the heat, stir in the butter until well blended, then stir in the baking soda.

2. In a mixing bowl, sift together the flour, baking powder, salt, and spices. Gradually stir these ingredients into the molasses mixture until completely blended and smooth. Allow to cool, then chill the dough until firm.

3. Preheat the oven to 350°F. Lightly grease baking sheets. Roll out the dough between two sheets of wax paper to a thickness of ¹⁄₁₆ inch and cut into shapes with floured cookie cutters. Bake the cookies until just firm, 5 or 6 minutes; do not overbake. Cool on wire racks and store in tightly covered containers in a cool place.

Note: Cookies can be decorated with pecan halves before baking. Or, decorate them by piping on decorative icing made by adding enough water to sifted confectioners' sugar to make it spreadable.

A romantic Strawberry Sweetheart Cake on a milk glass cake stand is garnished with whole berries.

An Old-Fashioned Chocolate Cake, served on an old-fashioned cake plate decorated with tulips.

Celebration Cakes for Special Occasions

◆

Old-Fashioned Chocolate Cake

Strawberry Sweetheart Cake

Mocha Buttercream Cake

Gift-Wrapped Chocolate Cake

Spiced Devil's Food Cake
with White Cloud Frosting

"Secret Ingredient" Spice Cake
with Cream Cheese Frosting

Mary Forquer's Astoria Cake

Sour Cream Coffee Cake

Perfect Wedding Cake

B irthdays, anniversaries, and other family celebrations happen all year, and for as long as I can remember every big celebration in my family was crowned by a cake. Not pies, or any kind of "fancy" dessert, but a big, glorious, homemade cake. This array of cakes can be used any time of the year, and as an alternative to any of the desserts in this book, making a special occasion an extra-special one. Celebrate anything from a birthday to the burning of the mortgage.

*Sparklers light up a birthday
Mocha Buttercream Cake.*

Classic Yellow Cake

MAKES TWO 9-INCH LAYERS

◆

I think cake mixes are silly; they don't really save much time at all, and they tend to include ingredients I can't even pronounce. If this delicious, perfectly textured, old-fashioned, *really* homemade "from scratch" cake takes more than 10 minutes to get into the oven, I'll eat my hat.

The basis for the three cakes that follow, this is a recipe that should be in anyone's standard repertoire.

- ⅔ cup (1⅓ sticks) butter, softened
- 1½ cups sugar
- 3 large eggs
- 1½ teaspoons vanilla extract
- 2¼ cups sifted all-purpose flour
- 1 tablespoon baking powder
- 1 teaspoon salt
- 1 cup milk

1. Preheat the oven to 350°F. Grease two 9-inch round layer cake pans.

2. In a mixing bowl, cream the butter and sugar together, then beat in the eggs and vanilla. In a separate bowl, sift together the flour, baking powder, and salt. Stir (do not beat) the dry ingredients into the wet mixture alternately with the milk, stirring until smooth with each addition.

3. Divide the batter between the two pans. Bake until the layers are nicely browned and a cake tester comes out clean, 25 to 30 minutes. Turn the layers out onto wire racks and cool them completely before frosting.

Old-Fashioned Chocolate Cake

MAKES ONE 2-LAYER 9-INCH CAKE

◆

The chocolate cake I grew up with wasn't chocolate at all, but a velvety yellow cake with a rich chocolate buttercream frosting.

- 2 tablespoons butter
- 4 ounces semisweet chocolate
- ⅓ cup half-and-half or milk
- 1½ to 2 cups confectioners' sugar
- 1 teaspoon vanilla extract
  Classic Yellow Cake (page 180)

1. Melt the butter and chocolate in a heavy saucepan over low heat or the top of a double boiler over simmering water. Remove from the heat and beat in the half-and-half. Beat in the sugar, ½ cup at a time, until the frosting is smooth, then beat in the vanilla.

2. While the frosting is still warm, place one cake layer on a cake plate and frost the top. Add the other layer and frost the top and sides, swirling the frosting with the back of a spoon. Once the frosting is firm, serve the cake in its unadorned simplicity.

Strawberry Sweetheart Cake

MAKES ONE 2-LAYER CAKE

◆

- 1 large egg white
- ½ cup sugar
  Pinch of salt
- 1 cup thinly sliced very ripe strawberries
  Classic Yellow Cake (page 180), baked in two 9-inch heart-shaped pans
  Whole unhulled strawberries, for garnish

1. Beat together the egg white, sugar, salt, and ⅓ cup of the sliced strawberries in the top of a double boiler until thoroughly blended, then place over simmering water. Cook, beating constantly, until the mixture stands in stiff peaks, about 4 minutes.

2. Remove the top of the double boiler from the heat and continue beating until the frosting is cool, about 5 minutes. Fold in an additional ⅓ cup strawberries.

3. Place one cake layer on a cake plate and frost the top. Arrange the remaining sliced strawberries over the frosting. Top with the other layer and frost the top and sides of the assembled cake. Garnish with clusters of whole strawberries.

Mocha Buttercream Cake

MAKES ONE 2-LAYER 9-INCH CAKE

◆

2 cups confectioners' sugar
2 tablespoons unsweetened cocoa powder
1/8 teaspoon salt
1/2 cup (1 stick) butter, softened
1/4 cup hot double-strength coffee
1 teaspoon vanilla extract
    Classic Yellow Cake (page 180)
    Shaved chocolate curls, for garnish

1. In a small mixing bowl, sift together the sugar, cocoa, and salt. Place the butter in a large mixing bowl and beat in 1/2 cup of the sugar mixture. Beat in the coffee and vanilla, then beat in the remaining sugar mixture, 1/2 cup at a time, until the mixture is smooth, soft, and spreadable.

2. Place one cake layer on a cake plate and frost the top. Add the remaining layer and frost the top and sides of the cake. Garnish with chocolate curls.

Gift-Wrapped Chocolate Cake

SERVES 12

◆

A little complicated but not at all difficult, this spectacular cake can turn the simplest dinner into a major event. It's the perfect Christmas or birthday present to anyone who's high on your list.

Chocolate Ribbons
    6 ounces semisweet chocolate
    1/4 cup light corn syrup

    Devil's Food Cake batter (see step 2, below)

Berry Filling
    2 cups cranberries or raspberries
    1 1/2 cups sugar
    1/4 cup orange juice concentrate
    1/4 cup heavy cream

Chocolate Frosting
    12 ounces semisweet chocolate
    10 tablespoons (1 1/4 sticks) butter
    1/2 cup sifted confectioners' sugar
    1 teaspoon vanilla extract

1. The chocolate ribbons should be started first. Melt the chocolate and corn syrup in the top of a double boiler over simmering water and stir until smooth. Transfer to a small bowl and cover with plastic wrap, placing the plastic directly on the surface of the chocolate mixture. Let stand about 6 hours, or until the paste is shiny and pliable.

2. Preheat the oven to 350°F. Grease a 9 x 13-inch cake pan and dust it lightly with cocoa or flour. Prepare the cake batter according to recipe directions (page 184), but omit the cinnamon, nutmeg, and allspice. Bake the cake according to recipe directions.

3. To make the filling, combine all ingredients except the cream in a small heavy saucepan over medium heat. Bring to a simmer and cook, stirring occasionally, until the berries soften and mixture is thick and syrupy, about 15 minutes. Remove from the heat, cool, and chill. In a small chilled bowl whip the cream with chilled beaters until stiff peaks form and gently fold the cream into the berry mixture.

4. To make the frosting, melt the chocolate and butter in a small heavy saucepan over low heat (or melt in the top of a double boiler over simmering water). Remove from the heat. Gradually stir in the confectioners' sugar until smooth, then stir in the vanilla.

5. To assemble the cake, cut it into three 4 1/3 x 9-inch rectangles; square off any rounded ends. Place one layer on a rectangular serving platter and spread the surface with half of the berry cream; repeat with the second layer. Top with the third layer and frost the top and sides of the cake with the frosting. Refrigerate the cake until the frosting is firm, about 1 hour.

6. To finish making the ribbons, form the chocolate paste into a flattened ball. Place it on a large rectangle of wax paper, top with another rectangle of wax paper, and roll out to a rectangle less than 1/8 inch thick. Cut the chocolate into 3/4-inch-wide "ribbons."

7. To decorate the cake, arrange the chocolate ribbons across the cake lengthwise and crosswise, letting the ends hang down the sides, simulating a ribbon-wrapped gift. Trim the ends. Make a multilooped bow with ribbon strips and place it on the center of the cake. Garnish the bow with a few whole berries or a red rose.

8. Store the cake in the refrigerator until a half hour before serving. To serve, cut into 3/4-inch-thick slices.

ABOVE: *A slice of rich and dense Spicy Devil's Food Cake with White Cloud Frosting.*

ABOVE RIGHT: *Gift-Wrapped Chocolate Cake is served on a silver tray and garnished with a long-stemmed rose.*

RIGHT: *Secret-Ingredient Spice Cake with Cream Cheese Frosting is garnished with a ribbon-tied bundle of fragrant cinnamon sticks.*

OPPOSITE ABOVE: *Astoria Cake has velvety, light chocolate layers and a fluffy white frosting.*

OPPOSITE BELOW: *Sour Cream Coffee Cake is lit up with candles for a surprise morning birthday celebration.*

Spiced Devil's Food Cake

MAKES ONE 2-LAYER 9-INCH CAKE

◆

Before there were "Chocolate Decadence," "Chocolate Sin," "Gone to Hades Cake," and all the other also-rans, there was dark, chocolaty, spicy, *rich* devil's food cake. As far as I'm concerned, there's no room for improvement.

> ⅔ cup (1⅓ sticks) butter, softened
> 1¾ cups sugar
> 3 large eggs
> 1 teaspoon vanilla extract
> 2 cups all-purpose flour
> ¼ teaspoon baking powder
> 1¼ teaspoons baking soda
> 1 teaspoon salt
> 1 teaspoon ground cinnamon
> ¼ teaspoon grated nutmeg
> ¼ teaspoon ground allspice
> ⅔ cup unsweetened cocoa
> ½ cup milk
> ½ cup cold strong coffee (it's okay to use instant)

1. Preheat the oven to 350°F. Grease two 9-inch layer cake pans and dust them lightly with cocoa or flour.

2. In a mixing bowl, cream the butter and sugar until light and fluffy, then beat in the eggs and vanilla. In a separate bowl, sift together the flour, baking powder, baking soda, salt, and spices. In a third bowl, blend the cocoa, milk, and coffee together until smooth. Stir this mixture alternately with the dry mixture into the butter mixture, stirring until smooth after each addition.

3. Divide the batter between the pans. Bake until a cake tester comes out clean, about 30 minutes. Turn the layers out onto wire racks. Cool the layers completely and frost with White Cloud Frosting or Chocolate Buttercream (page 180).

White Cloud Frosting

> 1 cup sugar
> ¼ teaspoon cream of tartar
>   Pinch of salt
> ⅓ cup water
> 1 large egg white
> ¼ teaspoon vanilla extract

1. Combine the sugar, cream of tartar, salt, and water in a small heavy saucepan over medium heat. Stir well and bring to a boil; remove from the heat.

2. Slowly add the egg white, beating constantly with a rotary or electric beater. Continue beating until the mixture has reached a fluffy, spreadable consistency, then beat in the vanilla.

"Secret Ingredient" Spice Cake

MAKES ONE 2-LAYER 9-INCH CAKE

◆

Don't let on that there's a secret here—this is a rich, dense spice cake that needs no explaining.

> ¾ cup vegetable shortening
> 1½ cups sugar
> 2 large eggs
> 2½ cups all-purpose flour
> 1¼ teaspoons baking soda
> ½ teaspoon salt
> 2 teaspoons ground cinnamon
> ½ teaspoon grated nutmeg
> 1 teaspoon ground cloves
> ½ teaspoon ground allspice
> 1¼ cups thick tomato puree
> 1 cup chopped walnuts
> 1 cup raisins

1. Preheat the oven to 350°F. Grease two 9-inch round layer cake pans.

2. In a mixing bowl, cream together the shortening and sugar until light and fluffy, then beat in the eggs. In a separate bowl, sift together the flour, baking soda, salt, and spices. Stir the dry mixture alternately with the tomato puree into the wet mixture, stirring until smooth with each addition. Stir in the walnuts and raisins.

3. Divide the batter between the pans. Bake until the layers are nicely browned and a cake tester comes out clean, about 30 minutes. Turn the layers out onto wire racks. Cool the layers completely and frost.

Cream Cheese Frosting

> ½ cup (1 stick) butter, softened
> 8 ounces cream cheese, softened
> 1 teaspoon vanilla extract
> 3½ cups confectioners' sugar
> 1 teaspoon grated lemon rind

Beat the butter, cream cheese and vanilla together until smooth. Gradually beat in the confectioners' sugar, about ½ cup at a time, beating until smooth after each addition. Beat in the lemon rind.

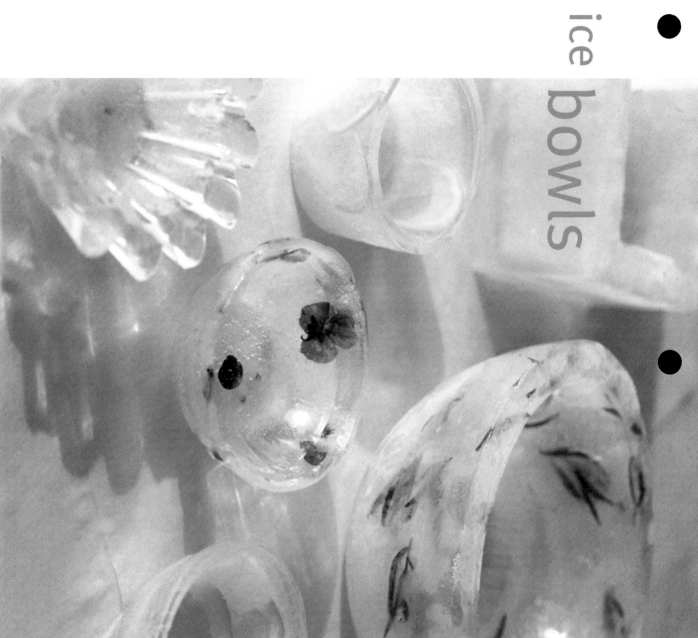

ice bowls

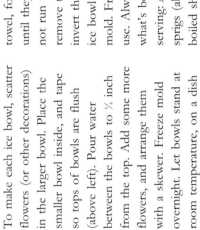

MATERIALS

1. Two glass or stainless-steel bowls; one should fit inside the other, with a ½- to 1-inch space between them

2. Fresh herbs, edible flowers, or citrus slices

3. Tape

ICE SCULPTURES ARE USUALLY CHISELED FROM HUGE BLOCKS OF ICE. TO MAKE THESE ICE BOWLS, DECORATED WITH EDIBLE FLOWERS, FRESH HERBS, OR CITRUS SLICES, DO IT AN EASIER WAY: FREEZE THE WATER INTO THE DESIRED SHAPE. THE RESULTS ARE AS USEFUL AS THEY ARE BEAUTIFUL ON ANY BUFFET TABLE.

To make each ice bowl, scatter flowers (or other decorations) in the larger bowl. Place the smaller bowl inside, and tape so tops of bowls are flush (above left). Pour water between the bowls to ¾ inch from the top. Add some more flowers, and arrange them with a skewer. Freeze mold overnight. Let bowls stand at room temperature, on a dish towel, for 10 to 20 minutes, until they separate easily; do not run under water. Untape, remove the top bowl, and invert the bottom bowl. The ice bowl will slide out of its mold. Freeze until ready to use. Always think about what's best with what you're serving: An ice bowl with dill sprigs (above right) holds boiled shrimp, while a smaller one with lime slices holds cocktail sauce, and a pretty linen towel between tray and napkin soaks up drips. Experiment with uses and shapes: Flower bowls can hold ice cream or sorbet; the fluted bowl (front of card) is plain, unadorned ice, made in brioche molds.

Photography: Fernando Bengoechea

ribbon board

Organize your cards, memos, and photos on a ribbon board

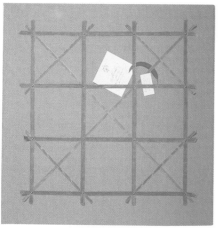

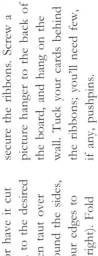

MATERIALS

1. Homosote board (a tackable surface available at home-supply stores and lumber yards)

2. Tight-weave linen (available at art-supply stores and fabric stores)

3. Twill tape (optional)

4. Ribbon

5. Upholstery tacks

6. Picture hanger

STOP TAPING BUSINESS CARDS TO THE COMPUTER SCREEN AND PROPPING INVITATIONS AND SNAPSHOTS AGAINST YOUR DESK LAMP. A RIBBON BOARD WILL PROVIDE YOU WITH A CLEANER, NEATER WORK SPACE—AND CLEARER THOUGHTS—WHILE KEEPING YOUR REMINDERS, PICTURES, AND MEMENTOS IN FULL VIEW.

Cut the board, or have it cut at a lumber yard, to the desired size. Pull the linen taut over the front and around the sides, and staple the four edges to the back (below right). Fold the corners neatly, and staple flush to the board. Glue twill tape over the staples to protect your walls, if you wish. Let your creativity loose in weaving a pattern with ribbons, like the tic-tac-toe pattern (above left), the argyle pattern (center), or the diamond pattern (right) inspired by the leaded windows of Victorian houses. The pattern on the front of this card is modeled after a garden trellis. Use upholstery tacks (look for ones with intriguing designs) to secure the ribbons. Screw a picture hanger to the back of the board, and hang on the wall. Tuck your cards behind the ribbons; you'll need few, if any, pushpins.

Photography: Stephen Lewis

ribbon board

ivy topiaries

Create tabletop topiaries using wire, moss, and live ivy branches

MATERIALS

1. Plastic-coated nineteen-gauge electrical wire

2. Florist's U pins, fine-gauge wire, or monofilament fishing line

3. Terra-cotta pots

4. Potting soil

5. Rooted ivy branches, dried sphagnum moss, and live moss

IF YOU CAN WIELD A PAIR OF PLIERS, YOU CAN MAKE A TABLE-

TOP IVY TOPIARY. SIMPLE SHAPES LIKE A HEART, FISH, MOON, OR

STAR WORK BEST, SINCE THEY WILL FILL OUT NICELY WITH LEAVES.

To make these small topiaries, choose small-leaved ivy varieties of *Hedera helix* like 'Ivalace,' 'Irish Lace,' or 'Spetchley.' You can also use trailing plants such as creeping fig, jasmine, or trailing abutilon.

1. Use pliers to shape a frame from plastic-coated nineteen-gauge electrical wire. Give the frame a wire stem with a forked base made from the same or a separate piece of wire so that it can be securely anchored in a pot.

2. Wrap the frame, section by section, with dried sphagnum moss, securing moss with the U pins, fine-gauge wire, or monofilament fishing line. Plant the frame stem in a terra-cotta pot, and bed potting soil around the base.

3. Plant three or four rooted branches of ivy in the pot, and wrap the trailers up around the frame to cover moss. Secure with U pins, wire, or fishing line. Tamp down live moss to cover soil. Water topiary daily, and prune often to preserve its shape.

Photography: Charles Masters

ivy topiaries

Mary Forquer's Astoria Cake

MAKES ONE 2-LAYER 9-INCH CAKE

◆

Whenever there was a large gathering of any kind in our neighborhood, everyone always expected Mary Forquer to bake her Astoria Cake. It's a light cake with a hint of chocolate flavor and a fabulous buttery frosting.

> ½ cup vegetable shortening
> 1½ cups sugar
> 2 large eggs
> 1 teaspoon vanilla extract
> 2¼ cups all-purpose flour
> 2 tablespoons unsweetened cocoa
> 1 teaspoon salt
> 1 cup buttermilk
> 1 teaspoon baking soda
> 1 tablespoon cider vinegar

1. Preheat the oven to 350°F. Grease two 9-inch round layer cake pans.

2. In a mixing bowl, cream the shortening and sugar together, then beat in the eggs and vanilla. In a separate bowl, sift together the flour, cocoa, and salt. Stir (do not beat) the dry mixture into the wet mixture alternately with the buttermilk, stirring until smooth with each addition.

3. Stir in the baking soda and the vinegar and divide the batter between the pans. Bake until the layers are nicely browned and a cake tester comes out clean, 25 to 30 minutes. Turn the layers out onto wire racks. Cool the layers completely and frost.

Astoria Frosting

> 1 cup milk
> 5 tablespoons flour
> Pinch of salt
> 1 cup (2 sticks) butter
> 1 cup sugar
> 1 teaspoon vanilla extract

1. In a small heavy saucepan, mix the milk, flour, and salt together until smooth. Place over low heat and cook, stirring constantly, until thickened, 5 to 7 minutes. Remove from the heat and cool.

2. Cream the butter and sugar until very light and fluffy, about 5 minutes. Gradually beat in the cooled flour mixture until smooth. Beat in the vanilla.

Sour Cream Coffee Cake

MAKES ONE 10-INCH TUBE CAKE

◆

If anyone wants to surprise me, serve me this rich and fragrant coffee cake as a birthday cake for *breakfast*, still warm from the oven. The only other thing I ask for is a hot cup of coffee, for dunking. For that, I'll even admit to being a year older.

Filling/Topping

> ½ cup sugar
> 1 tablespoon ground cinnamon
> 1 cup chopped walnuts or *pecans*
>
> 2 cups all-purpose flour
> 2 cups sugar
> 1 tablespoon baking powder
> ¼ teaspoon salt
> 1 cup (2 sticks) butter, softened
> 2 cups sour cream
> 2 large eggs
> 2 teaspoons vanilla extract

1. Preheat the oven to 350°F. Generously butter a 10-inch tube pan, preferably one with a removable bottom.

2. To make the filling/topping, stir the sugar and cinnamon together in a small mixing bowl, and then stir in the nuts. Reserve.

3. To make the batter, sift together the flour, sugar, baking powder, and salt in a large bowl. Add the butter, sour cream, eggs, and vanilla and beat for two minutes.

4. Spoon half of the batter into the prepared pan, then sprinkle half the filling/topping mixture over it. Carefully spoon the remaining batter into the pan and top with the remaining filling/topping.

5. Bake the cake for about 50 minutes, or until a cake tester comes out clean. Transfer to a wire rack and cool for 30 minutes. Remove the cake from the pan and serve warm, or cool completely before serving.

Variations Add 1 cup blueberries or coarsely chopped cranberries to the batter. Add 1 cup of sliced apples over the bottom layer of batter. Sprinkle ½ cup chocolate chips over each layer of batter.

Perfect Wedding Cake

SERVES 60

◆

Wedding cakes were traditionally dense fruitcakes. This recipe for orange-flavored layers studded with pecans and dates carries on the tradition in a lighter adaptation. The idea for the lacy coconut-covered frosting came about when I made a cake for a bride who just loved coconut. I like this cake because it's unusual and beautiful yet doesn't require hours of tedious decorating.

The pans I use for a three-tiered cake are 7, 10, and 13 inches in diameter and from 2¼ to 2½ inches deep; I make one batch of batter for the small and medium pans and one batch for the large pan. The frosting recipe, too, needs to be doubled. A bit of special equipment is needed here: before baking, cut three circles of clean, heavy cardboard the size of the pans; before assembling the cake, have ready ten 3½-inch-long ³⁄₁₆-inch dowels. Use large-scale seasonal flowers to decorate the finished cake, such as white and pale lavender lilacs in the spring, pale yellow and pink old roses in the summer, or white spider mums in the fall and winter. The cake layers freeze well, so they can be made in advance. Thaw the layers completely and assemble the cake no more than 12 hours before serving.

Cake Layers

      3 cups finely chopped pecans
      3 cups chopped dates
   1½ cups orange juice
      3 cups (6 sticks) butter, softened
      3 cups sugar
      6 large eggs
         Grated rind of 4 large oranges
         Grated rind of 2 lemons
      7 cups all-purpose flour
   2½ tablespoons baking powder
   1½ teaspoons baking soda
      ½ teaspoon salt
   1½ cups milk

Glaze

      1 cup sugar
      ½ cup orange juice
      ½ cup Grand Marnier

1. Preheat the oven to 350°F. Grease cake pans and line them with wax paper; grease the wax paper. Combine the pecans, dates, and orange juice in a small bowl and let stand for half an hour.

2. In a large bowl, cream together the butter and sugar, then beat in the eggs and the grated orange and lemon rinds. In a separate bowl, sift together the flour, baking powder, baking soda, and salt. Drain the orange and lemon juices from the fruit and nuts into the butter mixture; add the milk and beat well. Gradually beat the dry ingredients into the wet mixture.

3. Fold the nuts and dates into the batter and fill the pans two-thirds full. Bake the cake until lightly browned and a toothpick or cake tester inserted in the center comes out clean (about 45 minutes for the small layer, an hour and 10 minutes for the medium layer, and one hour and 40 minutes for the large layer). If the edges of the layers begin to get too brown, cover the edges loosely with aluminum foil. When done, transfer the pans to wire racks.

4. To glaze the cake, combine the ingredients in a small bowl and brush the mixture over the top of the layers while they are still warm. Allow the layers to cool 20 minutes in the pan, then invert them onto the rack. Brush the surfaces of the layers with more glaze and allow the layers to cool completely.

Frosting and Assembling

      1 cup (2 sticks) butter, softened
      1 cup vegetable shortening
      2 tablespoons Grand Marnier
      6 cups confectioners' sugar
      ½ teaspoon salt
      ½ to 1 cup milk

   10 cups shredded coconut, approximately
         Flowers, for decorating (see introductory text)

1. In a large mixing bowl, beat the butter and shortening together, then beat in the Grand Marnier. Gradually beat in the confectioners' sugar and salt. Beat in the milk, ¼ cup at a time, until the frosting is a smooth, spreadable consistency.

2. Place each cake layer on its corresponding cardboard circle. Place the largest layer on a large round tray or platter. Frost the cake, smoothing the icing with the spatula, and then cover with coconut.

3. Push six of the dowels into the cake, evenly spaced about 2½ inches from the edge, so they stand erect as support pillars for the next layer. Frost the dowels.

4. Frost the middle layer and cover it with coconut as in step 2. Push 4 dowels into the middle layer, evenly spaced and about 2 inches from the edge. Frost the top layer and cover it with coconut. (If the cake is to be transported, it should be moved in sections and assembled on site. Take along a little extra frosting and coconut for any necessary touchups.)

5. Center the middle layer over the bottom layer, letting it rest on the dowels. Center the top layer over the middle layer. Decorate the cake lavishly with groupings of flowers, masking the dowels.

A beautiful wedding cake, covered with lacy white
coconut and decorated with delicate pink roses,
white lilies, and lavender and white lilacs.

Basic Recipes

◆

Basic Pastry

MAKES ONE CRUST FOR A 9-INCH
OR 10-INCH PIE OR TART

◆

Use this basic pastry crust recipe as is for desserts—for a savory crust omit the sugar. I like using a combination of two shortenings, vegetable shortening for flakiness and butter for flavor. I use my fingers or a pastry blender for pastry making; the texture of the finished product is never quite as good when it's made in the food processor.

For a 9-inch pie
1½ cups all-purpose flour
    Scant ½ teaspoon salt
1½ teaspoons sugar
¼ cup vegetable shortening, chilled
¼ cup (½ stick) cold butter
3 to 4 tablespoons very cold water

For a 10-inch pie
2 cups all-purpose flour
½ teaspoon salt
2 teaspoons sugar
⅓ cup vegetable shortening, chilled
⅓ cup (⅔ stick) cold butter
4 to 6 tablespoons very cold water

1. Sift the flour, salt, and sugar together in a large mixing bowl, then add the shortening and butter. Using your fingertips, rub the dry ingredients and fats together until coarse and crumbly in texture. Do this quickly to keep the fats cold and solid, and do not overwork. Or use a pastry blender to combine the dry ingredients and shortenings.

2. Starting with 3 tablespoonfuls (4 for a 10-inch crust), add the water and work it into the flour-shortening mixture to form a ball of dough. Add 1 or 2 more tablespoons of water if necessary to hold the dough together. Wrap the dough ball in plastic wrap and chill for 1 hour before using.

3. Roll out the chilled dough ball on a floured pastry board or marble pastry slab into a circle about ⅛ inch

thick. For small tartlets, divide the dough and roll out each piece separately.

4. To line the pan, fold the dough into quarters and center the point in the bottom of the pan. Gently unfold the circle and press the dough into the pan without stretching. For pies, trim off the edges and crimp with your fingers. For tarts, simply trim off the excess dough. For further directions, follow the individual recipes.

Orange Pastry Double the sugar, substitute orange juice for the water, and add the grated rind of a small orange.

Red Wine Vinaigrette

MAKES 1½ CUPS

◆

½ cup red wine vinegar
1 teaspoon Dijon mustard
    Pinch of salt
½ teaspoon freshly ground black pepper
1 cup light olive oil

Whisk together the vinegar, mustard, salt, and pepper in a small mixing bowl, then gradually whisk in the oil. Or combine all the ingredients in a jar, cover tightly, and shake well. Refrigerate the vinaigrette for up to one week, tightly covered.

Homemade Mayonnaise

MAKES ABOUT 2½ CUPS

◆

2 large egg yolks, at room temperature
1 large whole egg, at room temperature
1 teaspoon Dijon mustard
¼ cup red wine vinegar or lemon juice
1 cup olive oil
1 cup vegetable oil
    Pinch of salt
    Ground black or red pepper

1. Combine the yolks, whole egg, mustard, and vinegar or lemon juice in the bowl of a food processor fitted with the steel blade. Process for 1 minute.

2. With the machine running, slowly add the oils through the tube in a thin, steady stream.

3. After the oil is completely incorporated and the mayonnaise is thick and fluffy, season it with salt and pepper to taste. Add more lemon juice or blend in more oil, depending on the consistency desired. Remove the mayonnaise to a jar, cover, and refrigerate up to a week.

Acknowledgments

When I began working on this project, I had no idea what a monumental task it would be. Having one cookbook under my belt, I knew this one would involve a lot of work, but creating more than one hundred and fifty pictures for this one was a task that could never have been accomplished without a lot of help. Luckily, I have a lot of good friends, and met some new ones along the way, who were always ready to offer help whenever I needed it.

Thanks again to my family and friends, who've helped create all my special occasions and continually offer their support. Some, too, have offered recipes, and their names are mentioned in the text.

Others offered both brains and brawn: Tom Barnes, Ken Daniels, Nolan Drummond, Lucille Hershiser, Katherine Hopkins, Joan Lindau, Mary Kranik, Genevieve Como, Rose Meola, Mary Ann Podesta, Al and Lorraine Stefanic, Linda Sunshine, Pam Thomas, and Dennis Varner.

While a good many photographs were created in my city apartment and country house, some were shot in other locations. Thanks to all those who graciously welcomed our crew into their homes: Amanda, Andrew, Fran, and Tom Barnes; Diane Cleaver; Jim Davis; Jim Fleming; the Handy family; Deborah Kass; Steve Magnuson; Chuck Nyhan; Carol and J. Barry O'Rourke; Michael Pritchard; Philip Stoehr; Janet Sutherland; Jim and Barbara Varner; and Judy and Michael Welch.

Thanks to Tony Fontana of Mantilia Motors in West Haven, Connecticut, for loaning us the Ford Taurus station wagon for the tailgate party, and Abercrombie & Fitch in New York for the picnic basket.

Again, many members of the Crown and Harmony family were particularly helpful. Special thanks to: my valued editor and good friend, Harriet Bell, who again smoothly guided me from beginning to end with her caring good judgment and careful attention to every detail; former editorial director Esther Mitgang, who supported me from the beginning and encouraged me to do a fully illustrated book this time; Crown's design director, Ken Sansone, who was instrumental in carrying it through, from helping me turn my ideas into pictures to designing the book; Claude Johnson, Peter Davis, and Kathy Belden in the art and editorial departments, who kept so many details in order; production editor Amy Boorstein, production supervisor Joan Denman, and managing editor Laurie Stark, who all kept me on (a very tight) schedule. Thanks, too, to Alan Mirken, Bruce Harris, Jo Fagan, Phyllis Fleiss, and the sales and marketing departments; and to Lisa Ekus and Sandy Konopka—without all their support of my last book, this one might never have happened.

Thanks to my agent, Diane Cleaver, who helped in every way she could, including running to the market when we took pictures at her house in the country.

Making all the food for the pictures was a huge task, especially working with tight schedules. Many, many thanks go to my mother, Clara Henry, for spending many weeks in my kitchen cooking and baking, and for helping to test recipes at home. Thanks, too, to Nancy Kenmore, for helping out in the kitchen with her special talents.

A year and a half ago, when Nancy Kennedy, food editor of *Ford Times*, was doing a piece on me, she brought along a young photographer named Randy O'Rourke. After working with him that day and seeing the resulting photographs, I knew I wanted him to photograph my new book. Working with Randy on this book has been a wonderful and rewarding collaboration. Through six months of hectic sessions, he remained patient, cheerful, and enthusiastic (and he likes my cooking!), always making the book his top priority, no matter how busy his schedule. Thanks, Rooster.

In every big project, there seems to be someone behind the scenes who never receives the credit they deserve. My heartfelt thanks go to Stephanie O'Rourke, Randy's wife and right hand. Her enthusiasm and energy never failed: she was always willing to help find a location, move a light, chop an onion, or do whatever needed doing to make a picture perfect.

Working on this book only emphasized something I realized long ago: special occasions can happen whenever good friends and good food come together —we certainly created a few during the course of the past year. I grew closer to old friends and made some new ones, and I thank them all for the memories.

Index

◆

For information on how you can have *Better Homes and Gardens* delivered to your door, write to: Mr. Robert Austin, P.O. Box 4536, Des Moines, IA 50336.